Island Tourism

Island Tourism

Management Principles and Practice

Edited by
MICHAEL V. CONLIN
Bermuda College, Bermuda
TOM BAUM
University of Buckingham, UK

JOHN WILEY & SONS
Chichester · New York · Brisbane · Toronto · Singapore

Baffins Lane, Chichester,
West Sussex PO19 1UD, England

Telephone: National Chichester (01243) 779777
International (+44) 1243 779777

Other Wiley Editorial Offices

John Wiley & Sons, Inc., 605 Third Avenue,
New York, NY 10158-0012, USA

Jacaranda Wiley Ltd, 33 Park Road, Milton,
Queensland 4064, Australia

John Wiley & Sons (Canada) Ltd, 22 Worcester Road,
Rexdale, Ontario M9W 1L1, Canada

John Wiley & Sons (SEA) Pte Ltd, 37 Jalan Pemimpin #05-04,
Block B, Union Industrial Building, Singapore 2057

Library of Congress Cataloging-in-Publication Data

Conlin, Michael V.
Island tourism: management principles and practice/Michael
V. Conlin, Tom Baum.
p. cm.
Includes bibliographical references and index.
ISBN 0-471-95556-6
1. Tourist trade. 2. Islands. I. Baum, Tom. II. Title.
G155.A1C65 1995
338.4'791—dc20 94–37087
CIP

British Library Cataloguing in Publication Data

A catalogue record for this book is available from the British Library

ISBN 0-471-95556-6

Typeset in 10/12pt Sabon by Vision Typesetting, Manchester
Printed and bound in Great Britain by Biddles Ltd, Guildford and King's Lynn

Contents

About the Contributors

Tom Baum is Professor of International Hotel and Tourism Management at the University of Buckingham, England. He is responsible for undergraduate, postgraduate and research studies in tourism and hospitality at the university. Dr Baum has researched and written extensively on international tourism matters, especially in the areas of human resource development and tourism policy. He has consulted widely on behalf of public and private sector organisations in Asia, the Caribbean and Europe. Tom edited *Human Resource Issues in International Tourism* (Butterworth Heinemann, 1993), and is author of *Managing Human Resources for the European Tourism and Hospitality Industry: a Strategic Approach* (Chapman and Hall, 1995).

Lino Briguglio is Director of the Islands and Small States Institute of the Foundation for International Studies at the University of Malta.

Peter Burns is with the Centre for Leisure and Tourism Studies at the University of North London and holds Masters degrees in the Social Anthropology of Tourism and Education. He is former Director of the Fiji Hotel School, advisor to the World Tourism Organization and the International Labour Organisation and has been consultant on a number of tourism master-plans including Romania and Sri Lanka. He is currently Education and Training advisor to the Tourism Council of the South Pacific.

Robert Cleverdon is a specialist in tourism development, policy planning and marketing. He has published extensively on tourism and the Third World and worked for a number of years with the Economist Intelligence Unit. He was director for several UNDP/WTO and Asian Development Bank tourism projects and missions, including the Cook Islands, Bonaire, India and Mauritius. He is currently Senior Lecturer in Tourism at the Centre for Leisure and Tourism Studies at the University of North London and maintains an active research/consultancy portfolio.

Michael V. Conlin is Dean of the Faculty of Hotel and Business Administration at Bermuda College and Director of the College's Centre for Tourism Research and Innovation. Mr Conlin is also the past chairman of the Council of Caribbean Hospitality Schools, a member of the Board of Trustees of the Caribbean Hospitality Training Institute and a member of the Board of Directors of CHRIE. In 1992, Mr Conlin was appointed to Bermuda's Tourism Planning Committee, a body charged with examining the island's tourism industry and making strategic recommendations about the industry's future development.

Klaus de Albuquerque is a Professor of Sociology at the College of Charleston in South Carolina. He has written extensively on the issues of sustainability and alternative tourism with reference to islands, particularly in the Caribbean region.

David L. Edgell, Sr. is the former Acting Under Secretary of Commerce for Travel and Tourism in the US Department of Commerce. In this capacity, Dr Edgell was the head of the US Travel and Tourism Administration which is the US government agency responsible for all governmental activities in trade in tourism. In addition, Dr Edgell, is a member of faculty at the George Washington University International Institute for Tourism Studies and the University of Hawaii's Executive Development Institute for Tourism. He is author of *International Tourism Policy*.

Diana Gevers is Research and Statistical Co-ordinator with the Tourism Corporation, Bonaire.

Donald Getz is an Associate Professor of Tourism and Hospitality Management at the University of Calgary. He specialises in tourism planning and impact evaluation as well as in festival management and event tourism. He is the co-author of the first comprehensive book on event tourism, *Festivals, Special Events and Tourism* (Van Nostrand Reinhold, 1990) and is co-founder of *Festival and Event Management: An International Journal*.

Larry Helber is Chairman of Helber Hastert and Fee, Partners, Inc., a consulting firm located in Honolulu, Hawaii and specialising in tourism/resort, community, waterfront and transportation master-planning. During his career as a planner, Mr Helber's work has included numerous projects in Asia, the Caribbean and the Pacific. Mr Helber is a past director of PATA and currently serves on the Advisory Council. Mr Helber has been an adjunct member of the faculty of the University of Hawaii's School of Travel Industry Management for the past 24 years and is co-author of *Tourism Planning and Development*.

Veronica Long is a doctoral student in Geography at the University of Waterloo, Canada. Her thesis research is concerned with the implications of tourism for community structure in Nusa Lembongan, Bali. She has previously conducted research on tourism impacts and mitigation strategies in Mexico.

Jerome L. McElroy is a Professor of Economics at Saint Mary's College in Indiana. Jerry has published widely in the area of island tourism and consults actively with a number of countries and agencies in the Caribbean.

Ram Mudami is Lecturer in Economics at the University of Buckingham and Course Director of the postgraduate Business Economics section. He has previously taught at a number of US universities. Dr Mudambi has published widely in economics and business journals and currently is taking an active research interest in aspects of the international tourism industry and its economic implications.

Peter Murphy is a Professor and Head of the Tourism Management Program in the School of Business at the University of Victoria, British Columbia. Dr Murphy has conducted tourism research for 17 years and is internationally respected for his work in the area of community participation in local tourism and for his book, *Tourism: A Community Approach*. Dr Murphy's current research interests centre on urban tourism and securing the appropriate blend of societal and business conditions to encourage sustainable tourism destinations.

Ronnie Pieters is with the Tourism Corporation, Bonaire.

Blair Poetschke is a Senior Consultant with Ernst & Young, Toronto, Canada, specialising in marketing strategies and competitive assessments for both private and public sector tourism organisations. He has in-depth experience with the effectiveness of Tourist Authorities from around the world, having assisted numerous government/industry coalitions to reach shared governance agreements and develop tourism industry strategies.

Sharr Prohaska is a visiting Professor at the International Insitute for Tourism Studies at the George Washington University. Sharr is also the Director of the Cultural Heritage Tourism Institute and Co-Director of the Pacific Northwest Institute for Tourism in Portland, Oregon. She has consulted widely in the area of cultural heritage tourism and is Advisor Emeritus to the National Trust for Historic Preservation in the US.

Chris Ryan is on the faculty of the Department of Management Systems at Massey University, Palmerston North, New Zealand. Prior to his current position, Dr Ryan was at the Nottingham Trent University, where he was Acting Head of the Department of Strategic Management and Marketing. He is author of *Recreational Tourism – A Social Science Perspective* (Routledge, 1991).

Alex Titcombe was the Field Co-ordinator for the Caribbean Hotel Training Programme, an EU funded project based in the Bahamas and Antigua from 1990 to 1994. Prior to his involvement with the Programme, Mr Titcombe was the Director of Training for Crest Hotels, a major UK and European hotel chain, and earlier had managed several Crest properties. Mr Titcombe has also served as the Vice Chairman of the Travel and Tourism Programme plc, which introduced the first industry/education sponsored secondary school tourism programme in travel and tourism in the UK.

Leslie Vella is with the National Tourism Organization of Malta.

Geoffrey Wall is Professor of Geography at the University of Waterloo, Canada, where he is cross-appointed with the Department of Recreation and Leisure Studies. Dr Wall's research interests concentrate upon the impacts of tourism and the consequences of different types of tourism development for tourism destinations. He has been providing input on tourism into the formulation of a sustainable development strategy for Bali.

Philippe Wing is Lecturer in International Tourism in the School of Leisure and Tourism at the University of Ulster. He has undertaken research on small developing island economies, particularly those located in the Indian Ocean and is currently completing a research project on tourism development in Mauritius.

Bert Winterbottom is a Principal of LDR International located in Columbia, Maryland, USA and Weybridge, England. Mr Winterbottom is a consultant in tourism development, a writer and speaker, and traveller. He consults with international public and private clients on a wide range of tourism issues ranging from resort planning to tourism strategic planning. He has recently contributed to the strategic planning process for tourism in Bermuda.

Preface

This book found its genesis in the First International Assembly of Tourism Policy Experts, hosted by Dr Donald E. Hawkins, the Director of the International Institute for Tourism Studies at The George Washington University, in November, 1990. The co-editors of this book, both of whom participated in the Assembly, came to realize the value of a small, interactive gathering of experts. This was the format which the Island Fora would later utilize.

Don, whose accomplishments have been recognized in his appointment in 1994 as the Dwight D. Eisenhower Professor of Tourism Policy at George Washington, spent the academic year 1991–92 as a Visiting Scholar at Bermuda College. During that time, we conceived and hosted the First Island Tourism International Forum. We had no idea whether it would be a success but did have a sense that island tourism was a niche whose time had come. The rest is history. Both the First Forum (1992) and the Second Forum (1993) were, by all accounts, highly successful and this book is just one of the tangible results of that success. The point is that none of this might have come to pass had it not been for the vision, leadership, and support of Don. In his role as Founding Co-Chairman of the Forum, he has worked tirelessly to ensure that the meetings are of the highest academic quality while incorporating a substantial practical component. In this way, the Fora have proven valuable to both academics, practitioners and public policy makers. For this, we are deeply appreciative.

The Fora also owe a great deal of thanks to Dr Archie Hallett, who is now the President Emeritus of Bermuda College. Without Archie's enlightened support for the Centre for Tourism Research and Innovation, the First Forum would not have happened. Dr George L. Cook, the current President of Bermuda College, has continued the College's support for the Centre and the Fora. Indeed, under George's leadership, the College is continuing its support of the Centre which is hosting the Third Island Tourism International Forum in December 1995 in Bermuda.

As anyone who organizes and implements conferences knows, they do not happen without the input and hard work of a great many people. It is not our intention to mention everyone who deserves individual mention: with the amount of support which the Fora generated, this would take an inordinate amount of space. We do, nonetheless, wish to recognize their valuable contribution and to thank them all for it.

Notwithstanding this, however, there are several people whose contribution was essential. Ann Parsons, who is the Acting Associate Dean of the Faculty of Hotel and Business Administration, served as a Co-Chair of the Second Forum. Her highly organized and energetic input was crucial to the Forum's success. In essence,

Ann ran it! Likewise, Patricia Trott and Cindy Hawkins, Don's wife, acted as administrative assistants for the Second and First Fora, respectively and without their constant vigilance and hard work, neither Forum would have been the well-organized events which they ended up as.

Several members of faculty made significant contributions to the organization and administration of the Fora, including Sue Klesniks, Barbara O'Shaughnessy, Sue Rhodes and Patricia Robinson. In the private and public sectors, David Dodwell, Dr Grant Gibbons, Buddy Franklin, Patricia Paynter, Gary Philips, Cordell Riley and Susie Wainwright all made substantial contributions in terms of raising support from the business sector for the Fora. In particular, John Harvey, the Executive Director of the Bermuda Hotel Association and his members made an invaluable contribution. For their collective efforts, we are truly grateful.

Putting together an edited work such as this is, at best, a challenging task. We would like to thank Dr Iain Stevenson, our publisher, and his team for their encouragement, forbearance and support.

Finally, the Co-Editors would like to thank Roxi and Brelda. Without their patience and encouragement, this project would not have come to fruition.

Michael V. Conlin,
Paget, Bermuda

Tom Baum,
Buckingham, England

Part I

ISLAND TOURISM MANAGEMENT PRINCIPLES

1 Island Tourism: an Introduction

MICHAEL V. CONLIN
Bermuda College, Bermuda

AND

TOM BAUM
University of Buckingham, UK

This book is about island tourism. The chapters consist, in the main, of papers originally presented at the Second Island Tourism International Forum held at Bermuda College, 17–20 May 1993. The Island Tourism International Forums are small, interactive gatherings of island tourism experts who meet to share current thinking and ideas about topical issues of importance for island destinations. Several additional chapters were commissioned in order to provide a more complete treatment of issues and exposure to island destinations.

The Second Forum brought together over 100 experts in island tourism to discuss the theme *Competitiveness Challenges for Island Destinations in the 1990s*. The theme was chosen because of the widely held belief in the tourism industry of the need to enhance competitiveness in all sectors in order to be successful. Born out of the economic downturn at the beginning of the 1990s, the importance of competitiveness continues to be one of the fundamental components for tourism success and will remain so, at least for this decade. To the extent that this is so, it is even more important for island destinations to focus on competitiveness strategies given the characteristics of islands outlined later in this chapter.

The delegates to the Second Forum represented a balanced mix of industry practitioners from the accommodation, cruise and transportation sectors; public-sector policy makers at the national, regional and local levels; tourism consultants in strategic planning, service quality, occupational standards, niche markets and promotion; and educators and researchers with a particular interest and expertise in island tourism. This mix of experts provides both theoretical and practical perspectives on island tourism and, specifically, island tourism competitiveness. It is this balanced perspective which gives this book its value and its title.

The purposes of this book are twofold. First, it is our intention to address the diversity of issues which face tourism in the island context through use of thematic and case study material which clearly illustrates these issues. Our contributors consider concerns which are both generic, within international tourism, and

Island Tourism: Management Principles and Practice
Edited by Michael V. Conlin and Tom Baum

specific to the island situation. In both cases, however, the discussion draws on experience from island tourism in Europe, North America, the Caribbean, the Indian Ocean and the Pacific. Thus, the book will be of interest both to readers with commitments to the growing field of island tourism as a specialism and to those who may wish to draw wider tourism themes from the material. Our second objective is to provide readers, and especially those with specific professional or academic interest in island tourism destinations, with applied business and management perspectives of a number of major themes, as they apply to islands.

It is hoped that this approach will enable the reader to translate the experience of our contributors, based on living, working and researching in diverse island situations, to their own environments. The book will have value for practitioners by providing examples of competitiveness in real settings. Public policy makers will find examples of innovative and effective planning models for developing competitive yet sustainable island tourism industries. The wide array of theoretical and applied discussion will provide educators and researchers with valuable contributions to curricula and the development of research agendas.

ISLAND TOURISM

Island tourism is not a recent phenomenon. The Romans used the Isle of Capri as a holiday destination two thousand years ago (King, 1993). Bermuda, the site of the Island Tourism International Forums and an island addressed from different angles by three chapters in this book, has been a popular tourism destination since the latter part of the 19th century. Bali, which is also discussed, has hosted tourists with a particular cultural orientation for most of this century. The allure of islands, be they in the Mediterranean, the Atlantic or the Pacific, as places where people go for relaxation and rejuvenation has a long tradition which continues unabated. Particular island destinations may come into vogue and then fall from favour, but the special attraction of islands in general continues.

What is recent is the interest which researchers have begun to show in islands and the role which tourism plays in their economic and social development. The recent spate of conferences dealing exclusively with the subject, including the Island Tourism International Forums (1992 and 1993) and the University of Malta's International Conference on Sustainable Tourism in Island and Small States (1993) are evidence of this interest. This professional interest has been matched in recent years by a parallel growth in interest by the general public, at least in Western countries. The plethora of popular magazines devoted to island tourism attest to this.

An analysis of island tourism must inevitably begin with a discussion of what constitutes an island. Surprisingly, geographers do not dwell much on this question. A number of general introductory texts on geography do not even ask the question nor do they attempt to provide a definition (see for example, De Bliji and Muller, 1992; and Stausfield and Zinolzak, 1990). Marshall, however, offers the following definition:

> And then there are the islands, which account for about a fifth of the UN's membership. Many are micro-states of less than a million people. Sometimes more, rather than less, vulnerable because of an isolation that produces poverty and instability (Marshall, 1991, p. 190).

This definition encompasses several of the characteristics which are generally associated with the notion of islands. Small scale, isolation and weak economies all play a role in forming our perception of islands. They also play a major part in the reality of island tourism, its opportunities and its problems. These characteristics and the manner in which island destinations deal with them will surface throughout this book.

The concept of the island has received attention by geographers and other academics within the context of social and economic development (Lockhart, 1993). What, at first, would seem to be a simple definitional problem, however, quickly turns into a more complex issue. King points to a number of complicating factors in defining islands including natural effects upon the shape, size and permanence of island coastlines, the impact of human construction such as causeways, thresholds of minimum and maximum size including overall mass and height, minimum and maximum population limits, and political and administrative contexts (King, 1993). He draws no definitive conclusions about what an island is.

Butler in his discussion of tourism development in small islands, highlights the characteristics of separateness and difference which inevitably come to mind when one thinks of islands:

> Their appeal may relate to the very real feeling of separateness and difference, caused in part by their being physically separate, and perhaps therefore different from adjoining mainlands. Where such physical separateness is accompanied by political separateness, the appeal can be expected to increase, and given people's desires for the different while in pursuit of leisure, different climates, physical environments and culture can all be expected to further the attractiveness of islands as tourism destinations (Butler, 1993, p. 71).

Island tourism itself is possibly more easily defined, both in terms which are generic and with reference to those characteristics described above which apply uniquely to islands. Tourism is generally more important in an economic sense to an island destination than is usually the case with mainland destinations. This is because it is invariably a larger and more significant part of the island destination's economy. Whereas tourism in, for example, Germany represents, in economic terms 0.7% of the GDP, in the United Kingdom 1.5% and in Spain 5.2%, tourism in an island like Bermuda represents approximately 50% of its economic activity. The economic impact of tourism on islands is felt in many ways. Obviously, the most direct impact is the generation of foreign exchange and investment. However, island tourism has a significant range of additional economic effects through employment and other forms of multipliers. The vagaries of the tourism industry hit harder in island destinations which do not have the capacity to generate alternative forms of economic activity and which do not, in many cases, have strong social insurance structures to deal with unemployment and retraining.

Tourism is also more pervasive in its impact on the small island community than it is on larger mainland resort destinations with good local communications to urban centres. The influx of large numbers of tourists to an island destination is likely to have a more profound effect on the destination in cultural, social and environmental terms because of the destination's small scale. Locals will have more contact with tourists than they might have in mainland destinations, particularly in large, developed metropolitan destinations. This contact can have negative effects. The phenomenon whereby locals begin to mimic the culture of their visitors, thereby diminishing the importance and permanence of their own culture and heritage, is well recognized as a cultural impact concern. The impact of employing locals in the hospitality industry may also have negative effects, particularly on those islands which have cultures and religions which are different from those of their tourists. The impact of shift work and other peculiarities of employment in the hospitality industry on the family unit and its traditions may also be negative in the ways in which it alters established family and community relationship and behaviour patterns. Finally, the small scale of an island's physical resources cause it to be far more susceptible to the negative effects of mass development and greatly increased usage which tourism brings. The impact of excessive water demand by tourism on agriculture in Phuket, Thailand is one illustration of this. Thus, islands can be significantly damaged for generations and perhaps forever by unplanned and uncontrolled tourism. Islands simply do not have the depth of resources to allow for recovery.

Finally, island tourism is more vulnerable to the vagaries of the market than mainland destinations. Being completely dependent upon providers of transportation, for example, islands find themselves in the unhappy position of having to rely on the services of airlines and shipping companies which make decisions in the best interests of shareholders and which do not consider the very real concerns of islands. Island destinations seldom have the strength necessary to influence significantly the corporate level decision making of airlines or cruise lines. Few small island states operate their own international airline—Air Mauritius is one successful example—and this further increases dependency on the outside world. In some situations, islands may seek to provide alternative transportation services which are generally not efficient and therefore only exacerbate an already fragile economic system. Notwithstanding these obstacles and concerns, islands generally embrace tourism as one of the best and in some cases the only development strategy available to them. The manner in which they do so, the degree of success and failure they experience, the extent to which they maintain control over their economic, cultural and social destinies as a consequence of embracing tourism, and the way they plan for the future within a rapidly changing international environment are all subjects which this book considers.

ISLAND TOURISM ISSUES

The following chapters attempt to address the most compelling issues facing tourism on island destinations. While clearly not exhaustive, the general areas of reference include the need for tourism planning and policy development, concerns about various forms of tourism within the context of sustainability, marketing issues relating to product, price and promotion strategies and, of course, the importance of competitiveness. Most of the chapters deal with several of these areas of concern and, in that sense, they mirror the pervasiveness of tourism in island destinations. In the island context, it is difficult to discuss any aspects of tourism without involving most aspects of the community's economic, cultural and social life. This will become quite clear as the reader progresses through this book.

Tourism planning and policy development

At the heart of effective development and management of tourism at a national level is the articulation of clear policy guidelines. These guidelines, in order to be effective, must recognize the often competing needs and expectations of the host community; the physical and cultural environment; the domestic and international investment market; and the visitors themselves. Traditionally, economic determinants have been the dominant factors in shaping policy. In a recent study, Baum (1994) identified the following as the priorities which determine why countries are in the tourism business:

1. generate foreign revenue/assist balance of payments;
2. provide employment—nationally;
3. improve local/regional economy;
4. create awareness about the country;
5. provide regional/local employment;
6. support environmental/public conservation;
7. contribute to infrastructural development;
8. create international goodwill.

There is, however, some evidence that tourism policy development is taking on a rather broader perspective and seeking to become much more responsive to the community and environment in all its aspects. Pieters' and Gevers' discussion of Bonaire, in Chapter 11, exemplifies such an approach.

Tourism policy themes feature strongly in a number of chapters in this book. David Edgell, calling upon his extensive experience at the helm of tourism policy development in the United States, in the next chapter discusses some of the major global trends and issues in international tourism, with a particular focus on market dimensions, and applies these to the peculiar, if not unique, island tourism environment. Edgell's "nine shadows" provide a backcloth to island tourism policy development at a national or trans-national level from which specific focus and priorities can be drawn. Edgell's perspective is, naturally, greatly influenced by his American base and, thus, his shadows have particular pertinence to islands with a traditional and heavy dependence on North American markets.

The Caribbean is a very good illustration of a region with this high level of dependence on the American market. However, recent evidence suggests that the Caribbean is increasingly looking elsewhere for its market growth while, at the same time, Americans seek out new destinations in other parts of the world. As a result, the share of the Caribbean market represented by American tourists is decreasing significantly as Table 1.1 shows.

Extrapolating the implications of Edgell's "shadows" into practically focused tourism policies may allow the island states of the Caribbean to reverse the stagnation in US arrivals to the region while, at the same time, maintaining impressive growth in other markets. Other destinations such as Bermuda, which have been heavily dependent upon the American market and which will probably remain so, can look to Edgell for guidance in maintaining their vital share of the American market. In Chapter 15 on Bermuda, Conlin discusses how that destination is seeking to do just that.

Chris Ryan's Chapter 7 complements Edgell's by reviewing tourism trends and formulating tentative market-related predictions from a strongly European perspective. Unlike Edgell, who is fairly incisive in his conclusions, Ryan rightly points to the diverse and, at times, contradictory lifestyle indicators which tourism planners need to analyse as part of their product development and marketing planning.

Pieters and Gevers (Chapter 11) present an excellent example of an integrated policy response, clearly consistent with both Edgell and Ryan's arguments, through their case study of Bonaire. This small island has experienced controlled development and growth in its tourism business, averaging 6% growth per annum between 1980 and 1992. The policy framework for Bonaire, intended to guide the

Table 1.1. Numbers ('000s) and Percentage Distribution of arrivals in the Caribbean by Region and Origin

	1980	1984	1985	1986	1987	1988	1989	1990	1991	1992
USA	4317	4710	4975	5288	5929	6116	6266	6532	6268	6310
	62%	62%	62%	62%	62%	58%	57%	55%	53%	52%
Canada	473	500	594	603	639	667	714	747	726	783
	7%	7%	7%	7%	6%	6%	6%	6%	6%	6%
Europe	878	716	732	817	1078	1348	1541	1643	1857	2041
	13%	9%	9%	10%	11%	13%	14%	14%	16%	17%
Caribbean	580	818	803	809	890	970	990	1070	1060	1070
	8%	11%	10%	10%	9%	9%	9%	9%	9%	9%
Other	720	849	859	946	1052	1393	1579	1817	1852	1896
	10%	11%	11%	11%	11%	13%	14%	15%	16%	16%

Source: CTO, 1992: *Statistical Report for 1988–92.*

development of tourism to the end of the century, is designed to ensure that tourism develops in a way which will allow "the people of Bonaire to benefit from the promotion and development of tourism by providing an optimum level of economic contribution consistent with the overall protection of Bonaire's environmental assets, cultural heritage, human resources and lifestyle". This overall objective translates into a practical set of policy guidelines which are unusually comprehensive in their consideration of tourism product, economic impact, socio-cultural matters, community response, employment and, perhaps most emphatically, environmental protection and preservation. The logic, of course, for this emphasis is compelling given the importance of reef diving to Bonaire's tourism industry and increasing international competition within the niche sports tourism market from countries such as the Caymans and Belize.

The articulation of a compelling and effective tourism policy is an important first step. Ensuring its implementation within the complex political, economic, cultural and tourism industry environment of most island destinations represents another challenge altogether. Natural resistance to change, the power of established elites, the very pervasiveness of tourism in island destinations, and the polarization of the private and public sectors all mitigate against effective implementation. Conlin (Chapter 15) discusses the challenges of policy implementation at the national level within the context of Bermuda's very recent attempt at creating a community-based national policy and at the regional level in his discussion with Titcombe (Chapter 6) of Caribbean human resource development strategy.

Various models exist to support the management of such implementation, ranging from strong, centralized, government-driven structures, such as in Malaysia and its islands, to approaches where virtually all aspects of policy determination and implementation are vested in the private sector as is the case in Gibraltar. In Chapter 5, Blair Poetschke puts the case for public–private partnership in tourism planning, implementation and management. Poetschke argues quite convincingly that such partnerships reduce antagonism between the public and private sectors, resulting in the generation of additional resources to support tourism development activities. Poetschke illustrates his argument with case material from a variety of partnership models from a variety of countries and locations including islands in the Caribbean and the Pacific.

Tourism and sustainability

The focus on environmental and socio-cultural sustainability which is prominent within the tourism policy of Bonaire is a theme which de Alburquerque and McElroy (Chapter 3) develop and extend considerably in their consideration of low-impact, alternative tourism. Reef diving, of course, need not be low impact, as a number of island locations have discovered to their cost. However, de Albuquerque and McElroy focus on approaches to the management of alternative, sustainable tourism which can allow destinations to guard against the destructive experience faced by islands such as Phucket in Thailand. The authors of this chapter are clear in their cautioning with respect to alternative tourism because, by its very nature, it locates in the most fragile and vulnerable of environments.

One example of the fragility of the socio-cultural environment, as opposed to the natural in Bonaire, is provided in Chapter 19 by Long and Wall in their consideration of small-scale tourism development in Bali. Bali could have been used to represent an example of planned and relatively effectively zoned mass tourism development but Long and Wall choose to consider the impact on traditional communities of small, locally owned and operated tourism accommodation units. Employing an interesting resident and observation-based methodology, the authors describe both the benefits and dangers of the impact of this form of tourism development on economic, cultural, community and family life in the *Banjar*, the local social and administrative unit in Bali.

Conlin and Titcombe's chapter on human resource development in the Caribbean (Chapter 6) focuses primarily on the issue of competitiveness. It can, however, also be viewed from the perspective of sustainability. Given the importance of human resources for tourism success in the region, the case can be made that a comprehensive human resource policy is essential if the region's inhabitants are to support, gain from and contribute to tourism. This sustainability argument has only recently received attention but is likely to grow in importance for island tourism as the role of human resources becomes more fully appreciated (Conlin and Baum, 1994).

Long and Wall are very aware of a sense of community in their discussion of tourism development in Bali. Equally sensitive, but from a very different standpoint, is Burns's controversial discussion of tourism in Fiji and the impact of two military coups during the 1980s (Chapter 20). Clearly political instability is a catastrophe to tourism in a way that is not experienced by other economic sectors; the examples of Grenada in the early 1980s and Thailand in the early 1990s, as well as Fiji, illustrate this point well. Burns goes beyond this level of impact in Fiji and considers the implications of political instability and change on the relationship between the tourism industry, its employees and its control and ownership by overseas interests. His conclusions clearly point to detrimental impacts on the host community in Fiji, particularly on those of Indian origin. The chapter raises a range of pertinent questions in relation to the political control of tourism development in the island setting and in that sense, while the experience elsewhere may not be as charged as that in Fiji, Burns does touch on wider, generic concerns.

Marketing issues

Marketing themes underlie much of the island hopping discussion within this book. Ryan, as already indicated, looks at tourism policy in the context of life-style analysis. From a practical perspective, in Chapter 8, Wing addresses the particular marketing considerations which small island states must address. He considers the key obstacles confronted by such states and proposes strategies, primarily driven by partnerships between governments and the international private sector or through trans-national co-operation as exemplified in the South Pacific, and Indian Ocean and the Caribbean.

Conlin's discussion of Bermuda in Chapter 15 focuses squarely on the problems of mature destinations and their alternatives for future development. In its planning, Bermuda has focused on a number of themes found throughout this book, including community appreciation, participation and gain through tourism. The emphasis on sustainable development through product evolution aimed at appropriate market niches is another theme which strongly influences Bermuda's tourism policy. Most importantly, Conlin stresses the need for comprehensive planning, which in an island context is absolutely essential given the pervasiveness of the industry.

In Chapter 9 Larry Helber continues the theme of mature tourism destinations and responsiveness to new consumer demands and expectations. Referring to a range of island destinations, Helber makes the case that mature island destinations need to go beyond superficial beautification campaigns, infrastructure improvements and aggressive marketing to retain competitiveness, needing to focus on the development of sustainability and on-going enhancement of both product and service. This chapter reinforces the obvious fact that a discussion of marketing within an island context must also consider the issues of sustainability and competitiveness.

Sharr Prohaska on cultural heritage tourism in islands (Chapter 4) underscores the opportunities which exist for niche market development. This is a generic theme, but in the context of islands presents a wealth of opportunities given the historically colonial, culturally fascinating and naturally exotic ambiences which many islands possess.

Three of the book's chapters maintain a product-focused theme. Donald Getz (Chapter 13) considers the contribution that festivals and events can make to island tourism. This strategy can represent a relatively low-investment and community-responsive approach to enhancing a destination's competitiveness. Getz considers the case of Newfoundland to illustrate the contribution that this dimension of product enhancement can make. Bert Winterbottom in Chapter 16 complements Getz with a discussion of revitalization strategies involving historical and urban places. He amplifies his discussion with the example of the development of Bermuda's historic Dockyard and the role it has played in rejuvenating tourism in the west end of the island. Whereas Getz approaches product enhancement from a cultural standpoint, Winterbottom is concerned with the practical logistics and facilities necessary to support this form of tourism. Taken together, both authors make a compelling argument for employing these strategies in island tourism. Finally, in Chapter 14 Murphy addresses the interplay between urban and island tourism, using Vancouver Island, in Canada, as his case resource.

Competitiveness

We have left competitiveness to the end of this introduction because it is at the core of many of the other issues and concerns. Virtually all the chapters already discussed have either explicit or implicit relevance for the competitiveness of island destinations. The delegates to the Forum reached that conclusion and it translates into their chapters. However, several chapters clearly attempt to focus purely on competitiveness as a strategic consideration.

Briguglio and Vella (Chapter 12) discuss cost and pricing dimensions of competitiveness within the family of Mediterranean islands and consider the problems that Malta faces in this context. Wing's case study on Mauritius (Chapter 18), also has competitiveness as an underlying theme. Mauritius represents an undoubted success story in developing a product and attendant markets which emphasizes quality tourism and high value added within the local economy. A strategy to assist tourism destinations in their pricing strategies, with a key focus on ensuring optimal occupancy on an island-wide basis and thus, competitiveness, is provided by Baum and Mudambi in Chapter 10 and demonstrated through the utilization of Bermudian data. Indeed, as Conlin indicates, the motivation behind Bermuda's recent assessment of tourism was a concern about the island's diminishing competitiveness. Finally, in their discussion of Caribbean human-resource development, Conlin and Titcombe (Chapter 6) make the somewhat radical argument that the level of competitiveness which an island destination strives for is fundamentally tied to its human resources and their ability and desire to produce a level of service quality which the destinations' visitors expect.

Thus, this book contains an eclectic collection of perspectives on some of the main themes that impact upon contemporary international tourism, addressed with specific reference to, arguably, the unique position of the small island destination. As is inevitable with such a collection and, indeed, constituting one of its main attractions, each author has prepared her or his material in an individual and non-standardized manner, resulting in the diversity of this volume.

REFERENCES

Baum, Tom (1994) "The Development and Implementation of National Tourism Policies". *Tourism Management*, **15**(3).

Butler, Richard W. (1993) "Tourism Development in Small Islands". In Douglas G. Lockhart, David Drakakis-Smith and John Schembri (eds), *The Development Process in Small Island States*. Routledge, London.

Caribbean Tourism Organization (1992) *Statistical Report for 1988–92*. Caribbean Tourism Organization, Christ Church, Barbados.

Conlin, Michael and Baum, Tom (1994) "Comprehensive Human Resource Planning: an Essential Key to Sustainable Tourism in Island Settings". In Chris Cooper and Andrew Lockwood (eds), *Progress in Tourism, Recreation and Hospitality Management, Volume 6*. Wiley, Chichester.

De Bliji, H.J. and Muller, Peter O. (1992) *Geography: Regions and Concepts* 7th ed. Wiley, London.

King, Russell (1993) "The Geographical Fascination of Islands". In Douglas G. Lockhart, David Drakakis-Smith and John Schembri (eds), *The Development Process in Small Island States*. Routledge, London.

Lockhart, Douglas G. (1993) "Introduction". In Douglas G. Lockhart, David Drakakis-Smith and John Schembri (eds), *The Development Process in Small Island States*. Routledge, London.

Marshall, Bruce (ed.) (1991) *The Real World*. Boston, Houghton Mifflin.

Stausfield Jr., Charles A. and Zinolzak, Chester E. (1990) *Global Perspectives: A World Regional Geography*. Merrill, New York.

2 Major Markets and Island Tourism: the US Perspective

DAVID L. EDGELL SR
US Department of Commerce, Washington, DC, USA

INTRODUCTION

This chapter will provide a general overview of some of the future challenges, problems and opportunities, alternatives and actions for island tourism. I want neither to overwhelm the reader with peripheral details nor to be overly simplistic.

In my book *International Tourism Policy*, I said that:

> international tourism in the twenty-first century will be a major vehicle for fulfilling people's aspirations for a higher quality of life . . . international tourism also has the potential to be an important stimulus for global improvement in the social, cultural, economic, political and ecological dimensions of future lifestyles. (Edgell, 1990:1)

Working together, we can all be better prepared to integrate the benefits of island tourism cohesively with people and destinations in order to improve our global quality of life and to learn from one another.[1]

The United States' perspective on its island destinations such as the US Virgin Islands, Hawaii, Puerto Rico, Guam, Northern Marianas, and American Samoa is to think quality, act globally and face up to the enormous competition. Recently, at the request of the US Congress, my agency has been working on a Caribbean Basin study aimed towards increasing tourism's contributions to the region's economic growth and development. I believe some of what this study suggests can be applied to many different island destinations around the world.

Islands must be aware of their similarities as well as their differences as they develop their competitive marketing strategies. Many islands share an abundance of natural resources: sandy beaches, warm climates, fresh seafood, fishing, natural harbours and coastal scenery. The industries and commodities that many islands have in common are tourism, boat building, agriculture, fishing, salt, sugar, rum, coffee, banking and real estate. Some of the shared differences include differing languages, religions, cultures, political systems and social and economic development. Aspects such as these, which islands share, are for the most part both positive and obvious, but unfortunately there also are major deficiencies which must be addressed.

Island Tourism: Management Principles and Practice
Edited by Michael V. Conlin and Tom Baum

Supply and quality control of food is a problem for many islands. Other concerns are the frequent hurricanes, earthquakes and tropical storms that often cause floods and physical damage. Frequently there is an insufficient supply of fresh water, poor quality soil, no permanent crops or the proper marketing of the produce, making the import of food necessary. Low rainfall in some areas, deforestation, water pollution and shortage of electric power supplies only add to this list of possible problems and challenges for island tourism.

Other problem areas are deficient maintenance of facilities. For example, many of the islands have hotels that are now 20–30 years old and need to be refurbished to maintain an appropriate level of quality and remain competitive. We should be aware of the obsolescence of the physical plant. When facilities are out of date and not refurbished, visitors will most likely not come back. An island infrastructure and how it effects the quality of the tourism product is linked directly to the economic stability of an island as a tourism destination.

These challenges of island tourism in today's global arena remind me of the words of a turn-of-the-century English poet, Thomas Campbell: "Coming events cast their shadows before". What are some of the shadows that can tell us about tomorrow's world of island tourism? Here are what I consider to be the "nine shadows of the 90s", which will address some of the tourism issues of concern to island destinations, issue areas at the core of international tourism. Learning to grapple with these shadows, to understand them and to recognize their implications and relationships to each other can provide keys to the major island markets and assist in formulating international-oriented island tourism planning and management programmes.

FIRST SHADOW: INTERNATIONAL CO-OPERATION

Various measures are taken by governments to encourage travellers from abroad to visit their respective destinations. Most developed and developing countries conduct their national tourism promotion under the aegis of a government tourism policy covering promotion and marketing infrastructure and training. Often this is in conjunction with associations of private-sector tourism interests, joint public–private consultative bodies and international and intergovernmental organizations.

Most governments in travel-receiving countries seek to stimulate the construction of essential tourist facilities such as hotels, highways and access roads, communications and visitor attractions. Significant efforts are also devoted to conserving areas of natural beauty—lakes, forest, rivers, mountains—and maintaining resort areas and cultural opportunities. Special events, entertainment and cultural activities are often supported by local and regional governments. Other services performed by governments are necessary to support tourism such as police protection and crime control, and maintaining good health and sanitary conditions. For tourism to develop in an orderly fashion and provide the social and economic benefits being sought requires a great deal of co-operation and co-ordination of programmes and policies at the local, regional and international levels. Sharing information, expressing our goals, co-ordinating some of our tourism efforts are all parts of that international co-operation which must take place if we are to grow and survive in the 1990s.

SECOND SHADOW: THE ENORMOUS POTENTIAL SIZE OF INTERNATIONAL TOURISM GROWTH

Islands have great potential for international market attractiveness and growth. Think about the shadow effect island destinations can have and the global opportunities cast on island destinations by the international tourism market. Island destinations are an important part of "global tourism". Consumption of travel and tourism's goods and services was expected to total over $2 trillion in 1993 and to employ over 126 million workers, according to the World Travel and Tourism Council. Island destinations, whether large or small, represent a major potential in the growth of tourism. It is projected by the year 2000 the tourism industry will grow to more than $3 trillion. Island tourism is of critical importance as an export product in both industrialized and less-developed island destinations. But the extent to which tourism contributes to an island's foreign-exchange earnings varies considerably. For example, in most of the Caribbean nations, trade in tourism is essential. In countries like the Dominican Republic, Jamaica and the Bahamas, tourism accounts for almost 70% of foreign-exchange earnings. In order for the enormous potential of international tourism to become a reality for an island destination, a greater public policy awareness of tourism as an integral force in the world economy is necessary. The stakes are clear but complex for properly marketing and promoting internationally renowned island destinations.[2] Perhaps a regional approach or some unique change could be considered when developing the international market.

THIRD SHADOW: THE SHADOW OF CHANGE

There are dynamic changes already taking place in the world today, which will be even more dramatic tomorrow, which will have an impact on the way the travel and tourism business will be conducted between now and the year 2000.

Those of us who have been involved with tourism have long accepted the fact that our industry is constantly changing. As buyers, suppliers, policy makers, managers and consumers, we know that this year's favourite island may suddenly be hit by a hurricane or that the rumble of an earthquake may send visitors to new destinations. Lack of access to one popular destination may simply shift travel to a nearby area, or it may dramatically redistribute tourism flows to entirely different island regions of the world.

In the words of the popular lecturer Tom Peters, author of the books *In Search of Excellence* and *Thriving on Chaos*, we in the tourism industry must learn to meet uncertainty by emphasizing a set of new basics. These include: ". . . world-class quality and service, enhanced responsiveness [to tourism consumers] through greatly increased flexibility, and continuous, short-cycle innovation and improvement aimed at creating new markets for both new and apparently mature products and services". In other words, we must learn to "cherish impermanence".

What is at work here is tourism's increasing interdependence with global affairs in every way you can think of—geographically, politically, economically, socially and culturally. Change is a necessary response to this increasing world-wide interdependence, and perhaps no industry in the world today is better adapted than tourism to weather the vicissitudes as well as to reap the benefits of change.

In this light, those industry sectors best prepared for and open to the total experience of contemporary tourism can seize upon change as an opportunity. The hotel industry, for example, is only one part of the infrastructure. The best marketing programme possible is to have a total quality tourism product which triggers repeat visits. This will be a measure of success in today's competitive island-tourism market. This will require what I call the six C's: commitment, co-operation, communication, contribution, and co-ordination—all of which can be summarized in the word "challenge".

FOURTH SHADOW: CHALLENGING THE COMPETITION

This is where the challenge of each island being unique comes in. Setting your island destination apart from the others, where and how you market are vital in this competitive industry.

International competition for tourism consumers and their revenues will heighten, something which the increasing numbers and sophistication of travellers will only intensify. World-wide population growth and increases in income and income distribution will make it possible for even more people of the world to travel. Changes in work habits and patterns of working conditions may yield greater leisure time for greater numbers of people to participate in tourism and recreation. As people become better educated and have greater exposure to other societies and cultures, they will want to visit the places about which they have read or heard.

In the 1990s, not only are there pressures from intensifying competition and a more demanding customer, there also is a protracted world-wide economic recession. This will cause those industry sectors which are not fully market-oriented and which are inefficient to suffer. Times are tight, and there will be winners and losers.

Demand for discretionary tourism, according to the World Tourism Organization, is likely to be most directly influenced during the 1990s by the fact that travel is rising in popularity and, as a consequence, greater attention is being paid to the human dimension of travel. Trends include expected growth in the proportion of holiday taking, especially to foreign destinations and growth in multiple, short-break holiday taking. These trends will lead to increased demand for new, more imaginative and innovative tourism products and services. Success also will depend on more extensive, aggressive and precisely targeted marketing of these services. Market segmentation of tourism consumers will become an essential marketing tool. As a consequence, marketing and promotional budgets will increase and a higher premium will be placed on professional tourism marketing expertise. In confronting this challenge of competition, island destinations must continuously incorporate change into management and operations strategy. For example, the increasing numbers of women business (40%) and pleasure travellers and greater travel by the growing numbers of mature travellers will require advance planning by the hotel sector to anticipate and accommodate their specialized needs. Additionally, as the opportunity for travel extends to both the leisure and business markets, island destinations will need to be able to address the sometimes unexpected assumptions of many first-time vacationers while meeting the sophisticated expectations—"high-tech" services, executive suites, telecommunications, small meeting facilities—of the increasingly more knowledgeable and demanding frequent-business-traveller group.

One specific area of new flexibility may be room rates. International travellers arriving late at night or leaving in the late afternoon may expect room-rate adjustments for late arrivals and departures and will be inclined to return to those hotels accommodating these new expectations. Knowing the type of services your customers want and providing them at a price they are willing to pay is essential.

Competition in the island-tourism industry will be especially high in the 1990s. Certain marketing and business objectives stand out as seminal in such an environment. Let me mention just a few: participatory executive leadership, total quality management, thorough information gathering, strategic planning and execution and a trained work force that is empowered to move heaven and earth, if need be, to satisfy customers. At the base of this quality management approach are committed employees. In fact, much of the responsibility of meeting high-quality guest services and customer-satisfaction goals rests with the employees. In other words, the aim of these and other customer-focused measures is not simply to meet the expectations of guests but also to provide them with a memorable visit that, if possible, fulfils even their unexpressed needs and wishes.

FIFTH SHADOW: COMMUNICATION AND TRANSPORTATION TECHNOLOGIES

Communication and transportation technologies will continue to revolutionize our knowledge base and ability and desire to travel. Advances in aeronautical engineering and aircraft technology, ground transportation systems, airline computer reservation systems, and electronic database systems will continue throughout the 1990s. Island destinations will remain dependent on international air travel. These developments, plus the development of new, aerospace airplanes, will make travel faster, more direct (on high-volume routes) and less expensive (in real terms).

The means for gathering information and making reservations for travel will be facilitated by airline and hotel computer reservation systems and other electronic databases to the point where privacy of information may become a central issue of the future in tourism. The question of who pays for updating computer databases for national tourism industries, as well as how these services and facilities are selected and distributed to include unbiased displays and objective data bases that are widely available, are among the concerns. Added to these will be ownership and control of technologies for electronically expedited inspection services, communication satellites which will improve the quality and reduce the cost of international telephone and teleconferencing services, and machine-readable visas and passports.

SIXTH SHADOW: HEALTH, SECURITY AND SAFETY

As island tourism increases, so travel security becomes more important and complex. It is clear that while all travel involves some risk, there are many ways in which the travel sector can help minimize the level of exposure of travellers to danger. Much is being done already, but more information dissemination and safeguarding actions are necessary. Above all, it is essential for governments and travel operators to work in unison on all travel security matters.

At the local level, the success of health and safety measures for a particular destination is often directly related by the customer to satisfaction with a specific accommodation. The increasing experience level and sophistication of international travellers as a consumer group may raise the level of expectations for hotel health, security and safety standards. The international hotel chain visibly incorporating these measures into its marketing and sales literature may be able to distinguish itself in the crowded international hotel market.

The matter of health, safety and security is an employee-wide responsibility. The positive image and utility of health, security and safety can be another important marketing tool.

SEVENTH SHADOW: HUMAN RESOURCES AND TRAINING

Training, education and general awareness will be in great demand to insure that workers understand the relationship between quality of service and an island's ability to compete successfully. Unfortunately the capacity of education in institutions has been inadequate in most countries to train staff at all levels and for the wide range of skills required for the travel and tourism industry.

The tourism industry has always been at the heart of the services sector. The development of human resources, of education and training, could emerge as the single-most important issue facing island tourism into the next century. Perhaps a co-operative partnership such as an island-destination training seminar could be proposed. Tourism industry leaders in the United States are seeking more ways and means to get policy makers and political leaders to understand tourism better. The publication *World Tourism at the Millennium* (Edgell, 1993) is one such effort.

EIGHTH SHADOW: DIVERSITY

Tourism's well-spring in the face of increasing interdependence and change is its strong recognition and promotion of diversity. By diversity, I mean, first, the diversity of the US islands as a top individual regional and world-wide destination which includes the expansive beauty and fragile intimacy and uniqueness of each island as for example Hawaii, within the US.

Additionally, with concern for the environment on a dramatic upswing, island destinations are in a position to capitalize on tourism's ability both to preserve and maximize diversity, from ecological to cultural.

For example, according to the Hawaii Visitor Bureau, 92% of US mainland visitors surveyed in 1991 rated their vacation to Hawaii as "excellent", the highest level in seven years. Ninety-eight per cent of mainland visitors said they would recommend Hawaii as a vacation destination to friends and relatives with 84% saying they were likely to return themselves within five years. Highest ratings of "excellent" or "above average" were given to scenery and weather, followed by water sports, golf, cleanliness, beaches, hospitality, activity variety and sightseeing.

It seems to me that there is a clear message here, and that is that there is the opportunity and responsibility to formulate policies and plans articulating a base of human resource development that provides for tourism development in an environmentally sound, sustainable manner. This involves working to preserve the diversity of an island as an important international destination as part of the larger core of diversity comprising global tourism . . . and this leads me to my ninth and final shadow.

NINTH SHADOW: INTERDEPENDENCE AND THE ENVIRONMENT

Tourism has a growing interdependence with global affairs. This shadow is complex and integrative and pulls many of the shadows and vectors of contemporary international tourism I have discussed together as a web.

I believe that if we can understand tourism's interdependent nature, we can both anticipate and become better managers of the rapid changes taking place within and outside of the tourism industry. As a result of this knowledge, we can better capitalize on island tourism's unique resilience and dynamism which can lead in the direction of new tourism products such as cultural and ecotourism.

We all know only too well the grave afflictions which can strike the tourist industry suddenly, with global significance, such as terrorism, crime, war and natural disasters. But there are other forces at work which move more slowly. For example, in the dynamics of transportation: we must remember that, in half a century, steamships gave way to airplanes as the essential travel mode over all the world's oceans, including the cruiseship resurgence of the eighties. Additionally, over the last decade alone, the integration of telecommunications technologies into tourism, too, has accelerated the pace and power of tourism-related capital and information across national boundaries.

Also, now, slowly, in similar dynamics of interdependence, the old-fashioned objectives of sandy beaches and scenic mountains are being modified by the inexorable threat to our natural environment and its scarce and diminishing resources. Island tourism is no longer just sunning and swimming and shopping for souvenirs. A new intellectual and complex component of interdependence has been added to the mix of island tourism: that the sky and the sea and soil are important; that rain forests and grasses are important; that fishing and whales are important, fresh water and volcanoes are important.

Above all, we also must not forget the core component of tourism—that people are important, that the residents of each island and ethic groups are important. And that if we disdain these concerns for the human dimension, for multiculturalism, and its relationship to the environment for only a few more decades, nothing that remains will be of any importance. But this does not have to be the outcome. We do have choice over our actions.

CONCLUSION

In summary, recognizing that we need to set priorities for developing quality island tourism, let me just paraphrase again from Tom Peters. He would tell us that to survive in the nineties we must provide top-quality tourism products, provide superior service, achieve extraordinary responsiveness to the consumer, be an internationalist, create uniqueness, become obsessed with listening (to the consumer), make sales and service forces into heroes, pursue fast-paced innovation and launch into a customer revolution. In brief, tourists have come to expect more from every country, business, organization and person employed in the tourism industry with respect to quality, accuracy, variety, convenience, value and professionalism. If we can meet these needs, we will be prepared for the tourism challenges of the nineties.

NOTES

1 For a more complete explanation of this concept, see Edgell (1990).

2 For a more detailed description of how to market a hotel internationally, see David L. Edgell Sr and James C. Makens (1990) "Internationalizing Your Hotel's Welcome Mat". *The Cornell H.R.A. Quarterly*, November, 64–70.

REFERENCES

Edgell, D.L. (1990) *International Tourism Policy*. Van Nostrand Reinhold, New York.

Edgell, D.L. (1993) *World Tourism at the Millenium—An Agenda for Industry, Government and Education*. US Department of Commerce.

3 Alternative Tourism and Sustainability

KLAUS DE ALBUQUERQUE
College of Charleston, South Carolina, USA
AND
JEROME L. McELROY
Saint Mary's College, Notre Dame, Indiana, USA

INTRODUCTION

The search is on in small-island destinations and elsewhere for softer, slower-paced, more durable nature- and culture-intensive tourism styles. This interest is fuelled by three primary factors: (1) growing disenchantment with the cumulative crowding, cultural disruption and ecosystem degradation associated with conventional mass tourism (Smith and Eadington, 1992); (2) the world-wide environmentalists' call for sustainable development, particularly in LDCs (de Kadt, 1992); and (3) an increasing demand among select vacationers for pristine natural and cultural experiences (Johnson, 1990).

There are other less obvious rationales for less-intrusive, lower-density tourism. Because of its vast scale and powerful drive (Lanfant and Graburn, 1992), international tourism exhibits an almost inevitable dynamic to overrun a destination's asset base (Butler, 1992). Visitor impacts on fragile assets are notoriously uncertain because of "spatial and temporal discontinuities between cause and effect" (Pigram, 1992: 78). Relatively large benefits accrue quickly while costs become visible only after long-run thresholds have been crossed. Particularly in small insular ecosystems, large-scale resorts cause irreversible outcomes, i.e. lost future options and—because of their transformational effects on habitats and endemic species—destroy both "existence values" for present generations and "bequest values" and biodiversity for future generations (Pigram, 1992). Finally, concern about global warming and sea-level rise suggests caution for long-term coastal development in general and island resort planning in particular (Connell, 1992).

In response, a host of so-called "new tourism" styles are being discussed and promoted under the generic label of "alternative tourism". Such tourism strategies especially appropriate for socially and environmentally fragile areas are variously called "responsible" (Johnson, 1990), "green" (Jones, 1987), "controlled" (Weaver,

Island Tourism: Management Principles and Practice
Edited by Michael V. Conlin and Tom Baum

1991), "nature" (Whelan, 1991), "soft" (Mader, 1988), "defensive" (Krippendorf, 1982), "sustainable" (de Albuquerque and McElroy, 1992), as well as "ecotourism" (Boo, 1990). These alternative approaches share certain commonalities that, in theory, distinguish them from conventional mass tourism: (1) an obvious focus on natural and cultural experiences in combination with specialized marketing; (2) small-scale facilities/infrastructure that strive to respect the native genius and heritage of the place; (3) attempts at positive host–guest interaction and mutual understanding; (4) an emphasis on local control and equitable dispersion of benefits; and (5), in the case of ecotourism, enhanced environmental quality, community cohesion and cultural revitalization (Johnson, 1990; Farrell and Runyan, 1991).

The fundamental allure and assumption behind alternative tourism is that it will overcome the distortions associated with high-density mass tourism: hectic pace, overcrowding, habitat destruction, landscape and coastline alteration, pollution, cultural debasement, inflation, inequitable and dependent development and so on (Smith and Eadington, 1992). Just as the academic literature of the past two decades has criticized the practice of mass tourism as economically beneficial but socially and environmentally harmful (Weaver, 1991), many recent proponents argue alternative tourism produces just the opposite with seemingly scant damage to the economy (see Butler, 1992 for a summary of these arguments). According to Pigram (1992: 87): "Alternative tourism is rapidly attaining the status of 'motherhood' as a desirable objective for tourist zones, although actual examples of the practical expression of the policy are not commonplace . . ."

SCOPE

This chapter attempts to examine these "alternative" claims by reviewing a growing but fragmented recent literature that is uneven in quality (Pearce, 1992). Such an assessment, even if preliminary and partial, is warranted especially if the wholesale adoption of alternative strategies may endanger the precious cultural and natural assets that remain the base of viability and competitiveness for insular destinations in the global tourist economy of the future. Such caution is particularly appropriate in light of the central conclusion of this overview, namely that alternative tourism's promises for sustainability are overly optimistic.

TOURISTS AND TOURISM

There are a variety of tourists and tourisms. Historically it has always been so (Smith and Eadington, 1992). Likewise, definitions of tourist forms have changed over time with technological shifts in transport, rising affluence and the emergence of global culture. What is now considered conventional mass tourism—the international tropical vacation—was alternative tourism in the 19th century. Some forms considered alternative today were mainstream in a bygone era. Such evolutions pose obvious challenges for sustainability and at least hint at the possibility that the conventional tourism of the 21st century may differ substantially from contemporary styles.

Such terminological amorphousness further suggests the need for more carefully distinguishing between alternative tourism that is truly "deliberate" as a result of conscious policies and that which is "circumstantial". The former would include, for example, planned village-based experiences or the establishment of low-density wildlife reserves. This contrasts with the merely "circumstantial", a type of indigenous, small-scale tourism characteristic of the incipient stage of the destination life cycle that may be eventually followed by large-scale, high-density, foreign-controlled development. According to Weaver (1991: 417), such tourism "is not deliberately cultivated as an alternative to conventional mass tourism but exists as its prelude".

Weaver illustrates this sometimes difficult distinction to draw (except with considerable hindsight) with the so-called "deliberate" case of Dominica. This Caribbean island is precluded from mass appeal because of limited transport infrastructure, black sand beaches and a rainy climate. This contrasts with the potentially "circumstantial" case of Belize—known for its small-scale but world-class diving and its wildlife sanctuaries—but possibly poised for major hotel expansion as its international visibility increases. In addition, this points up the difficulty of broadly characterizing any given destination as either alternative or conventional since each area can encompass a variety of assets, styles and visitors who participate in both mainstream (sand, sea, sun and sports) and other more adventurous and less accessible experiences.

Another complication involves the catch-all nature of alternative tourism. While sometimes useful in very generic discourse, the term's diffusiveness evades empirical testing. It may even be misleading if, as the evidence suggests below, most alternative types may inevitably create many of the same problems of mainstream mass tourism with significantly reduced or skewed economic benefits. Instead, it is preferable and more informative to assess specific forms of alternative tourism and remain faithful to the varieties of touristic experiences associated with postwar modernization (Nash, 1992). This approach also avoids the use of subjective purist terms like "responsible tourism". (Perhaps the most responsible form of tourism would be to stay home and send money instead to preserve a nature reserve, a monument, a culture, a rain forest.) It further avoids the risk of elitist, imperialist discourse that would unwittingly seek to redefine other environments, human societies and historical remains—mostly in poor countries that might prefer the economic promises of conventional tourism—as part of a new "global patrimony" of the privileged (Daltabuit and Pi-Sunyer, 1990).

To clarify various non-conventional tourisms for the discussion to follow, we have borrowed a relatively conventional typology with the three basic classifications of nature, cultural and adventure tourism, although there is certainly some overlap. Nature tourism is further divided into "hard" forms—academic and scientific types where research and student field experience are primary—and "soft" forms, i.e. rain forest visits, bird watching, wildlife viewing and certain types of low-key fishing and marine activities. Cultural tourism includes at least five distinct sub-types: (1) archaeological digs and site visits; (2) heritage, i.e. visits to monuments, sites, etc.; (3) sex tourism which in some areas (Bangkok, Manila) also retains a "mass" element; (4) anthropotourism/ethnic tourism involving village stays, ceremonials, etc.; and (5) religious tourism which also involves a "mass" quality in certain world-renowned sites such as Lourdes and Mecca. Finally, adventure tourism includes various athletic types of nature experiences like hiking, trekking, rafting, climbing, hunting, caving and so on.

IMPACTS

Are these various alternative forms of tourism sustainable? A partial review of the most recent literature readily available concerning alternative experiences from around the world suggests things seem to be going awry.

Nature tourism

Regarding "hard" forms, examples such as the tropical research installations in the Costa Rican rain forests (La Selva and Monteverde) and along the north coast of Jamaica (Discovery Bay), indicate that "science tourism" tends to foster a pattern of creeping commercialization and environmental stress. Though scientists retain their conservation ethic, they invariably become tourists and regular repeat visitors exploring cultures and engaging in various adventures. In addition, they attract a relatively substantial inflow of other visitors who are less ecologically sensitive (Learman and Perdue, 1989).

Compounding the impact, pressures to maintain research sites and programmes, as well as the general search for "eco-dollars" to support conservation efforts, often result in opening up these delicate areas and scientific expeditions to amateurs and lay persons to assist in the work and even to "cocoon tourists" with associated problems of control. In Antarctica, for example, where most pollution still stems from the continent's 57 scientific research stations (Warner, 1991), Chile has opened up a hotel, the so-called "Antarctica Riviera", and resident scientists are often appalled by careless visitors (Farrell and Runyan, 1991). Clearly tapping the tourism potential of these places to provide dollars for conservation and science is a difficult dilemma to resolve (Hill, 1990), and despite imaginative initiatives (debt-for-nature swaps), and the well-intentioned donation of some of the proceeds from ecotourism ventures to help sponsor conservation, reforestation, trail clean-up, etc., the economic potential of science tourism is relatively limited.

The popularity of "soft" nature tourism is fuelled by the environmental movement, rising affluence and hundreds of tour companies and conservation organizations specializing in every conceivable kind of nature experience. These tours involve mostly sophisticated urban, ecologically aware, professionals seeking new natural and cultural experiences as a spur to their naive activism (recycling, save the forests/whales). However, because of their rapidly expanding numbers in some heretofore sheltered areas, their presence is disturbing habitats, spawning pollution, disrupting bird-nesting sites and turtle-hatching grounds, interfering in animal breeding and foraging patterns and so on.

In Rwanda's Parc National des Vulcans made famous by Diane Fossey's *Gorillas in the Mist*, increasing numbers of visitors, despite strict controls and high fees ($170 a day) (Warner 1991), have disrupted gorilla breeding patterns, increased miscarriages and fostered more aggressive behaviour. In Malaysia, out-of-control tourists frequently produce a circus-like atmosphere while witnessing the egg-laying of giant leatherback turtles, "with children riding on their backs, kicking sand over the creatures, pulling at their flippers" (Elegant, 1991: 18). Such intrusion is partially responsible for the drastic decline in turtle beach arrivals since the mid-1980s.

In Kenya, "the world's foremost ecotourist attraction" (Whelan, 1991: 23), seasonal tourist pressure is altering the natural ecosystems of some game parks (Dieke, 1991). Sometimes 50 vans/safari buses crowd around a single pride of lions. Parks are riddled with vehicle tracks and choked with exhaust fumes as vehicles plough across savannahs with abandon. Among other results, cheetahs are migrating away as their foraging grounds are irrevocably damaged. In 1989, Amboseli Park in Kenya, one of the largest wildlife preserves in the country, saw its cheetah population drop from 15 to five (Winokur, 1990).

Marine parks particularly suffering from heavy traffic in the Caribbean are also experiencing cumulative degradation despite stringent controls, trained guides and reef etiquette postings. The Virgin Islands National Park in St. John continues to undergo mounting damage to coral from divers and snorkellers. The water quality of Francis Bay has been "virtually destroyed" by careless anchor dragging (Allen, 1992). The story is the same for Cayman Island reefs where an estimated 2100 square metres of coral have been pulverized by boat moorings and other tourism-related activities. In the Holchan Marine Reserve in Belize, black-band disease, a killer algae which attacks damaged corals, has begun appearing (Cates, 1992). World-famous Bucoo Reef in Tobago had to be temporarily closed to divers to allow time for recovery, usually a slow process that in severe cases can take half a century. The long-run problem is that there are so few accessible near-pristine resources that they inevitably succumb over time to unsustainable demand levels. Even Jean-Michel Cousteau acknowledges the role he and his father have played in bringing about the deterioration of some marine ecosystems. He relates seeing tourists on barges and glass-bottom boats in Australia tossing junk food like cheese puffs to grossly overweight fish (Cousteau, 1990).

Cultural tourism

In the case of *archaeotourism*, evidence suggests that the increasing number of groups and organized digs are leaving perverse footprints. It is difficult for scientists to monitor paying guests in the same way they control student assistants and employees. As a result, some sites are being disturbed and overrun by amateurs. In addition, many former hidden sites are being made accessible. The example of Coba in Quintana Roo, Mexico is instructive. It is proximate to the remains of a major classic Maya metropolis dominated by Nohoch Mul, the tallest pyramid (42 metres) in Yucatan. Presently, the area is suffering from visitor spillover from Cancun, mounting garbage and sewage pollution and sanitation problems. Without trained local personnel to prevent indiscriminate visitors trampling over ruins, the prognosis for sustainability is not favourable in an area that has grown from fewer than 500 villagers to over 50 000 inhabitants in two decades.

According to Daltabuit and Pi-Sunyer (1990), the same fate may befall the much-touted *La Ruta Maya* (the Mayan Route) planned to wind some 1500 miles through five Central American countries. It would provide visitor access and exploration of heretofore inaccessible pyramids and rain forests through a series of parks and reserves and low-impact (footpaths, boats, mules) transport systems that would encompass much of the known Mayan civilization (Warner, 1991). Similar concerns of despoliation are being expressed about the opening up of Angkor Wat in Cambodia now that the political situation has improved.

In case of *heritage* travel, many of the world's great monuments have been devastated by tourism as well as by industrial pollution and general urban development. Egyptian monuments are not only suffering from a rise in the water table since the construction of the Aswan but also from the physical effects of thousands of visitors. As Hochfield notes (1991: 119):

> Too many tourists have climbed up the pyramids and crowded into the tiny rooms of the ancient tombs. The press of half a dozen people in a small underground room is enough to raise the humidity by five or six degrees. Eventually salt crystals flower on the damp walls and dislodge the paint.

Other examples abound. The Lascaux caves in France now restrict visitors to five per day. To avoid damage, tourists to Stonehenge in England must now keep to a path that rings the site. Many monument-rich sites are being buried by accumulating mass visitation. In a typical holiday weekend some 80 000 tourists descend upon Venice. As a partial consequence of these pervasive impacts, the World Heritage Committee under UNESCO supervision has had to call a moratorium on its campaign to save endangered sites because the tourism-related deterioration is so extensive that the funding earmarked for this campaign is totally inadequate.

Assessing the impacts of *anthropotourism/ethnic tourism* is especially difficult given the range and intensity of human interaction and the subjective conditioning role that host–guest reactions play. Analysis is further complicated by the inherent conflict between commercial interests to preserve native culture and the subjects themselves who have undergone significant change through outside contact. The situation is additionally compounded by the age-old conundrum between real and staged ceremonial authenticity (Cohen, 1989).

What is clear is that tourism can revive forgotten traditions and arts (Johnson, 1990). It is also clear that there have been early documented examples of successful village-based enterprises that have achieved the triad of economic profitability, social compatibility and environmental stability. Examples include Senegal's Lower Casamance region (Saglio, 1979) and the Tufi guest houses in Papua New Guinea (Ranck, 1987). What is not well known is the durability of these cultural tourisms over time.

To illustrate, in Tufi as early as 1985 when individuals began to claim ownership of communal guest houses, there was bickering over responsibilities toward guests, things had fallen into disrepair, advertised services were not being offered and visitors were being fed Western rather then traditional foods. In hill-tribe trekking in Thailand, Cohen (1989) notes the inevitable decline over time in host–guest spontaneity and an increasing tendency towards reduced authenticity. In other places modest modern standards of comfort and hospitality are deteriorating. According to Adams (1990), in Tana Toraja, Indonesia locals and their shrines and rituals are treated as objects by tourists, and their ancestral homes and religious landmarks are cavalierly disrespected and/or expropriated by government decision makers. Internecine conflicts have forced temporary closure of certain villages to outsiders.

Adventure tourism

Trekking and mountain hiking is the most popular form of international adventure tourism. The example of Alpine ecosystems provides an instructive background. Years of development, complex roadways and overuse have produced the most altered mountain system in the world (Denniston, 1992). As a result, over half the endemic species are threatened in the more heavily trafficked northern and western European regions. Most primary forest is lost and what remains is being destroyed by atmospheric pollution sourced in industrial activity as well as intense vehicular traffic. Large-scale damming has upset the hydrological balance and climate in some places, and erosion, mudslides, avalanches and floods are on the rise.

In Third-World trekking, the outcome is similar. In both moist rain forests and dry desert elevations, the more popular the destination/expedition and the more sustained the activity through time, the greater the degree of visible degradation. The trekking boom in Nepal has induced a host of unforeseen impacts. The Annapurna Himalayan region, destination of over 250 000 annual visitors, has suffered deforestation to provide cooking fuel and warm bathing water for tourists, water scarcity, trampled vegetative cover, persistent litter and the loss and defacement of monuments (Karaw and Mather, 1985; Lueck, 1991). Since 1970 the demand for wood to heat mountain lodges there has "lowered the tree line by several hundred feet" (Warner, 1991: 42). According to Sill (1991), economic benefits have been severely vitiated by local inflation in basic commodities, high import leakages (over 60%) from visitor spending, and the disruption of traditional social cohesion by new occupational and income shifts. In other Nepalese locales, high-handed government park set-asides have caused resentment, encroachment and poaching by displaced groups.

Similar impacts are commonplace in other favoured adventure destinations. The high-altitude Indian desert of Ladakh, where visitors tour a preindustrial Buddhist culture and enjoy mountain vistas, has experienced rising levels of inflation, shortages of basic commodities, water contamination and disease, economic inequality and heretofore unheard of theft and begging among native youth (Goering, 1990). Northern Thailand, where there has been a sustained trekking boom for over a decade, has also suffered trail erosion, soil compaction, litter, increased deforestation and human waste disposal problems (Dearden, 1991). Even in low-land and formerly inaccessible beach areas, the impact of rising tourism densities has produced nearly identical environmental despoliation and cultural pollution as Smith (1992) notes has occurred in the offshore Philippine island of Boracay. Such evidence world-wide suggests that the search for the exotic and the pristine is ultimately self-defeating. As partial confirmation of the overgrowth propensity of tourism, apparently some of the least damaged and most unspoiled areas are likewise the least visited because of inadequate infrastructure and poor promotion (Chapin, 1990) or some other kind of unplanned protection.

CONCLUSIONS

Despite its broadbrush and cursory nature, this chapter suggests some scepticism about alternative tourism's claims for sustainability. Put simply, "successful" destinations, assets, and expeditions spawn rising visitor densities, cumulative deterioration and socio-cultural change. This creeping commercialization tends to infest even the most delicate and remote assets/experiences and is partly fed by international tour and travel interests, fostered by local governments, villagers, guides and suppliers and, often unwittingly, championed by global conservation groups and their world-wide clientele.

The "alternative" lessons suggest that what was once the authentic and unique adventure of the sophisticated and intrepid traveller becomes eventually the more staged, familiar prosaic pastime of the less affluent and less daring vacationer, i.e. the "tourist" by name. Since there are literally hundreds of tour organizations promoting this form of "travel", it has become really quite indistinguishable in form and experience from conventional tourism.

Many forms of alternative tourism create the self-same set of problems as conventional tourism and often at a faster pace with more irreversible consequences because the assets are more fragile and lack protective infrastructure and the technical controls that accompany large-scale more complex developments. Clearly in some cases the cure may become worse than the disease (Butler, 1992).

There are scattered examples of successful and potentially sustainable alternative tourism forms; however, alternative tourism should not be uncritically accepted as a panacea for all the ills of Third-World tourism. The associated cultural and ecological intrusions and often minor and mal-distributed economic benefits provide no positive sustainable alternative to mass tourism. In fact, a mix of alternative and conventional forms seems the most realistic alternative, with the more popular and accessible assets "sacrificed" to provide revenues to support historical preservation, park systems and so on and thus provide economic participation for locals in more remote areas. The key, in so far as possible, is that the two types remain somewhat exclusive, a difficult balance that Kenyan, Costa Rican, and Yucatan examples illustrate. Determining this mix and maintaining this balance is even more critical in small island states that are heavily tourism dependent, since, as our earlier research has shown (de Albuquerque and McElroy, 1992), these island states appear to be the most vulnerable to the overgrowth propensities of international tourism.

Additionally, all the well-known bromides that have been touted for years, and that curiously enough make for successful theme park tourism, must be seriously considered and meticulously implemented: stringent controls on visitor numbers and behaviour, continuous funding for upkeep, long-term local participation in site planning, frequent professional monitoring and enforcement and so on. But most importantly, local residents, guides, tour organizations, policy makers, etc. must identify together and early on a consensus vision of the shape of the asset/expedition over the next generation that will simultaneously achieve their agreed-on economic, cultural and environmental goals. Without this vision, the untrammelled market will continue to erode our natural and cultural patrimony across the globe and jeopardize the economic livelihoods of future low-income generations.

REFERENCES

Adams, K. (1990) "Cultural Commoditization in Tana, Toroja, Indonesia". *Cultural Survival Quarterly*, **14**(1), 31–34.

Allen, W. (1992) "Increased Danger to Caribbean Marine Ecosystems". *Bioscience*, **42**(5), 330–335.

Boo, E. (1990) *Ecotourism: the potentials and pitfalls. Vols 1 and 2.* World Wildlife Fund, Washington, DC.

Butler, R. (1992) "Alternative Tourism: the Thin Edge of the Wedge". In V. Smith and W. Eadington (eds), *Tourism Alternatives*, 31–46.

Cates, E. (1992) "Profits from paradise". *Geographical Magazine*, March.

Chapin, M. (1990) "The Silent Jungle: Ecotourism among the Kuna Indians of Panama". *Cultural Survival Quarterly,* **14**(1), 42–45.

Cohen, E. (1989) "Primitive and Remote: Hill Tribe Trekking in Thailand". *Annals of Tourism Research,* **16**(1), 30–60.

Connell, J. (1992) "The Problems of Stoll States: Meeting the Threat of Global Warming". *Insula*, **1**(1) 19–25.

Cousteau, Jean-Michel (1990) "The World of Jean-Michel Cousteau". *Visavis (The Magazine of United Airlines),* **4**(7), 50.

Daltabuit, M. and Pi-Sunyer, O. (1990) "Tourism Development in Quintana Roo, Mexico". *Cultural Survival Quarterly*, **14**(1), 9 13.

de Albuquerque, K. and McElroy, J. (1992) "Caribbean Small-island Tourism Styles and Sustainable Strategies. *Environmental Management,* **16**(5), 619–632.

Dearden, P. (1991) "Tourism and Sustainable Development in Northern Thailand". *The Geographical Review,* **81**(4), 400–413.

de Kadt, E. (1992) "Making the Alternative Sustainable: Lessons from Development of Tourism". In V. Smith and W. Eadington (eds), *Tourism Alternatives*, 47–75.

Denniston, D. (1992) "Alpine Slide". *World Watch,* 5(5), 36–38.

Dieke, P. (1991) "Policies for Tourism Development in Kenya". *Annals of Tourism Research,* **18**, 269–284.

Elegant, S. (1991) "The Plight of Malaysia's Leatherback". *New York Times*, 19 May, 16–18.

Farrell, B. and Runyan, D. (1991) "Ecology and Tourism". *Annals of Tourism Research,* **18**, 26–40.

Goering, P. (1990) "The Response to Tourism in Ladakh". *Cultural Survival Quarterly,* **14**(1), 20–25.

Hill, C. (1990) "The Paradox of Tourism in Costa Rica". *Cultural Survival Quarterly,* **14**(1), 14–19.

Hochfield, S. (1991) "Mortal Monuments". *ARTnews,* **90**,(6) 114–128.

Johnson, B. (1990) "Introduction: Breaking Out of the Tourist Trap". *Cultural Survival Quarterly,* **14**(1), 2–5.

Jones, A. (1987) "Green Tourism". *Tourism Management,* **26**, 354–356.

Karaw, P. and Mather, C. (1985) "Tourism and Environment in the Mount Everest Region". *The Geographical Review,* **75**(1), 93–95.

Krippendorf, J. (1982) "Towards New Tourism Policies". *Tourism Management,* **3**, 135–151.

Lanfant, M.F. and Graburn, N. (1992) "International Tourism Reconsidered: the Principle of the Alternative". In V. Smith and W. Eadington (eds), *Tourism Alternatives*, 88–112.

Learman, J. and Perdue, R. (1989) "Science Tourism in Costa Rica". *Annals of Tourism Research,* **16**(1), 205–214.

Lueck, T. (1991) "The Annapurna Experiment". *New York Times.*

Mader, V. (1988) "Tourism and Environment". *Annals of Tourism Research,* 5(2), 274–276.

Nash, D. (1992) "Epilogue: a Research Agenda on the Variability of Tourism". In V. Smith and W. Eadington (eds), *Tourism Alternatives*, 216–225.

Pearce, D. (1992) "Alternative Tourism: Concepts, Classifications, and Questions". In V. Smith and W. Eadington (eds), *Tourism Alternatives*, 15–30.

Pigram, J. (1992) "Alternative Tourism: Tourism and Sustainable Resource Management". In V. Smith and W. Eadington (eds), *Tourism Alternatives*, 76–87.

Ranck, S. (1987) "An Attempt at Autonomous Development: the Case of the Tufi Guest Houses, Papua New Guinea". In S. Britton and W.C. Clarke (eds), *Ambiguous Alternative: Tourism in Small Developing Countries*. University of the South Pacific, Suva, Fiji, 154–166.

Saglio, C. (1979) "Tourism for Discovery: a Project in Lower Casamance, Senegal". In E. deKadt (ed.), *Tourism: Passport to Development?* Oxford, Oxford University Press, 321–335.

Sill, M. (1991) "On the Development Trail". *Geographical Magazine,* **63**(9), 4–7.

Smith, V. (1992) "Boracay, Philippines: a Case Study in 'Alternative' Tourism". In V. Smith and W. Eadington (eds), *Tourism Alternatives*, 133–157.

Smith, V. and W.R. Eadington (eds) (1992) *Tourism Alternatives: Potentials and Problems in the Development of Tourism*. Philadelphia, University of Pennsylvania Press, 253.

Warner, E. (1991) "Ecotourism: New Hope for Rainforests?". *American Forests,* **97** (March/April), 37–44.

Weaver, D. (1991) "Alternatives to Mass Tourism in Dominica". *Annals of Tourism Research,* **18**, 414–432.

Whelan, T. (ed.) (1991) *Nature Tourism: Managing for the Environment*. Washington, DC, Island Press, 223.

Winokur, Julie (1990) "Access and Conservation: the Paradox of Ecotourism". *San Francisco Chronicle*, 18 March, Section T, 5.

4 Trends in Cultural Heritage Tourism

SHARR STEELE PROHASKA
George Washington University, USA

A dream vacation! A sun worshipper's paradise! From the Caribbean Sea to the Gulf of Mexico, from the Pacific Ocean to the China Sea, there are thousands of beautiful islands and miles of coastline lined with glittering resorts, quaint indigenous villages and quiet hideaways surrounded by spectacular stretches of sand that a visitor can temporarily call their very own. The weather is warm and tropical, the clear blue waters perfect for every kind of water sport known to man or woman, and an abundance of world-class restaurants and exotic night life are exceptional by any standard. The loudest sounds a person may hear are the songs of the colourful birds or the lapping of gentle waves against the sandy shore.

Even with all of these extraordinary sensual leisure activities that may lure someone to escape to an island destination, studies show that tourists are seeking even more from their travel experience. This insatiable quest for "more" presents exciting and challenging times for islands whose businesses cater to the tourism industry. The evolution of "sun and sand" vacations into the integrated development of cultural heritage tourism is one area of growth opportunity for all island destinations.

Professional studies demonstrate how cultural heritage tourism can be used to fill the educational and cultural void which often accompanies an island vacation. Heritage tourism is gaining widespread acceptance as a special-interest tourist attraction and as part of overall tourism planning. Island communities are discovering how the planned integration of historic, cultural, and natural resources can help sustain local economies and contribute to a greater appreciation of each island's unique heritage.

The benefits of community-based cultural heritage tourism are a new phenomenon. Communities are discovering how the direct linkage between the tourism industry and cultural resources can encourage sustainable local economic development. Cultural heritage tourism—a shared visitor experience—is the key to identifying the distinct culture of each island and at the same time to sustaining the heritage for future generations of travellers to enjoy.

In a recent study on Special Interest Tourism by Weiler and Hall (1992), they found that the interest in cultural tourism is growing throughout the world. For example:

Island Tourism: Management Principles and Practice
Edited by Michael V. Conlin and Tom Baum

England and Wales	22% increase in heritage site visitation; 68 million visitors/year at cultural heritage sites
Scotland	570% increase in tourism with shift to cultural heritage emphasis
Australia	$30 million increase in tourism revenues with native cultural focus
China	150% increase in room demand in heritage site area
United States	Virginia—63% of visitors come to single heritage site Texas—45% increase in heritage tourism over 3 years New Mexico—79% increase in heritage tourism in 3 years Overall—estimated 100 million visitors drawn to heritage-based sites across the nation

Other studies examining the relationship between cultural heritage and tourism have determined that:

- a National Tour Association of travellers over 50 years of age indicates that 52.3% favour trips to historical sites and 62.4% travelling on group tours favour visits to sites associated with America's heritage;
- 91% of tourists travelling to Virginia do so because of its historic atmosphere.

WHAT IS CULTURAL HERITAGE TOURISM?

The definition of cultural heritage tourism has evolved during the last 25 years. During the 1969 ICOMOS Congress in Oxford, England, it was stated that "cultural tourism, by creating the conditions for a new humanism, must be one of the fundamental means, on a universal level, or insuring man's equilibrium and the enrichment of his personality".

During the 1970s historic sites and monuments were beginning to experience overcrowding and people began to express concern about the impact of tourism on cultural and natural resources. Within ten years, the ICOMOS Committee on Cultural Tourism issued a charter on cultural tourism. The charter stated that "tourism is an irreversible, social, human, economic and cultural fact. Its influence in the sphere of monuments and sites is particularly important and can but increase."

Cultural tourism is that "form of tourism whose object, is, among other aims, the discovery of monuments and sites. Cultural tourism exerts a very positive effect insofar as it contributes to their maintenance and protection—it calls for the respect of the world's cultural and natural heritage." The charter outlined several action steps. Some steps important to the development of cultural tourism on island destinations include:

- the integration of cultural assets into the social and economic objectives which are part of the planning of resource protection;
- co-operation among agencies and communities to implement policies which protect mankind against the effects of tourism's anarchical growth;

- the development of educational programmes which lead to understanding and respect for monuments, sites and cultural heritage;
- to work for the protection and against the destruction of historic resources.

In 1980 the Manila Declaration on Tourism was adopted by 107 countries and 57 organizations. The Manila Declaration stated that "there were social and cultural as well as economic implications in tourism and that tourism had an educational role to fulfill in a larger global context." In 1985 the World Tourism Organization at a meeting in Bulgaria defined cultural heritage tourism in a broader context:

> Cultural tourism may be defined in broad and narrow terms. In the narrow sense it includes movements of persons for essentially cultural motivations such as study tours, performing arts, cultural tourism, travel to festivals, visits to sites and monuments, folklore, pilgrimages—in the broader sense, all movements of persons might be included in the definition because they satisfy the human need for diversity, tending to risk the cultural level of the individual and giving rise to new knowledge, experience and encounters.
>
> This emphasis on cultural heritage tourism and communication between people is increasing. The interaction of tourism within a social and cultural context will result in an enriched educational experience.

WHO ARE THE CULTURAL HERITAGE TOURISTS?

In the vast mosaic of the tourism industry, the history and arts bring culture, beauty and a sense of continuity to the way of life on each island. Arts can turn traditions and languages into paintings and interpret change in lifestyles. Arts and cultural resources help define the tourism product and give greater insight into the different characteristics of each island. The diversity of historic and cultural resources within a specific area has created a major niche in special-interest tourism development. Cultural heritage tourism differs from mass tourism in that the travel experience must be educational, adventuresome and personally enriching. For many visitors, the excitement of visiting a historic site is the opportunity to experience a different time or place—to escape and capture a feeling which cannot be experienced any other place on earth.

Visitors to historic sites travel to be educated—they want to learn about history and events of cultural significance. The resurgence of interest in sites associated with Christopher Columbus, Ellis Island, pathways of the early pioneers or areas of ethnic settlement is a relatively new phenomena in the tourism industry. However, visitors to these sites no longer want the typical history tour; instead they want to be entertained as they "step back in time".

Special-interest tourism studies in the United States show that cultural heritage tourists are usually professionals or managers with college or graduate school education and a higher than average income. Cultural tourists are more outgoing, adventurous and interested in new experiences. A study conducted by the United

States Travel and Tourism Administration (1991) demonstrated that aside from the first three favourite tourist activities of shopping, dining and sightseeing, the overseas traveller to the US preferred to take part in water sports or sunbathe, tour the countryside (36.1%), visit historical places (34.0%) or visit a theme park or national park (31.9%). The number of households participating in cultural activities while travelling in 1991 include 30% who visited a historic site, district or building, 24% who visited a museum or art gallery, 17% attended a play or concert, 25% went to a festival or craft fair and 28% purchased local/ethnic foods or crafts.

In 1989 a market study on pleasure travel to North America was prepared for the United States Travel and Tourism Administration and Tourism Canada (see Tables 4.1a and 4.1b). Research was conducted in Japan, the United Kingdom, West Germany and France including approximately 1200 personal, in-home interviews. Respondents in each country were people aged 18 or older who had taken a vacation trip of four nights or longer by plane in the past three years, or intending to take such a trip in the next two years. For European travellers, trips were defined as going to destinations outside of Europe and the Mediterranean. For Japanese travellers, trips were to destinations outside of Japan and South Korea.

The four markets examined represent a large and quickly growing number of travellers world-wide with a potential for attracting visitors to inland destinations. For travellers leaving the United Kingdom, the United States is currently the most popular long-haul destination, Canada and the Far East/Asia tied at 16% each of trips taken. Canada's advantages were given as its outdoor opportunities, cleanliness, personal safety and interesting and friendly people; the United States' advantages included its national parks and forests, public transportation and beaches for swimming and sunning. While on vacation travellers to Canada visited scenic landmarks (70%) or visited galleries and museums (56%); travellers to the US were likely to visit amusement or theme parks (65%).

SEGMENTATION

Evaluating visitors to Canada and the United States is one way to help island destinations understand their needs in the areas of cultural heritage product development, promotion and marketing activities. The study was divided into product segmentation, travel philosophy and benefit segmentation.

In terms of product segmentation, a total of five groups were identified.

- *Culture and Nature* travellers (16% of the total market) have an interest in such culture-related features as historical sites and buildings, historic cities and museums and art galleries. They are also interested in nature-related features like national parks and forest, wildlife and birds and wilderness areas. Accordingly, their cultural interests extend to visiting rural small towns and villages, viewing local crafts and handiwork, participating in local festivals, and meeting unique native cultural groups.

Table 4.1. Pleasure travel markets to North America, 1989: (a) Activity visits in the US (%)

	UK	France	West Germany	Japan (to US mainland)
Concerts/plays	32	38	24	20
Festivals/special events	39	35	39	29
Museums/galleries	37	63	32	27
Historic places	53	57	54	21
Commemorative places	38	57	43	11
Archaeological places	18	20	26	6
Military history sites	31	21	20	9
National parks	53	53	61	28
Market size (in '000s)	1540	1240	2740	1130

Source: US Travel and Tourism Administration and Tourism Canada

(b) Highlights report

Country	Market ('000)	Culture and nature		Culture and comfort	
		% of market	Number ('000)	% of market	Number ('000)
United Kingdom	4 700	16	750	19	890
France	5 900	13	750	18	1060
West Germany	11 200	17	1900	21	2300
Japan	10 200	23	2300	26	2650
Subtotal, 4 nations	32 000	18	5700	22	6900

Source: US Travel and Tourism Administration and Tourism Canada

(c) Overseas travellers to the United States, January–December 1989, actual activities (%)

Activity	All overseas	Western Europe	UK	France	West Germany	Japan
Arrivals (in millions)	14.0	6.1	2.2	0.6	1.1	3.1
Shopping	86.3	83.4	84.5	74.9	83.9	90.0
Concert, play or musical	19.0	21.3	17.0	20.8	22.2	13.0
Art gallery or museum	26.0	33.4	28.5	36.3	34.1	12.8
Sightseeing	68.0	70.4	73.7	64.3	69.0	79.4
Guided tours	25.0	23.5	25.2	22.1	20.0	39.5
Nightclub dancing	19.7	23.5	22.7	18.9	23.8	13.0
Water sports	24.4	27.8	34.0	20.6	31.6	35.4
Tennis, golf	12.9	11.0	12.2	12.9	8.7	22.4

Source: US Travel and Tourism Administration, Inflight Survey. Based on twelve activities plus "other".

Table 4.1. Continued

(d) Overseas travellers to the United States, January–December 1989, ranking of actual activities

Activity	All overseas	Western Europe	UK	France	West Germany	Japan
Shopping	1	1	1	1	1	1
Concert, play or musical	7	7	7	5	6	6*
Art gallery or museum	3	3	4	3	3	8
Sightseeing	2	2	2	2	2	2
Guided tours	4	5*	5	4	7	3
Nightclub dancing	6	5*	6	7	5	6*
Water sports	5	4	3	6	4	4
Tennis, golf	8	8	9	8	10	5

*Tie.
Source: US Travel and Tourism Administration Inflight Survey. Based on twelve activities plus "other" (eight shown).

(e) Long haul pleasure market to the United States for 8 selected countries with an interest in native cultural groups and immigrant cultures

	Germany	Japan	Mexico*	France	UK	Italy*	Australia*	Brazil*
Potential market for the USA ('000)	10 000	8800	7800	4900	4200	4100	3500	2200
Interest in unique and different native cultural groups* (%)	70	32	57	73	55	72	64	81
Volume of potential travellers ('000)	7000	2800	4500	3600	2300	2900	2200	1800
Interest in unique and different immigrant cultures (%)	54	36	NA	59	48	NA	NA	NA
Volume of potential travellers ('000)	5400	3200	—	2900	2000	—	—	—

*For Mexico, Italy, Australia and Brazil the estimates are for "Interested in unique and different cultural groups", in 1989 the questions were changed to the ones displayed.
Source: USTTA Pleasure Travel Markets to North America series reports 1988 and 1989.

- *Beach* travellers (19% of the total market) are interested in beaches, the seaside and water sports.
- *Developed resort* travellers (16% of the total market) enjoy resort areas with beaches, seaside and reliable weather. They also are concerned about some forms of entertainment, hospitality, personal safety and standards of cleanliness.
- *Sports and entertainment* travellers (21% of the total market) give high ratings to a number of sports-related product items such as water sports, golf and tennis, fishing and hunting.
- *Outdoor and native cultures* travellers (9% of the total market), like the culture and nature segment, enjoy nature-related products, but they are more interested in participating in outdoor activities and experiencing unique and different native cultural groups and cultures different from their own.

Looking at the relationship between the different segments offers a greater understanding of visitors who would be attracted to island destinations. Demographically, the culture and nature segment is 16% of the target market, more likely than average to be female (60%), 55 years of age or older (45%) , married or divorced/separated/widowed (86%), in a professional or technical occupation (29%) and travelled by plane within Canada (41%).

The product segments describe what features are desired by travellers on their vacation. Identifying these segments helps island destinations understand what products they should be developing and how to market those products in the most appealing manner.

NATIONAL SURVEYS

France

The study of travellers from France revealed that the United States was the most popular long-haul vacation destination and was visited on 28% of all trips, followed by Central/South Africa, Far East/Asia and Canada.

Culture and Nature travellers (13% of the total market) were interested in such culture-related items as historical and archaeological sites and buildings, historic cities, museums and art galleries, local crafts and handiwork, interesting small towns and villages, local festivals and so on. They were also interested in native cultural groups, immigrant cultural groups, and in cultures different from their own. In addition, they were interested in a number of nature-related products such as wildlife and birds, national parks and forests, lakes and rivers, and wilderness.

Culture and Comfort travellers (18% of the total market) have cultural interests such as museums and art galleries, historical and archaeological sites and buildings, theatre and concerts and historic cities. They also value their comfort and want first-class hotels, excellent restaurants and high standards of cleanliness.

Demographically, the Culture and Nature segment is more likely to be female

(61%), 55 years of age or over (35%), married or divorced (67%) and living in a household without children under 18 years of age (63%).

West Germany

The most popular long-haul vacation destination among West German travellers was the United States. It was visited on 42% of the long-haul trips taken in the past three years, followed by the Far East/Asia, Central/South Africa, Canada, Australia/New Zealand and the West Indies/Caribbean.

Activities that differentiated trips to Canada and the US from trips to other destinations were as follows:

Canada

- visiting scenic landmarks (78% of visitors to Canada)
- visiting places of historic interest (61%)
- visiting amusement or theme parks (57%)
- visiting sites commemorating important people (49%)
- visiting galleries and museums (29%)
- attending concerts or theatre (18%)

United States

- shopping (81% of visitors to US)
- sightseeing in cities (80%)
- visiting amusement or theme parks (61%)
- visiting galleries and museums (32%)
- attending concerts or theatre (24%)

Culture and Nature travellers (17% of the total market) were interested in native cultural groups, immigrant cultural groups and generally in cultures different from their own. They were also interested in nature-related features and areas of outstanding scenery.

Culture and Comfort travellers (21% of the total market) had different cultural interests than the previous group. They share an interest in native cultural groups and are more interested in such attractions as historical, archaeological and military sites and buildings, museums and art galleries and historic cities. This group demands high standards of cleanliness, personal safety and good restaurants.

The German Culture and Nature segment was more likely to be aged between 18 and 34 (49%), single (46%) and educated. They were more likely to have been independent travellers (61%) or sought to have adventure travel (64%). Promoting indigenous cultural groups would provide a strong appeal to their cultural interests.

One interesting aspect of the study is that within a three-year period (1986–1989) the cultural interests of the Culture and Nature segment changed from historical sites, museums and art galleries to native and immigrant cultural groups.

Japan

The most popular destination was the US (43%), most of which was accounted for by Hawaii/Guam/Samoa (29%) as opposed to the US mainland, followed by the

Far East/Asia, Europe, Australia/New Zealand and Canada. Some of the weaknesses in the Canadian and US product identified by the Japanese were the lack of historical sites, buildings, museums and art galleries in Canada: in the US, the lack of historical sites and buildings was also considered a weakness.

The Japanese visitors to Hawaii/Guam/Samoa were likely to sunbathe at the beach (59%), swim (56%), take part in water sports (27%) or take a day cruise (19%).

Culture and Nature travellers (23% of the total market) were interested in native cultural groups, immigrant cultural groups and in cultures different from their own. They also enjoyed small towns and villages and historical and archaeological sites and buildings. In addition they enjoyed nature-related features and outdoor activities such as hiking and climbing.

Culture and Comfort travellers (26% of the total market) had a variety of cultural interests including historical and archaeological sites and buildings, museums and art galleries, historic cities and local crafts and handiwork. The comfort aspect of this group placed high emphasis on first-class hotels and standards of cleanliness.

The Culture and Nature segment were more likely than average to be a student (16%) or in a professional/technical occupation (14%) and university educated (44%). They were more likely than average to spend more nights away on their trip (mean of 19 nights), take a trip that combines business and pleasure (14%) and travel on a non-package vacation (31%).

The United States: Travel Industry of America's Travelometer

The Travel Industry Associations' (TIA) Travelometer is a unique seasonal forecast of what Americans think about the US economy and how it will relate to their travel plans. In January 1994, TIA's research affiliate, the US Travel Data Center, surveyed 1500 US adults regarding their intentions to travel during the spring of 1994. Travelometer is unique because if focuses on forecasting trends. Normally "Trends" surveys study past behaviour. Another feature is that it correlates travellers' confidence in the economy and their personal finances with upcoming travel plans. It also targets those who have actually taken a trip during the past year and asks them about their travel plans for the upcoming travel season.

Some of the highlights of the 1994 study that relate to island destinations are as follows:

- Approximately one-third of US travellers (35%) were very or somewhat likely to travel on business compared to 30% last spring.
- Almost three-fourths of US travellers (73%) were very or somewhat likely to take a pleasure trip this spring compared to 68% last spring.
- Travellers planned to spend an average of 7.6 nights away from home on their longest pleasure or vacation trip this spring.
- Pleasure travellers planned to spend more on their spring 1994 pleasure trip, $990 mean, in comparison to past seasons.

- Visiting friends and relatives is the most popular activity planned among spring travellers reported by 70%. Certain activities which registered higher interest for spring 1994 visits than for winter 1993 or fall 1993 included: visit a city (68%), visit an historical site (40%), attend a cultural event (31%), go to a gambling casino (19%) or take a cruise (12%).
- When travellers named their top three choices for a US destination for a spring or vacation trip, Florida (40%), California (30%) and Hawaii (17%) were names most frequently mentioned.

Looking at the trends in these reports which cover a five-year span, it is apparent that the interest in cultural heritage tourism continues to grow at a significant rate.

WHY IS CULTURAL HERITAGE TOURISM IMPORTANT TO THE VISITOR?

> Every culture represents a unique and irreplaceable body of values, since each people's traditions and forms of expression are its most effective means of demonstrating their presence in the world. All culture form part of the common heritage of mankind. The cultural identity of a people is renewed and enriched through contact with the traditions and values of others. Cultural identity and cultural diversity are inseparable. The international community considers it its duty to ensure that the cultural identity of each person is preserved and protected. The neglect or destruction of the culture of any group is a loss to mankind as a whole.
>
> The cultural heritage of a people regardless of where they may live includes the works of its artists, architects, musicians, writers and scientists, and also the expressions of the people's spirituality and of the system of values which give meaning to life. It includes both tangible and intangible works through which the creativity of that people finds expression: languages, rites, beliefs, historic places and monuments, literature, works of art, archives and libraries. [Mexico City Declaration of Cultural Policies].

IMPACTS OF TOURISM

The cultural heritage of many islands around the world has suffered severe degradation and in some cases been destroyed as the consequence of too many tourists and changes imposed on a culture through insensitive development and improper tourism planning. Of even greater concern is the change to an island's heritage as the result of military intervention, foreign domination or unplanned mass tourism. These factors can lead to the loss of the indigenous culture or lack of appreciation for former traditions and values.

By planning for sustainable development, policies can be developed which will protect and interpret each island's cultural and historic identity. The intrinsic value of all island culture must be identified in order to provide for the educational tourism experience that so many international travellers are seeking. Every island has a unique history and each island has the opportunity to showcase their culture and at the same time provide the visitor with a special experience. It is memories of the people, their food, the cultural traditions and local festivals that the island guests will share with their friends when they return home.

Throughout the last decade there has been an increasing awareness of the role that cultural heritage contributes to the development of international tourism destinations. One reason is that the cultural resources of any city or rural community on any island differ from those on other islands. Attractions developed for the tourist market such as shopping malls, theme parks and zoos are not that unusual and can be found almost anywhere in the world. Cultural resources are unique to each destination and cannot be duplicated in other places within the same context. With good interpretation cultural resources provide the visitor with an authentic experience and help maintain the identity of each island.

Cultural heritage tourism should be used as an approach to protect, interpret and enhance all the island's significant resources, architecture, performing and visual arts, local traditions and values. At the same time cultural resources can encourage quality economic development by planning for sustainable use of resources for tourism product development. It is the responsibility of the local community to decide which of the island's resources—the folklife, historic sites, handicrafts, festivals, songs or dances—are to be shared with the visitor. The strength and flexibility of local traditions and culture determine the ability of the host community to separate what is traditional but sacred from what is to be shared with the tourist. The integration of historical and cultural resources into a tourism product can provide a profitable alternative or complement sun/beach tourism.

As we approach the 21st century, the conservation and protection of every island's heritage is essential. Every tangible form of local expression such as abandoned sugar mills, historic forts, industrial buildings, handicrafts, historic towns and archaeological sites, rituals, songs and dances must be identified and preserved. Not everything can be saved and some cultural traditions may already be lost, but the tourism industry working with local communities must take an interest in counteracting their loss.

HERITAGE AREAS

One of the most exciting trends for the future that plans for and integrates the concepts of cultural heritage, conservation, interpretation and recreation into a quality tourism product is the designation of heritage areas based on partnerships of local, state and national organizations. The significance of heritage areas is that the public and grassroots groups have turned to the government with a request: preserve our cultural heritage.

The reasons behind the demands are:

- The growth of cultural heritage tourism
- The rise in cultural preservation concern
- The decline in post-industrial regions.

When heritage preservation is integrated with strategic planning, it may create a demand for heritage tourism which can lead ultimately to the revitalization of an entire region. Heritage areas can be defined as: "Places with unique identities which have evolved over generations." Heritage areas often cover large regions with varying natural landscapes and numerous jurisdictions. They are not museums or monuments but can be termed "eco-museums or living landscapes". They offer total immersion where the visitor becomes, even for a brief time, a living part of the experience. Not only does the experience educate and entertain, it is living history and the visitor is part of the experience. At the present time over one hundred heritage areas have been identified across the United States, and several pieces of legislation are proposed at the national level entitled *Heritage Partnerships*. The process being used to develop heritage areas is based on the National Park Service planning process created in response to a grassroots demand for a standardized framework in which to determine the significance of a site. When significance has been determined, then the process for preservation and tourism interpretation can be established. Once the cultural and historic resources have been identified and assessed, policies can also be developed for their protection.

The Heritage Preservation Process involves six steps:

1. Identify the resources that are important to heritage.
2. Develop a preservation plan driven by grassroots efforts.
3. Co-ordinate a co-operative approach for implementation of the plan.
4. Provide technical assistance for implementing the plan.
5. Market the implementation effort and its results.
6. Monitor, evaluate and fine-tune the plan as it progresses.

The criteria for significance of resources are identified in the first step of the process. This first stage is when the resources are assessed and their preservation value determined. The assessment should be done by a professional who understands the context of the resource and includes not only its historic merit but its current use within the community. Two examples of heritage partnerships and how they have been integrated within the tourism industry are described below.

Lowell, Massachusetts

The first experiment in modern partnership came in the city of Lowell, Massachusetts, in 1978. With the decline of the US garment industry, Lowell was a prime example of post-industrial urban decline; however, it still retained a strong local culture that was worthy of preserving. The federal Department of the Interior joined with state and local governments and the private sector to form a National Historical Park—a 583-acre preservation district.

America's Industrial Heritage Project

A few years later another post-industrial nine-county region in southwestern Pennsylvania was identified as an area of special significance. The region already had four National Park Service sites and represented the nation's earliest industrial development through the post-industrial period. America's Industrial Heritage Project was formed by federal mandate in response to requests from the private and public sector. The Industrial Heritage Project contains more than 8000 square miles and 999 municipalities, three urban areas and hundreds of small industrial and rural communities.

The nine-county region has a rich heritage. One of the country's largest canal systems was designed and built here. The world's first steel rail was rolled here and then laid across the mountains. Coal mines in the area supplied fuel and food for the nation. The miners and steel workers brought their cultural heritage to Pennsylvania from across the ocean and that heritage is reflected in the style of homes, social halls and churches built in the local communities. The Industrial Heritage Project was first proposed in 1985. In 1988 a law was passed to establish the Southwestern Pennsylvania Heritage Preservation Commission whose responsibilities were to guide the project. A 21-member Commission included members from regional tourism and economic development agencies, state government, along with private-sector representation.

The success of the partnership is beginning to show. In 1991 a series of summer events drew an estimated 167 000 visitors in an area where previously 20 000 visitors had been considered a great success. The following year they began holding National Folk Festivals funded by state and local agencies. Building on the previous festivals, these events drew increasing crowds, resulting in more than 200 000 people in 1992. Within the area are 45 identified heritage sites and 200 supporting amenities—each with its own story to tell based on local significance. The beauty of heritage areas for cultural heritage tourism is that although the heritage area is a mosaic of many pieces, they are united by a common thread. In 1994, a Heritage Tour Route will connect a series of sites that tell a variety of stories important to the development of American's industrial heritage.

The significance of the heritage areas to the tourism industry—whether it is a small archaeological dig, restoration project or artists' show—is that: (1) the public is learning about the significance of the area; and (2) the economic impact that visitors can bring to an economically distressed area.

In 1992, 73% of the visitors to the five American Industrial Heritage sites came from outside the nine-county region. Nearly 60% travelled a distance of 90 miles or more. Most people spent one (66%) or two (26%) days on the Heritage Route. More than half (52%) visited multiple sites. Eighty-five % said they were likely to return, and 66% of those returnees hope to spend two or more days on the next visit.

In addition to the social, educational, economic, environmental and cultural benefits:

- two national historic landmarks have been preserved and three additional landmark properties have been recognized;
- more than 700 individual properties have been identified as potentially eligible for the National Register of Historic Places;
- four National Historic Districts have been nominated for the national register;
- the region's folk traditions have been documented through photo collections and oral histories;
- heritage curricula have been integrated into the region's schools.

The concept of heritage areas is very relevant to the future success of island tourism. In fact, heritage areas should work best in an island setting because islands are a self-contained area.

AMERICA'S HERITAGE TRANSPORTATION CORRIDORS

A series of broader heritage corridor pilot projects have recently been established. These heritage corridors focus on a single geographic or man-made feature and often extend across state lines. Their existence is recognized in the unique heritage that has developed around that feature.

Historic transportation corridors have much in common: (1) they are linear land areas; (2) they were and may still be used to transport people and their goods; and (3) the routes, or sites or structures along them are significant in history and culture. These routes are defined by their natural terrains; thus, the advantages of following a water course were frequently exploited by successive generations of travellers. Historic transportation routes may be rivers or canals, footpaths, wagon trails, rail lines or roads and highways.

Transportation routes are often long and narrow but provide an opportunity to interpret the surrounding landscape to the visitor. Through the identification and preservation of such routes as linear parks, the tourism industry can focus on an island's historical identity and at the same time provide new opportunities for outdoor recreation based on an historical or cultural association. The links with the past provide visitors with an opportunity to extend their vacation and at the same time contribute to an appreciation of the historical development of an area. One good example of an historic route that links an entire area's cultural and natural resources is Patriot's Path in New Jersey which connects numerous Revolutionary War sites and creates an identity for the communities along the route.

Another example is the Chesapeake and Ohio Canal Historic Park which includes several forms of transportation in the Potomac River Basin, the gateway to the western frontier. The towpath of the C & O Canal is the centre of a network of trails. In 1984, the Illinois and Michigan Canal region was established as the first National Heritage Corridor to preserve transportation links between the Mississippi

River, the Great Lakes and the St Lawrence River. In 1986, a second corridor was recognized in the Blackstone River Valley of Massachusetts and Rhode Island. A third corridor, the Delaware and Lehigh Navigational Canal, was created in 1988.

Some of the most significant historic transportation corridors are occupied by rail lines, which defined the growth patterns in the 19th and early 20th centuries. Rail corridors are particularly suited to the tourist who enjoys biking, jogging or horseback riding. In some cases the historic rail line has been restored for the development of tourism as in Georgetown, Colorado. The Colorado Historical Society has sponsored the reconstruction of a 95-foot high trestle spanning Clear Creek and a four-mile section of track between two mining towns. The reconstruction project is part of an Historical Mining Park Loop and is used to demonstrate railroad and mining history.

FESTIVALS AND SPECIAL EVENTS

Conch fritters, soft-shell crabs, curry and paprika, mangoes and papaya quickly bring to mind the culinary pleasures of some islands. Carnivals and festivals create visions of artists, songs and dances, an exhibition of local arts where people come together from different backgrounds and perform according to traditions passed down from one generation to another. Most festivals embody an aesthetic rooted in earlier times. Festivals and special events have become big business and provide islands with another opportunity for strengthening the cultural heritage of their people. Many people throughout the world are aware of many national and international festivals and island cuisine through travel marketing and they want to visit the festivals and taste the foods. Some festivals have become so large that they are now the focus of major cultural productions—a basis for celebrating shared values, myths, lifestyles and views of cultural expression. In some cases cultural forms have been renewed based on traditions or memories of the older people.

Most quality festivals continue to grow in attendance each year. For instance, since 1977 the city of Charleston, South Carolina has hosted the Spoleto Festival, considered by many to be "the world's most comprehensive arts festival". During a 17-day celebration, chamber music, jazz bands, clowns, jugglers, performing and visual artists fill the city squares, parks and public buildings. Spoleto attracts an international audience and has been a major factor in establishing Charleston as a tourist destination. The festival generates approximately 50 million tourist dollars for the local community and attracts about 125 000 visitors.

In San Antonio, Texas, economic development and tourism working together are producing very dramatic results. San Antonio has established itself as a major tourist destination based on its cultural heritage. A Night in Old San Antonio celebration which showcases every ethnic group in the city attracts approximately five million visitors each year. The Arts and Cultural Affairs Department offers almost $2 million in grants, including a category for cultural tourism projects. Target 90, San Antonio's vision for the future, includes turning the local festivals into international events, having the city museums serve as interpreters of the region's culture and history and turning San Antonio into the nation's leading centre for Hispanic music, visual and performing arts.

Hawaii has started a $500 000 Cultural Tourism programme. The Office of Economic Development will promote tour programmes based on Hawaii's culture, arts and local people. The fund will provide money for festivals and events highlighting local arts, historic entities, ethnic attractions and celebrations. They are also assessing the possibility of starting a performing arts company to showcase the native Hawaiian heritage.

INTERPRETATION AND EDUCATION

A carefully planned, well-organized tourist destination can benefit both the residents and the visitors through exposure to new ideas, people, languages and other cultural traditions. Good planning can add a greater dimension to the tourism experience by stimulating an interest in an island's history through the preservation and restoration of historical sites and areas. The revitalization of many ethnic communities has been based on their cultural heritage, landmarks, museums, music, parks and architectural design. As a result they have become places people want to visit.

As cultural heritage tourism gains in popularity, it is important for the local governments to interpret the history of the community and at the same time develop a code of ethics for responsible tourist behaviours. Ethnic groups on each island need to develop a policy on such things as photography of individuals and sacred sites, photographing religious ceremonies, tape recording special ceremonies, sketching of sites and people, visiting homes, visiting sacred places and generally acceptable behaviour. One of the most critical concerns facing indigenous island cultures revolves around the privacy of the villagers and a protection of their lifestyle. Island people need to be able to lead a normal life yet still be willing to welcome visitors. Interpretation by trained community guides or through written materials will help prevent problems. Education plays an important role in informing visitors about the host culture and the traditions of the people. The development of a brochure that emphasizes the history and social structure of the community will help alleviate negative impacts. The important key to success is to involve visitors in the community, make them feel wanted and that they are experiencing the community as the original residents did.

One way to make visitors feel welcome is through living history presentations where the visitors become involved directly with the people. One good example of this is at Williamsburg in Virginia where the visitor is taught methods of earlier construction, dress, arts and crafts. Visitors watch the interpreters make guns, glass, pottery, bread, etc and can interact with the interpreter at the actual site where the event took place. Most visitors feel they have had a positive experience if the interpreters are costumed in period clothing and can tell interesting stories about the people who lived and worked at the site. Visitors are more interested in people and their culture than they are in historical details.

This will continue to present a challenge for the tourism industry. On one hand we want to protect island cultures in order to promote authentic tourism. On the other hand, people change when their community becomes a living museum with living history programmes. Caution must be exerted so when cultural identity becomes part of the tourism product, the local community does not change to meet the demands of the visitor industry.

CULTURAL CENTRES

One opportunity often overlooked in the development of tourism products is local cultural centres which interpret the cultural and natural resources of each island. Cultural centres offer the best opportunity to educate visitors about the island's diversity, its people, their history and customs. On smaller islands, cultural centres may serve as a central orientation facility, where visitors first meet with local guides and learn about the customs and environment they are visiting.

HOW DO WE PROTECT AND DEVELOP THESE RESOURCES FOR TOURISM?

According to the National Trust Heritage Tourism programme, sustainable cultural heritage tourism is developed by understanding the capacity to service visitors and then capturing the economic impact from outside markets while not endangering the very resources which attract visitors. Heritage tourism strives to balance the short-term economic gain with the long-term preservation, protection and promotion of historic and cultural resources within the tourism industry.

To accomplish this goal certain standards must be encouraged. The following five principles were developed:

1. *Authenticity and quality*: Tell the true stories of historic sites and the culture of the area. The specific development of an area and contributions made by previous generations are what distinguish one place from another.
2. *Education and interpretation*: History can be fun. Names and dates don't bring a place or event alive but the human drama of history does. The interpretation of historic sites should be creative and exciting.
3. *Preservation and protection*: Take care to maintain historic places, and the historic buildings of neighbourhoods and towns for residents and visitors both now and in the future. A community wanting to attract tourists must safeguard the future by establishing measures to protect the very elements that attract visitors.

4. *Local priorities and capacity*: Help communities build strong, comprehensive protection and tourism programmes to achieve local priorities and ensure that tourism is of economic and social benefit to the community.
5. *Partnership*: Co-operation among business leaders in tourism, operators of historic sites, local governments and many others is important to achieve tourism objectives. Historic sites and districts deserve special funding consideration for operations and maintenance since they are often the reasons why people visit a community.

Once a community or an entire island has committed itself to long-term, sustainable cultural heritage tourism, the process of product development can begin based on an assessment of the cultural resources and their potential for tourism, strategic planning, product development and research and marketing.

CONCLUSION

As cultural tourism becomes an increasingly important factor for islands interested in expanding their tourism product and attracting more international visitors, there is merit in assessing how tourism can be better managed through planning with local communities in order to ensure greater local economic benefits, fewer social impacts and increased international educational opportunities.

Any new product development should take into account the important changes in the world economy, changes in tourism development priorities, and the growing concern about the impact of mass tourism on cultural and natural resources. Increasingly, the trends in tourism need to stress the need for sustainability and balanced growth, a more equitable distribution of benefits to the local community and environmental projection. Any future development needs to take into account the cultural impact of any proposed projects and increase local participation in the decision-making process.

Unlike other industries, tourism depends upon the protection of the culture and the environment. Although tourism may manifest itself differently on an island compared to an industrialized country where visitors have more opportunities to visit museums, churches, etc., it is the local island culture and the interaction with the host population that will make an island vacation memorable and encourage repeat visitation. With planning and education, cultural heritage tourism will contribute to a greater understanding, knowledge and appreciation of ourselves and of other cultures. Cultural heritage tourism allows us to appreciate other cultures which differ from our own and at the same time understand the common aspirations of all mankind. Cultural heritage tourism can create a sense of identity for the people living on the islands and a greater awareness of the shared responsibility we have to protect all natural and cultural resources. The beautiful heritage of the past is the basis of quality tourism for the future.

REFERENCES

National Trust for Historic Preservation (1985) Routes of History: Recreation Use and Preservation of Historic Transportation Corridors. Information Series No. 38.

National Trust for Historic Preservation (1990) *Heritage Tourism Initiative Fact Sheet.*

Railroaders Memorial Museum (1993) The Heritage Partnership Challenge.

Tighe, Anthony J. (1991) Research on Cultural Tourism in the United States, National Endowment for the Arts.

Travel Industry of America, Spring (1994) *TIA TRAVELOMETER.*

United States Travel and Tourism Administration (1989) *Pleasure Travel Market to North America: United Kingdom, France, West Germany and Japan.* US Department of Commerce.

Weiler, B. and Hall, C.M. (1992) *Special Interest Tourism.* Bellhaven Press, London.

5 Key Success Factors for Public/Private-Sector Partnerships in Island Tourism Planning

BLAIR POETSCHKE
Ernst & Young, Toronto, Canada

INTRODUCTION

This chapter focuses on the reasons behind the creation, success and failure of various forms of tourist authorities and the impact of these authorities on tourism planning and marketing. A growing number of islands, countries and regions around the world are now adopting this type of organization structure for directing the future development and marketing activities of their tourism industries, particularly since traditional sources of funds (i.e. governments) are no longer as readily available.

The essence of a tourist authority is a private/public-sector partnership, often taking the form of a board of directors with representation from both sectors. Key benefits commonly derived from the creation of such an authority are:

- reduced antagonism between the public and private sectors;
- more effective use of resources (money and time);
- new sources of funds; and
- additional profits, jobs and tax revenues.

This approach to governance of a country or region's tourism industry is rapidly becoming essential to being competitive in today's global tourism industry. It is particularly relevant to island destinations, given their relatively isolated situation and often smaller financial resources, to overcome many of the unique challenges they face from mainland (and cruise) destinations.

THE PROBLEM

The world-wide tourism industry is becoming increasingly competitive. Not only are travellers becoming more discerning in choosing their destinations, but the number of destinations to choose from are multiplying as more governments

Island Tourism: Management Principles and Practice
Edited by Michael V. Conlin and Tom Baum

recognize that the tourism industry is a significant engine for economic growth and therefore worthy of receiving substantial resources dedicated to its development.

Key challenges for individual destinations include the ability to offer a "suitable" array of tourism products, develop an "appropriate" promotional message and ensure that this message is heard. "Suitable" products must take into account the increased sensitivity of travellers to receiving value for money, their desire to have active/educational experiences and the current interest in experiencing the unique "culture" that a particular destination has to offer. An "appropriate" message is one that selectively presents a destination's tourism products in a manner that appeals to the new discerning traveller. Focused target marketing is essential, matching specific types of products to specific tastes.

Finally, ensuring that this "appropriate" message is heard is becoming increasingly difficult as more and more destinations realize the economic potential of their respective tourism industries and devote resources to attracting prospective travellers. At the same time, many destinations which have traditionally promoted tourism are faced with declining resources for tourism development and promotion.

A message from any one destination will only be heard among the "noise" created by the promotional efforts of all the other destinations if it is:

- consistent (i.e. different organizations from the same destination do not present conflicting messages) and innovative;
- repeated frequently; and
- seen by many people ("reach").

Consistency requires co-operation among the numerous tourism organizations which operate within any given destination, while high frequency and reach require spending money, a resource that many destinations are finding increasingly scarce. On the other hand, if insufficient promotional money is spent, too few economic benefits result for a "suitable" array of products to be developed, making it more difficult to attract new travellers.

RELEVANCE TO ISLANDS

Islands have particular difficulty in this competitive environment because typically they face a number of inherent disadvantages. These include difficult access (often by air only), fragile ecosystems, undiversified economies and difficulties in offering a comprehensive range of products. Difficult air access implies that travellers must make an extra effort to visit a particular destination. Given the decision-making criteria of today's travellers, that extra effort will need to be met with additional value in the form of an island's tourism products.

Second, fragile ecosystems may require that islands place further constraints on travellers, in that they may not be able to do all of the activities that they could do at some other destination. Thus protecting the ecosystem, a key component of any island's tourism product, makes it potentially more difficult to satisfy the traveller's sense of value.

Third, islands that have one- or two-industry economies typically do not have the ability to make substantial investments in tourism marketing or in the creation of a more comprehensive range of products. Again, this impacts on their ability to compete with the thousands of other destinations trying to attract travellers.

Thus islands face even greater challenges than most mainland destinations in attracting and retaining travellers. Their lack of resources, specialized tourism products and justifiable environmental concerns, in the face of increasingly strong competitive forces, make tourism industry development a daunting task.

THE SOLUTION

These difficulties make it apparent that the future of island tourism demands better product planning and marketing than ever before. No longer can money be spent at anything less than maximum effectiveness or with sub-optimal co-operation among the various tourism organizations in any one destination. In addition, there is always a need for more resources to add to tourism development and marketing efforts. Each destination can accomplish this through increased partnership efforts between all of the key tourism "stakeholders" (all groups directly impacted by tourism). In particular there must be representation from both the private sector and the public sector in a single organization charged with tourism development planning and marketing for that destination.

Non-integrated tourism planning efforts, where customer expectations are not properly shaped through appropriate marketing and product development, may not succeed or will at least make an island more vulnerable to competing destinations. Thus, it is critical for all island governments to work more closely with private-sector tourism interests in order to perform this tourism industry planning role at a time when more resources are required for development and promotion but fewer are available.

The following section illustrates some of the approaches various destinations have taken in the past to this type of partnership effort and my rating of the effectiveness of their efforts.

SELECTED PARTNERSHIP MODELS

Willing and active co-operation between the public and private sectors is often difficult to achieve due to fundamentally different operating philosophies. As a starting point it is useful to examine briefly the various types of partnership models which are currently used. The following diagram illustrates the typical range of approaches to co-operation between the public and private sectors:

Figure 5.1 divides these approaches into four categories, or partnership models.

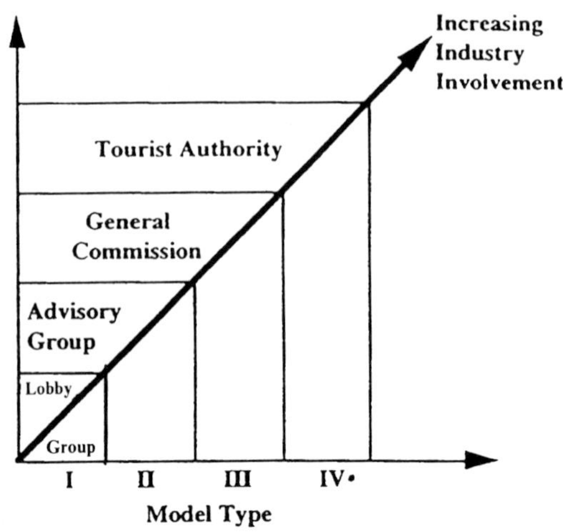

Figure 5.1. Partnership models

Models I through IV represent increasing levels of industry involvement and control over planning for tourism development and marketing.

Characteristics

- *Type I—Lobby Group*: A Type I governing structure, where the private sector provides input through a lobby group which it has formed, is the traditional form of government. The government sets and implements tourism policies and the private sector often finds itself in a position where it must lobby for change—usually a somewhat antagonistic process.
- *Type II—Advisory Group*: A Type II relationship is usually characterized by the participation of the private sector in an advisory council. In this case, the government still sets and implements the policies but actively seeks advice from the private sector. This advice may or may not be followed.
- *Type III—General Commission*: Here the private sector gains some degree of formal control over the strategic decision-making process. A general commission is often made up of prominent members of the community and is charged with overseeing the strategic planning function for a country or region's tourism industry. Decision making by the Commission is at the broad, strategic level only.
- *Type IV—Tourism Authority*: A tourism authority is typically controlled through a board of directors and is a distinct entity, separate from the government. Board composition is usually some mix of business people drawn from the tourism industry and government officials. The board takes responsibility for carrying out strategic planning at a more detailed level than commonly found in a Commission.

For the purposes of this chapter only the Type IV (Tourism Authority) example will be discussed as this is the organizational structure which goes furthest towards establishing such partnerships. In the following sections, selected countries with tourism authorities in place are evaluated with respect to the degree to which they are reaping the benefits inherent in private/public-sector co-operative efforts. First, however, a fuller discussion of these inherent benefits is necessary.

BENEFITS OF PRIVATE/PUBLIC-SECTOR CO-OPERATION

There are five major potential benefits of having a tourist authority in place in a particular country or region. These are:

1. *Reduced antagonism*: Because a tourist authority by definition brings all stakeholders together to make key strategic decisions, policies which are decided upon meet significantly less controversy and opposition. Of course, the tourist authority decision-making process itself may not be easy since there will be many different points of view around the table; however, given a strong base of facts and a clear sense of direction for a particular objective, difficult decisions can surprisingly often be reached with unanimous consent.
2. *Avoiding duplication*: Again, because all of the various tourism industry stakeholder organizations (e.g. hotels, restaurants, government departments, attractions etc.) are ideally represented on the board of directors for the tourism authority, channels of communication between these organizations are enhanced. When these representatives make decisions as part of the tourism authority board, they carry the rationale for these back to their own organizations. Thus the overall tourism authority strategy will act as a guide when setting objectives and priorities for their own organizations. Conflicting actions between stakeholder organizations are therefore less likely to occur.
3. *Combined areas of expertise*: One of the key benefits from bringing together private and public partners is the creation of a powerful pool of expertise. The private sector brings a sound understanding of market and customer needs, as well as efficient operating methods and a demand for accountability, to the table, while the public sector is best suited for matters such as guiding infrastructure development and ensuring that economic benefits to the country as a whole are maximized.
4. *Increased funding potential*: Additional resources will result from the creation of an effective tourism authority for two reasons. First, the reduction in duplication of effort among the variety of tourism stakeholders ensures that existing resources will be spent more effectively (item 2, above). Second, as the private sector gains a voice in how money is spent to benefit their tourism industry, it will be more willing to contribute, either directly or, more likely, through new taxes. The key is that accountability, with respect to how this money is spent, must be present.

5. *Create a "win/win" situation*: In a tourism authority both parties win through more effective investment of perhaps more money or other resources: the private sector wins through more profits and the public sector wins through increased tax revenue and a stronger economy.

Bearing in mind this array of potential benefits inherent in tourism authority partnership arrangements, we now turn to a discussion of selected examples of tourism authorities in operation around the world.

SELECTED TOURISM AUTHORITY CASE STUDIES

There are many examples of tourism authorities around the world—in fact they seem to be emerging from practically every corner of the globe. It has become an increasingly sought after system of governance, driven by the need to be globally competitive. Countries and regions which have adopted some form of an authority include Britain, the Caribbean, Canada and some of its provinces, various US states, Jamaica, Barbados, New Zealand, Australia, Tahiti, Singapore and many others.

This section briefly discusses and evaluates some of these existing tourism authorities and shows to what extent they have been able to realize each of the five major benefits from having an authority in place. Three broad categories of tourism authorities are discussed, including tourism authorities which focus solely on carrying out marketing efforts, authorities which carry out tourism development planning as well as marketing and authorities which are mandated to carry out still broader activities. A "report" card scoring system is used to highlight the overall effectiveness of each category, with grades of "A", "B" and "C" being given to represent the various degrees of excellence (a mark of "A+" is outstanding, whereas a "D" is poor).

The British Tourist Authority and Jamaica—a focus on marketing

The first example is perhaps one of the best known examples of a tourist authority—the British Tourist Authority (BTA). Many islands, including Jamaica, the Canadian province of Prince Edward Island and a number of others have also recently adopted this organizational model. The BTA is an organization appointed by the secretary of state, and is a private-sector board with five directors—each with some significant tourism industry experience. The primary mandate of the board is for foreign overseas marketing, with secondary responsibilities to advise the British government on tourism matters that "affect Britain as a whole" and to "encourage the provision and improvement of tourist amenities and facilities". The BTA in fact concentrates on overseas marketing to the virtual exclusion of the other two, more development-oriented, considerations.

This concentration on marketing efforts, virtually excluding tourism product

Reduced antagonism	B
Avoiding duplication of resources	B
Combined areas of expertise	
private-sector input	B
public-sector input	A−
Additional resources	B
Creation of win/win situation	B+

Figure 5.2. Britain's "report card"

planning and other key considerations, is the main reason why it did not earn a straight "A" report card. While there is less antagonism than in many other jurisdictions, the board of the BTA is not representative of the variety of stakeholders in the tourism industry and therefore the full potential benefit is not achieved. "Resource duplication", "private-sector input" and "additional resources" also received "B" grades.

The BTA does eliminate much of the duplication of resources with respect to overseas marketing, although some of the individual country boards such as Scotland (and recently Wales) carry out overseas marketing as well. However, the BTA appears to provide no overall direction to the numerous other tourism groups involved in other aspects of the British tourism industry and there still seems to be significant duplication in these areas.

"Private sector input" appears to be confined to marketing issues, and aside from the board of directors providing overall strategic direction, there is no formal input mechanism. However, it does appear that industry agrees with much of the BTA's marketing directions since the industry contributes a substantial amount of co-operative advertising money to Britain's tourism efforts. "Additional funding" is given a "B" because of the degree of success achieved in co-operative marketing. A higher mark could have been awarded if the BTA were able to generate additional funding for non-marketing activities. "Public sector input" was given an "A−" as the British government seems to be very supportive, providing the BTA with additional funding for marketing when required. "Creating a win/win situation" was scored as a "B+". The private sector definitely wins from the co-ordinated marketing efforts, as does the public sector in terms of additional revenues and a stronger economic base for the region. The private sector has sufficient confidence in the management and board of the BTA to place money voluntarily in the BTA's marketing fund. In return, the public sector also demonstrates its positive view by continuing to contribute money to the BTA.

Returning to Jamaica and Prince Edward Island as our examples of islands following in the footsteps of the British Tourist Authority, it is interesting that both of these relatively new authorities have recognized the importance of guiding the tourism development function but have formed a second organization, separate from the tourist authority, to deal with these issues. In Jamaica this organization is called the Tourism Product Development Company while in Prince Edward Island it is still primarily a government-controlled issue. The key to these destinations' success for the future will be how well their respective marketing and product development organizations communicate and integrate their activities. The danger is that the marketing efforts of the tourist boards will create expectations unmatched by tourism products presently available.

The Colorado Tourism Board and Tahiti—tourism development planning and marketing

The second example is the Colorado Tourism Board, a tourism authority for the state of Colorado which oversees both tourism development planning as well as marketing. The Colorado Tourism Board's directors are appointed by the State Governor and are drawn from each of the state's five major tourism industries:

- skiing;
- attractions;
- transportation;
- restaurants;
- hotels.

In addition to the five private-sector board members, there are also two political members, one member of the house and one member from the senate, for a total of seven. The board, representing Colorado's entire tourism effort, is funded through a three-tenths % tax on each of the five tourism industry areas.

Tahiti is a present-day example of an island trying to implement the structure of the Colorado authority. It has formed a board of directors separate from the island's government, composed of both private- and public-sector representatives, and is currently emphasizing co-operative private-sector funding for its tourism marketing and development efforts. However, because it is too early to be able to evaluate the effectiveness of this new structure, the following ratings refer only to Colorado (but might also be reasonably expected of Tahiti).

Because the Colorado Authority oversees both development planning and marketing efforts, it scores generally higher in all categories over the British Tourist Authority and the Jamaica model. "Reduced antagonism" still does not receive an "A" due to the formal structure of the relationship between the private and public sector. The selection of board members and the mandate of the Colorado authority have been very clearly laid out in law, and these boundaries may not be crossed.

Reduced antagonism	B+
Avoiding duplication of resources	A
Combined areas of expertise	
private-sector input	B+
public-sector input	B−
Additional resources	A
Creation of win/win situation	A−

Figure 5.3. Colorado's "report card"

This illustrates each party's wariness or mistrust of the other's actions, thereby taking away some of the efficiency of this organization.

Similarly, while this authority receives only a "B+" for "private-sector input", it is still superior to the BTA/Jamaica model because of its broader mandate. The private sector has good representation, but there seems to be some deficiency in terms of individual businesses and the various state travel regions being unable to communicate to the board exactly what they think needs to be done. "Public sector input" was given a "B−" since the Colorado government was very much pro-tourism when it created this tourism board in 1982, but a recent legislative technicality (31 December 1994) allowed current legislators to remove its dedicated funding. A replacement system is currently being negotiated. The board is also limited in its ability to influence the actions of other departments with respect to tourism-related decisions (e.g. agricultural policies, land management issues, fishing issues, taxes, etc.), making a lower "Public-sector input" score. "Additional funding" is given an "A" because the board directors place a strong emphasis on return on investment and accountability from their staff. It is important to note that all facets of the industry represented by the directors, are investors through the dedicated state sales tax. Also, the staff are state employees—something which they consider to be a disadvantage (do not have the power to hire and fire). Finally, in terms of the win–win situation, Colorado earns an "A−" rating as it is an extremely efficient organization.

The New Zealand Tourism Board—more than development planning and marketing

A third example is New Zealand. It too has a private-sector board which manages its tourism development efforts, also appointed by the government. The New Zealand Tourism Board is a crown agency and is similar to the BTA in that it has an overseas marketing role. However, a key difference is that the Board is evolving into a much broader role in the industry.

There are nine members on the tourism board in New Zealand, brought together for the purpose of more effective marketing of the country. The board discovered that in order to meet their ambitious target of tripling their tourism visitation over the remainder of the decade, they needed to take into account a number of things including:

Reduced antagonism	A+
Avoiding duplication of resources	A
Combined areas of expertise	
private-sector input	A+
public-sector input	B+
Additional resources	A
Creation of win/win situation	A

Figure 5.4. New Zealand's "report card"

- existing tourist attractions were overcrowded and visitors needed to be encouraged to visit other regions of the country;
- new attractions and other tourism product development was needed in order to make this re-distribution happen;
- in order to get these new attractions built, foreign investment was required;
- in order to bring in foreign investment the profitability of the existing tourism industry had to be increased.

The bottom line is that they discovered that their job could not just be restricted to marketing—they had to become involved in every aspect of tourism industry development in order to try and reach their target of boosting visitation. This included travelling through Asia trying to source investment money.

The ratings given to the New Zealand Tourist Authority show that this organizational arrangement has worked out very well; most of the points are in the "A" range as a result of very little duplication of resources; strong private-sector input from its board and excellent public-sector support. In fact, many additional resources were made available as a direct result of the Ministry of Tourism, both in terms of funds making strategic appearances to encourage investment and the increasing of public-sector funds when appropriate. The reason for the generally extraordinary level of support from both the private and public sectors in New Zealand can be traced to the fact that the board sets out specific targets and holds itself accountable to industry. All in all, it is definitely a "win/win" situation for all concerned.

CONCLUSION

This chapter has discussed the challenges specifically facing islands and all destinations generally. An increasing number of destinations are actively promoting themselves to much more discerning travellers. Thus more resources need to be dedicated to tourism development and marketing for any one destination to stand out "above the crowd". At the same time, governments, particularly island governments, are finding that they do not have these additional resources to do this. Closer partnership efforts, between private- and public-tourism sector interests, are an answer to this dilemma and tourist authorities appear to be the organization of choice for these efforts.

To summarize, the key success factors for creating a successful tourist authority include the following:

- a significant degree of private-sector control over how the authority spends its money;
- an understanding of the need to accommodate public-sector objectives in order to gain the appropriate match between marketing and the development of tourism products;

- the existence of a dedicated revenue stream for use by the tourism authority which is not subject to annual government control;
- strong accountability as a key ingredient in obtaining private-sector funds for investment in the tourism industry as a whole, either through a membership system or increased taxes; and finally
- a broad, integrated, mandate encompassing all functions critical to the development of a strong tourism industry, including marketing, education and training, research, infrastructure development and much more.

Those destinations who wish to be leaders in the competitive world-wide tourism industry must address all of these key success factors. Destinations which act first will gain a competitive edge; those who wait will fall behind.

6 Human Resources: a Strategic Imperative for Caribbean Tourism

MICHAEL V. CONLIN
Bermuda College, Bermuda
AND
J. ALEX TITCOMBE
Nassau, Bahamas

It is a commonly held view that human resource development will become the single-most important issue facing world tourism by the year 2000. Arguably, it is already a fundamental issue, particularly when considered in the context of service quality (Baum, 1992; Conlin, 1992). However, tourism has a poor image among those who might become the leaders of tomorrow's industry, particularly in the Caribbean (Charles, 1992). In island tourism, industry fails to attract the best young people and both the private and public sectors have lagged in their support of the infrastructure necessary for the development of educated, professional human resources. This results, in part, from the private-sector's view of human resources as an operational, tactical consideration and public policy on many islands, particularly those with a colonial heritage, which implicitly views service as servitude.

Human resource development, however, should be seen as a competitive strategy for island tourism. Service quality and value are related and are human resource-based (Baum, 1992). The quality of service received rests in the hands of individuals employed in the sector, whether they are employed in hotels, resorts, restaurants, casinos, as taxi drivers or at the airport, car rental agencies, banks, immigration or customs. The extent to which they do their jobs well will contribute dramatically to how successful a destination will be.

Accordingly, the role of well-educated, trained and motivated employees becomes crucial to the industry's success. Without skilled employees, island tourism will not be able to compete effectively with other destinations, and a deterioration in the profitability of the industry will follow. Although there are other factors in play, this is exactly what has transpired in the Caribbean. Failure to act will result in other destinations which have invested in the development of human resources gaining share at the expense of the region.

This chapter will argue that this perspective needs to be broken, that industry and government need to consider the development of human resources as a

Island Tourism. Management Principles and Practice
Edited by Michael V. Conlin and Tom Baum

strategic, long-term investment which is absolutely necessary for the survival and growth of tourism. It will make this argument through an analysis of the current state of development of the tourism educational and training infrastructure in the Caribbean. The chapter will also provide evidence that the region's treatment of human resources is changing in a positive direction. It will examine an example of a strategic, integrated, regional model currently being adopted in the Caribbean and conclude with recommendations for further action aimed at strengthening the development of human resources in the tourism industry.

THE CURRENT STATE OF HUMAN RESOURCE DEVELOPMENT IN THE CARIBBEAN

Most Caribbean islands have programmes of education for the tourism industry. These programmes vary considerably in their objectives, structure and quality. In total, there are approximately 20 national programmes which have hospitality management as their principal focus. The University of the West Indies has a degree programme in regional hospitality and tourism at its campus in Nassau, the Bahamas. Some American universities, including Johnson and Wales University, have attempted to establish satellite campuses in the region and have met with mixed success. Several non-English-speaking islands have branches of European universities, most notably the French and Dutch territories in the region. A number of other islands, including Puerto Rico, Dominica and Haiti, have indigenous programmes at the university level. Venezuela, Guyana and Mexico are members of the Caribbean Hotel Association (CHA) and have a range of tertiary programmes in the hospitality and tourism areas. A number of these are of high quality and are recognized as such by both the private and public sectors. However, it would be a valid observation that the majority of programmes are not particularly well regarded, particularly by the tourism industry.

Several regional organizations play a role in the planning and delivery of education and training on a regional basis. The Caribbean Hospitality Training Institute (CHTI) is the training arm of the CHA. CHTI offers a broad range of courses and custom-designed training activities throughout the Caribbean. The Caribbean Tourism Organization (CTO) is active in the area of tourism awareness and training. The Caribbean Regional Hotel Training Program (CRHTP) is a major training initiative of the CHA and other constituents in the region and is funded by the European Union (EU). Two regional tertiary educational organizations exist. The Association of Caribbean Tertiary Institutions (ACTI) was formed in 1990 to develop a regional institutional accreditation scheme within the region's colleges and universities. The Council of Caribbean Hospitality Schools (CHOCHS) was also formed in 1990, in large part through the support of the CRHTP. Two of the primary objectives of CHOCHS are the development of a regional programme-accreditation scheme for the region's college and university programmes in hospitality and tourism and the creation of a regional occupational standards and certification scheme. The membership of CHOCHS represents the majority of hospitality programmes in the English-speaking Caribbean (see Table 6.1).

A number of funding agencies are active in supporting tourism education and training in the region including the United Nations Development Programme (UNDP), the EU, the Organization of American States (OAS) and the World Bank. A number of countries outside the region have also been active in supporting training for the Caribbean tourism industry including the United States through its AID Programme and Canada through its Training Awards Programme. The private sector has also begun to support education and training in the region with the American Express Company being the dominant force to date. American Express contributes significant amounts each year to the CHTI to fund regional training activities. Of course, the industry plays a major role through its in-house training programmes.

WEAKNESSES IN THE REGION'S EDUCATION AND TRAINING INFRASTRUCTURE

Generally, education and training in the region can be characterized as fragmented, unco-ordinated, and occasionally redundant. Weaknesses consistently reported by the membership of CHOCHS with respect to educational programmes are as follows.

Table 6.1. Member Colleges, Programmes, Schools and Universities of the Council of Caribbean Hospitality Schools

Albena Lake Lodge School	Anguilla
Aruba Hotel School	Aruba
Bahamas Hotel Training College	The Bahamas
Barbados Community College	Barbados
Belize Tourism Industry Association	Belize
Bermuda College	Bermuda
Caribbean Hotel Training Institute	Antigua
College of Arts, Science and Technology	Jamaica
College of Further Education	St. Kitts & Nevis
Community College of the Caymans	Cayman Islands
Curaçao Hotel and Tourism Training Centre	Curaçao
Grenada National College	Grenada
H.L. Stout Community College	British Virgin Islands
Hotel Training Centre	Antigua
Monserrat Hotel Programme	Monserrat
National Hotel School of Venezuela	Venezuela
Runaway Bay HEART Academy	Jamaica
Sir Arthur Lewis Community College	St. Lucia
The Hotel School of Bonaire	Bonaire
Trinidad and Tobago Hotel School	Trinidad and Tobago
University of the West Indies	The Bahamas

- The difficulty in attracting high-calibre students due to the poor image of the industry as a career choice and as an employer.
- The difficulty in attracting appropriately trained and experienced faculty, primarily due to a universal faculty shortage and the financial terms and conditions of appointment.
- The lack of development programmes for existing faculty. Research carried out by the CRHTP suggests that many teachers employed in hospitality programmes lack any formal teacher training, appropriate academic qualifications and industry experience. As a result, faculty are ill-equipped to develop new curricula and tend to rely on dated or inappropriate material.
- The failure of the public sector to invest sufficiently in physical facilities. Virtually all schools in the region report that they do not have the physical plant appropriate to their programmes. Laboratory space, classrooms and student facilities are generally inadequate. Figure 6.1 shows the inadequate level of facilities which the University of the West Indies, the only regional university, was able to provide for its hospitality and tourism programme until recently. For many years, the programme was housed in a small, residential building located in the back of Nassau alongside the Bahamas Hotel Training College which is seen in Figure 6.2. In addition to inadequate facilities, many schools are unable to obtain sufficient and appropriate textbooks and other learning materials.
- The failure of the public sector to invest sufficiently in operating budgets to support hospitality and tourism education and training. In addition to the problems mentioned above, inadequate funding tends to divert attention away

Figure 6.1. For years, the Centre for Hospitality and Tourism Studies at the University of the West Indies Campus in Nassau was housed in this residential building

Figure 6.2. This block of teaching rooms was typical of the facilities of the Bahamas Hotel Training College for many years

from the improvement of curricula and the development of links with industry and colleagues. Rather, they focus instead on day to day survival.

- The relative isolation within which most schools in the region operate. Because they are generally founded on traditional and colonial philosophies and structures, there is little consistency in programme design or standards and they do not share the growth generated in other educational systems by regular communication and collaboration with colleagues and industry partners. Communication and collaboration does take place, but it is the exception and not the rule. This results in schools not meeting the needs of the industry, and industry not understanding and consequently not supporting the role of hospitality programmes. Indeed, the only real opportunity for communication is the annual CHOCHS conference.

The following issues relate to weaknesses in the provision of training in the region. Most are common to tourism training everywhere, but some are Caribbean-specific.

- Research into the identification of training needs is patchy. On a local level, research is often unscientific and politically motivated, resulting in short-term, short-duration programmes with little impact. While all experts recognize that there are clearly defined needs, those needs are not always supported by demand. Clearly, the economic climate during the early 1990s has had an impact, but there is also a suspicion that many managers in the region do not understand the true nature of training and its potential benefits, particularly when it applies to their own development.

- A significant number of managers and supervisors working in the industry have had no formal hospitality education or training. Many are reluctant to accept that they need any further development. This attitude devalues training in the eyes of employees, stifles new thinking and the development of modern management skills and techniques.
- There is no system in place in the region which accredits the prior learning and experience of those in the industry or provides a route for further development. The result is that many are ill-prepared for the role they are undertaking, and those who aspire to higher positions within the industry are unable to ascertain what further skills and knowledge they require or how they can obtain them. This weakness, however, will be increasingly offset in the future as the recently introduced HOST Programme described later in this chapter provides a regionally accepted set of occupational standards for the industry.
- With the exception of the HOST Programme, there have been no occupational standards in place that are recognized nationally or regionally, and there has been no means of assessing whether people are "competent". Certification programmes currently available tend to recognize attendance, not achievement. Training programmes need to be designed to be more quantifiable and supportive of what the industry requires.
- Trainers have a critical role to play in the continuing development of human resources. There are a number of regional trainers who provide training through a number of outlets or organizations. However, there is little consistency of approach and standards, resulting in variable quality. There is no means of accurately assessing training from a qualitative viewpoint. Also worth noting is the uneasy relationship between project-driven trainers, who usually are appointed from outside the region, and regional trainers, many of whom feel that "outsiders" do not have a sound enough understanding of the region and its particular characteristics.
- Most training providers in the region work in isolation. This results in an unco-ordinated approach. Commercial training initiatives inadvertently compete with funded initiatives. Equally, the funding agencies fail to communicate with other providers of education and training which leads to confusion, duplication of effort and the lack of any strategic approach to human resource development. Therefore, while it may be true that significant investment has been made in training in the region, the efficacy of this investment is very much in doubt.
- In most cases, the private sector views training as a cost rather than an investment for the future. This frequently prevents adequate resources being allocated at the planning stage. The result is that training is almost always underfunded or cancelled during a recessionary period.

In short, training attracts a great deal of "lip service" but little prioritization.

PROGRESS TO DATE

While the above paints a fairly bleak picture of human resource development in the Caribbean, there are some encouraging signs emerging. Indeed, some progress has been made in addressing several of the issues raised above. What is particularly encouraging is the extent to which recent developments have been strategic in their scope.

In February, 1992, the CARICOM Heads of State Summit on Tourism convened in Kingston, Jamaica. Included on its very heavy agenda were recommendations included in a paper prepared by the Human Resource Group of the CHA's Product Development Committee. The following conclusions were reached and endorsed by the Heads of State.

Governments [would]:

- Make every effort to up-grade or facilitate the up-grading of their national hotel schools, The Caribbean Hospitality Training Institute, and the University of the West Indies Centre for Hospitality and Tourism Management . . .
- . . . expedite the issue of Work Permits and in the case of qualified Caribbean nationals, remove or significantly liberalize requirements for Work Permits for management staff in the tourism sector, wishing to take up employment in other Caribbean countries.
- . . . encourage and facilitate the exchange of employees within the Caribbean and from/with operations outside . . .
- . . . encourage the establishment of a Regional Tourism Education Council and National Tourism Education Councils which could have among their functions the co-ordination of training programmes and the accreditation and articulation of programmes (Caribbean Community, 1992, 4–5).

Further recommendations were made in November 1992 by the Human Resources Sub-Committee of the CTO/CHA Tourism Product Development Task Force which met in St. Lucia. These called for governments, international funding agencies, the industry and educational institutions to prioritize human-resource development with respect to the survival and growth of Caribbean tourism.

Since the Summit, some progress has been made in complying with these conclusions, but it has been painfully slow. A number of hotel schools in the region, including Antigua, Barbados and the Bahamas have or will benefit from EU and World Bank funded projects. Notwithstanding that these projects were already in the pipeline prior to the Summit, they represent major improvements in the educational infrastructure in the region. In particular, the World Bank funded Bahamas Tourism Training Centre, which houses the University of the West Indies programme and the Bahamas Hotel Training College, is a vast improvement over the facilities these programmes once occupied (see Figure 6.3). The government of

Figure 6.3. The new Bahamas Tourism Training Centre houses the Centre for Hospitality and Tourism Studies of the University of the West Indies, the Bahamas Hotel Training College and various other agencies concerned with training in the Bahamas. This is typical of the various buildings which comprise this new facility

Bermuda continues to prioritize hospitality education and has invested heavily in the development of facilities at the Stonington Campus, including the College's training hotel (see Figures 6.4 and 6.5).

There has been some progress within the Organization of Eastern Caribbean States (OECS) in liberalizing immigration procedures within those states. However, there has been little progress with the establishment of a Regional Tourism Education Council or National Councils. Several other developments indicate that a regional strategic view of human-resource development may be growing. The CHA, CHTI and CRHTP formally recognized CHOCHS as the representative body for tertiary programmes of hospitality and tourism in the CHA region. This provides the CHOCHS with regional legitimacy, thereby strengthening the profile of its members and providing a foundation for the regional improvement of hospitality education. The CRHTP also began work in 1992 on the development and implementation of regional occupational standards to be linked with a regional certification scheme. This work has now been completed and the HOST Programme was launched in December, 1993.

Figure 6.4. The Faculty of Hotel and Business Administration at Bermuda College is located in purpose-built facilities on the College's Stonington Campus

Figure 6.5. The facilities for hospitality education and training at Bermuda College include the Stonington Beach Hotel, a luxury 64-room resort hotel purpose-built for training and adjacent to the Stonington Campus. The Hotel has grounds and a pool area typical of Bermuda's fine small hotels

THE HOST (HOSPITALITY OCCUPATIONAL STANDARDS FOR TRAINING) PROGRAMME

The Programme, designed at this stage of its development for the hotel and restaurant sectors, is unique in that it is a truly regional effort, incorporating input from over 200 individual managers, chefs, supervisors, educators, industry association executives and public-sector representatives in 11 countries in the Caribbean. This input has been used to create occupational standards in four major areas of work: food production, food and beverage service, housekeeping and the front office. The standards are grouped together in units at five levels of competency: foundation craft, skilled craft, advanced skilled craft, supervisory management and divisional management.

The assessment process for the Programme is a good example of a regional approach to maintaining occupational standards. Attainment of the standards is assessed initially by internal assessors within a candidate's place of employment. When the internal assessors conclude that the candidate has met the standards required for each unit, an external assessor examines the candidate's ability to meet the standards. External assessors are usually recognized experts in a country and, along with internal assessors, are trained in the assessment and administration of the Programme. The National Supervisory Body, which may be an already existing organization or a new entity created specifically to administer the HOST Programme, with the approval of the Programme, awards the certificates and diplomas which have been earned. In this way, the regional standards are assessed and recognized through local members of the industry.

The Programme sets policy through its Occupational Standards Council, which consists of representatives from 12 regional and international organizations. The membership of the Council provides a wide range of guidance skills from a variety of relevant sources and imparts a high degree of credibility on the Programme. The membership is listed in Table 6.2 and includes all the major industrial and educational organizations involved with the hospitality industry in the region and its major markets.

Table 6.2. Members of the Occupational Standards Council of the HOST Programme

Members
Council of Caribbean Hospitality Schools—Chair
Caribbean Hospitality Training Institute—Vice Chair
Hotel Catering and Institutional Management Association—Treasurer
American Culinary Federation Educational Institute
Association of Caribbean Tertiary Institutions
Canadian Tourism Human Resources Council
Caribbean Hospitality Industry (2 representatives)
Caribbean Hotel Association
Caribbean Tourism Organization
Council for Hotel, Restaurant and Institutional Education
University of the West Indies

During its first year of operation, the HOST Programme has enjoyed broad regional support. It is being actively utilized in 14 countries and by 22 companies. In addition, many of the regional schools are examining the standards with a view toward incorporating them into their curriculum in order to allow students to work toward the regional qualifications and to provide training for persons working in the industry who are working towards a HOST qualification. The creation of National Supervisory Bodies for the Programme may assist in the growth of National Tourism Education Councils as called for by the 1992 Tourism Summit. The HOST Programme provides a model for regional co-operation in the development of human resources for Caribbean tourism.

Finally, a second Summit on Tourism is being planned for 1995. This meeting will serve to strengthen the regional recognition of the importance of tourism for the Caribbean and build upon the success of the 1992 Summit. What is particularly noteworthy is the importance which human resources are being given in the planning for the Summit. Rather than being viewed as a component of product development, as was the case with the 1992 Summit, the organizers plan to designate human resources as a separate category for consideration by delegates. This will be the first time that human resources has received this level of attention and is an indication that the industry and public sector are increasingly understanding the strategic importance of human resources to the success of Caribbean tourism.

FURTHER ACTION STEPS

As has already been stated, a strategic approach to human-resource development is essential for the survival and long-term growth of the Caribbean tourism industry. In a region like the Caribbean, this is indeed a challenge. However, where 8 out of 10 persons are employed in or are dependent on tourism, it must be a priority if the quality of service in the industry is to improve, waste and duplication to be eliminated and the image of the industry as an employer to improve. Notwithstanding the signs of progress discussed above, the following action steps need to be taken:

Recognition of the strategic importance of human resource development for the long-term success of the region's tourism industry

Industry, governments, funding agencies and educational institutions must move towards this goal. Although they stated such commitment at the 1992 Summit and at the annual industry conferences, they must demonstrate their commitment to the goal by prioritizing human-resource development, particularly with respect to funding. The achievement of this goal would be the development of a regional, integrated human-resource strategy with commitment for funding and on-going support for education and training.

The establishment of a Regional Tourism Education and Training Council

To make any progress in terms of action, the appropriate infrastructure needs to be in place. While there are a number of regional organizations which have a vested interest in promoting tourism education and training, there is no one organization that would be appropriate to oversee this activity. The establishment of a Regional Tourism Education and Training Council with the support of the public and private sectors in the region would be the cornerstone for any progress. This has already been endorsed by the CARICOM Heads of State at the 1992 Summit but has yet to be established. The Council should be made up of representatives of regional bodies such as the CHA, CTO, CHOCHS, CHTI, ACTI, University of the West Indies (UWI), regional governments and regional and national unions. The Council would need to have the power to co-opt other members and it would be responsible:

1. for the co-ordination of regional tourism education and training at the tertiary level;
2. for the encouragement of tourism as a core subject in primary and secondary curricula;
3. for the development of a long-term strategy for the strengthening of the region's tertiary programmes in hospitality and tourism;
4. for playing the lead role in the development of national tourism education and training councils.

The Occupational Standards Council of the HOST Programme is, to some extent, a model for the Regional Tourism Education and Training Council but the body would need expanded regional representation in order to achieve the objective listed above.

Strengthening of hospitality schools in the region

The current state of many hospitality schools in the region is worrying. There is much work to be done which needs to be tackled at a national level before regional issues can be addressed. Certainly CHOCHS is able to represent schools from a regional perspective but it will require funding if it is to be able to do this effectively. Many schools, particularly the smaller ones, are simply unable to fund their involvement in regional issues. Governments are urged to give this matter priority consideration in their support of the conclusions reached at the 1992 Summit.

The creation of a centre of hospitality educational excellence for the region

The strengthening of the region's hospitality schools should be accompanied by the development of a regional world-class centre for hospitality and tourism education and research. The aim should be to provide the region with a school on a par with the world's top schools and provide leadership for the region's other schools. This centre would make a statement about the professionalism of the industry and assist in the changing of attitudes which will be necessary if the industry is to attract the best and brightest of people. Whether the centre would be a completely new facility and organization or an upgrading of an existing regional school is a matter to be decided. However, the creation of such a centre would represent the adoption of a strategic, multi-constituent perspective which would be a radical departure from past practice.

Tourism education at the primary and secondary level

If the industry is to attract the best students in the region, it will be necessary for tourism awareness and appreciation to form part of primary and secondary curricula. There are several good examples of this already in place in the region, including the Bahamas where tourism awareness is part of the secondary curricula. This objective would be a priority for the Regional Tourism Education Council.

The strengthening of training in the region

It has already been stated that training in the region comes from varying sources and at varying levels of competency. The region needs comprehensive, competency-based training standards and a regional certification scheme to allow trainers to earn internationally recognized training qualifications. The 1992 Summit singled out the CHTI for support. However, there is a need for closer links between regional training providers and the various funding agencies. The assessment of regional training needs, the planning of programmes to address these needs and the co-ordination of their delivery should be another priority of the Regional Tourism Education Council.

CONCLUSION

This chapter has presented an analysis of tertiary education and training in the Caribbean. The analysis leads to the conclusion that human-resource development still does not attract the strategic attention necessary for it to function effectively as a cornerstone of the industry. Human-resource development has been identified as a major component of the industry by the region's governments, and a model for strategic development has been endorsed. However, the commitment from industry, government and education is still not at a level where significant change can be projected.

Failure to act now will threaten the competitiveness of the region in the world tourism arena. While sun, sea and sand is an irresistible combination for many, it is no longer enough. The tourism industry is complex and sophisticated. It needs professionals to run it. As the tourism client becomes more and more demanding and is presented with a growing array of choices, those destinations which have invested in human-resource development will have a competitive advantage. The private and public sectors in the region must realize that this linkage between people and success is fundamental and make the necessary level of investment in recommended regional and national structures for implementing strategic human-resource development.

REFERENCES

Baum, T. (1992) "Human Resources: The Unsung Price-Value Issue". *Proceedings of the First Island Tourism International Forum*, Centre for Tourism Research and Innovation, Bermuda College, Paget, Bermuda.

Caribbean Community (1992) *Summary of Conclusions of the Caricom Summit on Tourism*. Kingston, Jamaica, 18 February.

Charles, K.R. (1992) "Career Influences, Expectations, and Perceptions of Caribbean Hospitality and Tourism Students: A Third World Perspective". *Hospitality and Tourism Educator*, **4**(3), 9–14.

Conlin, Michael V. (1992) "Human Resource Development In Caribbean Tourism: Issues for the 1990's". In Tom Baum (ed.), *Human Resources in International Tourism*. Oxford, Butterworth Heinemann, 145–160.

7 Islands, Beaches and Life-stage Marketing

CHRIS RYAN
Massey University, New Zealand

INTRODUCTION

This chapter considers the degree to which conventional life-stages can still be used as a means of market segmentation. It therefore differs from other chapters because (1) it considers issues pertinent to many tourist destinations and not simply islands; and (2) it is not destination specific. It presupposes that market segmentation is an important element in devising tourism market strategies, and so the first part considers why this should be the case. The second part examines some of the evidence for and against life-stages as a means of identifying tourist categories, and argues that, at least in the short to intermediate term, it is a valid predictor for the traditional tourist-generating areas of North America and Western Europe. Third, some implications for marketing islands as tourist attractions are considered.

THE NEED FOR SEGMENTATION—THE GLOBAL CONTEXT

Although it is a cliché to note that tourism may be, by the end of the millennium, the world's largest industry, what is not always noted is that in the last part of the 1980s the supply of tourism facilities grew as fast, possibly faster than, the growth of tourism demand. While, in the longer term, it is possible to point to the emergence of more Asian countries (including India and China) as tourist generators, in the short-to-medium term the traditional tourist-generating countries of North America and Western Europe are possibly beginning to show diminishing growth rates of outgoing tourist activity. Partly this might be due to the recent, and still lingering, recession, but equally it can be hypothesized that outside of that recession, emergent post-industrialized trends can lead to shifts in the tourism–leisure ratio that begin to diminish the role of international tourism as a source of escape from daily routine. Short weekend stays and increased day-trip activities in association with new leisure trends will undoubtedly continue to grow, but these are primarily intra- rather than international in context, subject to one proviso noted below. As early as 1985 the Economist Intelligence Unit indicated that

Island Tourism: Management Principles and Practice
Edited by Michael V. Conlin and Tom Baum

saturation levels within the traditional tourism-generating countries of Europe were being approached. Traditionally, shorter working weeks and increased holidays have been noted as permitting increased holiday taking, but in the last decade the growth of holiday entitlement within northern Europe has significantly slowed, and for many individuals, data do not support contentions of growing leisure time. Furthermore, for those who have experienced some growth in leisure time, the pattern of the immediate postwar period to the 1970s, where there was increased income per hour of available leisure time, can no longer be automatically assumed to be the case.

In Europe, international tourism statistics may also hide a growing trend of a larger number of trips of short duration and journey time. For example, the completion of the Channel Tunnel is expected to lead to a new demand for international travel, but in many respects its duration and nature is expected to be a substituted domestic weekend or short vacation (Jefferson, 1993). Again, the opening of Eastern European countries such as the Czech Republic has led to an increase in international tourism, but on closer examination, the journey patterns of many Germans are those of short weekend breaks. Hence, within a European setting, an apparent growth in international tourism does not, in itself, give lie to the contention that there are real changes in patterns of leisure and associated travel.

The position in North America is partially different. Americans are important as international tourists by reason of their numbers and levels of high daily expenditure, but it remains true that most Americans holiday within their own country, and for many older Americans the cliché that the overseas trip is a once-in-a-life-time trip is not without truth. It might be expected more Americans will travel abroad, but none the less a number of factors still exist to inhibit the development of mass international travel as it is understood in Europe. One of these factors is that the United States' authorities are appreciating the impact that tourism is having on their own balance of payments. As Edgell (1993) makes clear, the United States Department of Commerce has identified the development of America's own tourist facilities as not only a way of securing more tourists to the USA in order to add to its balance of payments' revenues, but also the improvement of its own tourist infrastructure acts as an import substitute, reducing expenditure overseas by its own citizens. Perhaps only in the ASEAN countries can a vast new demand for tourism be identified, but this may not, in the short term, directly affect many islands in the Mediterranean or Caribbean that are traditionally dependent upon the slower-growing north European or American markets.

In consequence, the position facing islands as they seek to compete for tourists at the end of the 20th century is one of increased competition not only from other islands and existing tourist attractions but also from new attractions both within and outside of traditional tourist generating and receiving areas. Further, to take one possible scenario as argued by Emery (1981), the future will be of more selective but possibly reduced overseas travel per capita in terms of the numbers of tourist trips or nights—a trend which might not only apply to traditional tourist-generating countries but one that may be learnt quickly by the new markets of south-east Asia.

The degree to which this will affect different islands is difficult to assess. For island destinations at the start of their particular life-cycle, it can be argued that they possess the advantage of novelty, an ability to compete for special niche markets based upon exploitation of cultures, facilities or specific activities new to the market place, but on the other hand they are forced to compete against well-established suppliers of the tourist product. Islands such as Bermuda, Aruba, the Bahamas, Malta and the Balearics which are in the mature stage of their life-cycle (de Albuqueque and McElroy, 1992) possess the infrastructure but also the problems of reinvestment to maintain quality and freshness of appeal while seeking to re-establish their market position to avoid the possibility of decline. And, as noted, each island has to do this at a time when competition for tourist expenditure is increasing and when the needs for employment and income generation are at their most pressing during the period of slow, fragile, recovery from the world recession that exists in the mid-1990s. Further, to state the obvious, geographical proximity *and* accessibility to major tourist-generating centres will be important. Majorca, only two hours' flying time from London Gatwick airport, could realistically seek to compete in a market in the London area for an extended week-end break. The same would not be true of, say, Bermuda.

Other factors make a complex scene even more confusing. Islands have traditionally depended upon an appeal of sun, sea and sand, but these appeals are losing their attraction to increasingly experienced and sophisticated tourists (Forbes and Forbes, 1992, 1993), while potential worries exist about the effects of the weakening of the ozone layer. Additional concerns about the environmental impacts of tourism might lead to tougher planning regulations which might inhibit the size of developments.

The impacts of such factors are difficult to assess. Societies within tourist-generating countries are not homogeneous. As incomes have tended to increase, previously low-income groups move into the habit of taking foreign holidays for the first time—indeed this is the very basis of the concept of successive class intrusion whereby a resort area experiences different social grouping (or nationalities) as it proceeds through its life-cycle. Resorts can retain their appeal for other reasons:

1. As a product begins to lose an appeal in one market, it may be successfully promoted in a new one. For example, as resorts like Brighton become less appealing to the British, its very traditional "Britishness" has allowed it to be marketed by the British Tourist Authority to the Japanese market.
2. If past behaviour has led to satisfactory holiday experiences, there is a strong reason for holiday-takers to repeat that behaviour as a risk-avoidance strategy.
3. As individuals pass through their life-stages, the demands of each stage might induce holiday-makers to change past patterns and to use existing holiday products designed for specific groups (e.g. those with young children). Unable to continue past holidays which require adventure or flexibility, they may turn, in relief, to holiday areas or products previously not considered.

Evidence for this might be seen in the continued popularity of the package holiday in the British market. Arguably the "package holiday" was a concept of the 1950s based on escape motivations, competitive pricing and a search for the sun. It has also successfully developed a number of resorts and hotels which cater for specific life-stage groupings based on the singles, young family and retired market segments. For example, in the Balearic Islands, Ibiza and Minorca tend to cater for different types of tourist based to some degree upon life-stages. These motivations and needs still help to sell over 11 million package holidays each year, and although changes have occurred, it can be contended that the basic core of the product has remained unchanged for 40 years. If therefore, higher-income groups have a pre-disposition to move out of the market to pursue new leisure interests and modes of behaviour, previously lower-income groups enter into the market seeking to emulate the holiday experiences others have had in the past. As this occurs against the background of increased competition already noted, a paradox can be shown to exist where traditional island products and resorts can continue to enjoy degrees of success even while others seek to change and meet new demands. Therefore, while on the one hand there may be the changes identified by the Forbes (1992, 1993), some islands might continue their product unchanged as they reach out to new markets and market segments. Indeed past patterns of tourist motivation and behaviour thought to be outmoded may in fact be repeated as new tourists enter the market. Islands thus face a complex pattern of increased competition, potential over-supply in the short-term, changed requirements by some market segments, a demand for existing products by large parts of its risk-averse clientele, and a demand from new groups of consumers for existing products which, however, might be used in new ways.

This poses considerable difficulties for planning authorities, hoteliers and tour operators at strategic and operational levels. To give one example. Research by the author found that in Magaluf, Majorca, in the winter of 1993, many British holiday-makers complained about the numbers of retired Spanish tourists who were taking advantage of the Spanish government's schemes to discount winter holidays for their pensioners. This was part of a campaign to aid the Spanish hotel industry over a period of falling occupancy levels resulting from the recession in northern Europe. Entertainment within some hotels was becoming orientated towards these longer-stay Spanish tourists, and British visitors returning to the island who had become to think of Magaluf as "their resort" found it difficult to readjust to these changes (Ryan, 1994). Majorca's authorities also have to maintain existing tourist products even while they seek to develop new resources geared to different markets. The result is a significant environmental impact on the area between Andratx and Santa Ponsa as it is developed with marinas and complexes for "up-market" segments. In other areas there is a prohibition on development to maintain pro-environmental policies to support new concerns and marketing images. Finally, there is the problem of upgrading existing facilities in, say, Magaluf, which, for the moment, continue to be used by Majorca's traditional markets.

One further point in this review of global change must also be noted. Although resorts can extend the mature stage of their life-cycle by enabling the product to meet traditional demands from new market groupings, there is a proviso. Both groups, the "experienced" and the "new" tourist, are practised consumers in other areas of their lives. They are today at ease with the marketing strategies employed by companies; they are no longer naïve in their reactions to television advertising and other promotional strategies. Their skills are not left behind when purchasing holidays or evaluating the product and experience. Consequently producers need to ensure that "value for money" is provided, and this extends not only to the design of the product but also to the interaction between the client and the members of staff at the hotel or resort. As Bitner *et al.* (1990) demonstrate, the "critical incident" can be important in the evaluation of the experience, the determination of repeat purchasing and the "word of mouth" recommendation. The complexity of the tourism marketing and planning task is thus evident.

SEGMENTATION—BASED UPON WHAT?

Producers in many industries, faced with increasing competition, have sought to define their markets more narrowly. As Richard Branson commented upon the launch of Radio 1215AM in the United Kingdom, he was not a "broadcaster" but a "narrowcaster"—seeking to appeal to specific types of listeners. Market segmentation has become a means of knowing customer profiles better, identifying their needs and securing a match between product and market positioning that utilizes the supplier's advantages *vis-à-vis* their competitors. Within tourism such a matching might be based upon specific natural attractions (e.g. unspoilt waters for scuba diving in the case of Bonaire), a specific cultural tradition (opera holidays at Verona) or a combination of man-made attractions that generates their own rationale (e.g. Disney World).

A "natural way" of segmenting holiday-takers is to base categories upon life-stage. The need of the young-singles market based on a supply of bars and discos is easily differentiated from the needs of those with young children or the desire of the older person for quieter pursuits. Yet, on the other hand, as a basis for marketing it might be regarded as "old-fashioned". Recently adopted approaches to marketing have yielded sophisticated versions of the tourist typologies described in textbooks of tourism. Whereas Cohen's (1974, 1979) classification of tourists as explorers, drifters, independent mass-organized and mass-organized tourists has for long been part of tourism literature, more recently authors have taken advantage of increasingly accessible computer power to use cluster analysis to produce statistically based psychographic profiles of tourists. For example, within 1992 alone, Mazanec developed a categorization of visitors to the "Euro-sports area", Yiannakis and Gibson considered typologies based on leisure-based tourist roles, while at a specific destination, Fielding *et al.* distinguished between intrinsically and extrinsically motivated tourists and their different behaviours at Ayres Rock, Australia.

From the commercial perspective, within the UK, tourist-attraction owners and tour operators are increasingly using commercially available geo-demographic and psychographic databases to help in developing mail-shots and to describe their customer profiles. Even where a company is selling to a specific age group, as is the case of Saga Holidays who undertake direct selling to the over-55s, use is made of these systems. In short, there is seemingly a greater use of profiles based on psychological concepts of motivation, attitude and lifestyle.

IS THIS BECAUSE MORE TRADITIONAL CRITERIA ARE LESS VALID FOR SEGMENTING MARKETS AND DESIGNING PRODUCTS?

The arguments for the use of other than conventional socio-economic and life-stage variables for marketing segmentation are well known. Throughout the period since the 1960s females have become a more important part of the work force, and a cliché of the 1980s was the emergence of the career-orientated, professional and single female. This was not without truth, as is revealed in the UK General Household and Census of Population figures for the United Kingdom. In 1961 76% of females between the ages of 18 to 49 were married; by 1991 the figure was 61%. Higher divorce rates have produced convoluted life-stage patterns as couples marry, divorce, remarry and hence might end up in extended family networks of children from either one or both marriages. Within the UK approximately one-fifth of all births are illegitimate in that on the birth certificate there is either the name of only one parent or the identified parents have different surnames. Single-parent families are, in some London boroughs, accounting for over one-third of all households with children. The UK has one of the highest divorce rates in the world, and over a third of marriages end in divorce, while, in any one year, approximately a third of marriages include a partner previously married. Nor are these phenomena restricted to the UK. In Denmark in 1992 46.5% of all births were outside of marriage. For the EC as a whole 19.5% of births are extra-marital, an increase from 1982 when the figure was 10.7%. The Danish and Belgian divorce rates are almost as high as those in the UK.

One impact of divorce and remarriage is that it delays the empty-nest stage and in future years might impact on concepts of an older affluent market, which, although it will still exist, might not be so numerous as was once thought. As it is, the relationship between age and predicted leisure expenditure becomes less certain given the delay in the empty-nest stage. Additionally, other factors such as delayed child bearing might create the "squeezed generation", as couples find that they have as dependants both their elderly parents as well as young children. In short, the conventional picture of life-stages moving to an "empty-nest" as described by Kotler (1967) in the first edition of his textbook on marketing, is giving way to one where the "empty-nest" stage is either maintained throughout marriage by couples not having children, is reached early by those marrying and having children young, is delayed considerably by a combination of later marriage and child bearing or through a process of divorce and having children in the second marriage.

Additionally, the traditional pattern described by Kotler will also continue, albeit as a shrinking percentage of the total population. For example, drawing upon the data in Social Trends, in the UK, the conventional advertising cliché of a family of two (married) adults and two children would appear to account for less than 10% of all households.

Another longer-term threat to the concept of the wealthy, leisure-orientated older empty nester might also lie in governments' growing realization of the costs of sustaining an increasing number of older people, with subsequent demands upon health services, at times of uncertain economic growth. The politics of the "new right" with advocacy of the "user pays" principle may mean that future generations of the elderly will be faced with the need to pay for hospital and welfare services previously considered to have been paid for through taxation. For the moment the impact upon saving ratios and leisure spending is one of surmise only, but its negative implications for the concept of the wealthy, older market spending more on travel are obvious.

Higher incomes, a greater diversity of goods and the creation of new leisure activities have all combined to produce more individualized lifestyles. In the area of leisure some sports such as mountain biking, windsurfing, hang gliding, and orienteering have only become recognized sports in the last two decades, while other, more traditional sports such as sailing, rock climbing, martial arts and road running have all enjoyed significant booms. Additionally, it is argued that the distinctions between work and leisure are breaking down, for the nature of work changes as advanced societies move into post-industrialized employment structures. Such occupational changes, combined with higher numbers of working women, change household income patterns to the extent where occupation is even less of a guide to income and expenditure than was the case some three or four decades ago.

All of this social change would seem to confirm the hypothesis that changes in the nature of demand for holiday-taking must surely occur. Thus commentators such as Emery (1981), and Forbes (1993) referred to above and others such as Pearce (1988) have written of the importance of concepts of self-actualization, the tourist career as tourists aspire to a need for more meaningful experiences and the "learning moment" as motivations for holiday-taking.

Yet the evidence from positivist studies is not entirely convincing. Detailed studies of large samples have indicated the strength of traditional motivations for holiday-taking, even if the classifications differ (for example, Laing, 1987; Yiannakis and Gibson, 1992, 1993). In a study conducted by the author of 1127 respondents, the motivations for holiday-taking as measured upon a seven-point scale where seven was the highest score continued to be the traditional ones of "to relax mentally" (5.96), "escape from the daily routine" (5.63) and "to relax physically" (5.51). The intellectual "pull" motivators scored less highly for the total sample. For example the item "to increase my knowledge" scored 4.39, and "to use my imagination" 3.45 (Ryan, 1993).

Positivist studies can be, and are, criticized from the perspective of deconstructionists. If consumers play games in shopping malls in the fulfilment of passing a pleasant moment or two, and thereby rendering a positivist explanation of their behaviour invalid (Urry, 1991), how much more ludic involvement is there in holiday-taking? Indeed, some commentators have specifically referred to the holiday as a means of regression into childhood, a sanctioned release from responsibility (Crompton, 1979; Ryan, 1991). The sought for "learning moment" may be a matter of play, a matter of no real concern. Indeed, studies of feeling of well-being would even indicate that the "peak experience" is comparatively unimportant in the development of life view when compared to the frequency of less-intensive experiences (Diener *et al.*, 1991). For a number of reasons, therefore, readily to dismiss the traditional explanations of holiday-making in favour of new scenarios of the importance of self-actualization seems, to this author, to be premature.

DOES TRADITIONAL MARKET SEGMENTATION STILL POSSESS VALIDITY?

If traditional motivations can still be utilized in the demarcation of holiday groupings, can the same be true of traditional classifications? Within the UK the Market Research Society and British Audience Research Bureau have monitored the validity of social class as predictors of consumer purchasing. It has been argued that there is a lack of stability over social-class membership. In a review of Granada's television panel O'Brien and Ford (1988) reported an apparent change of social-class membership by 41% of the respondents in a six month period. On closer examination, this was corrected to 10%. Thus, it seems that the discussion of consumer behaviour is bedevilled by both social-class movement and mistakes in class attribution.

Cornish and Denny (1989) argue that social grade often under-performs because "individuals will often be graded in the field on a shortened and subjective version of the measure". A combination of socio-educational grade, income and life-stage is, they argue, a powerful predictor of consumer behaviour, while they also point out that (based on data drawn from the National Readership Survey) for package holidays disposable net household income is a strong discriminator. O'Brien and Ford (1988) did include holidays as a purchase item in their survey of the effectiveness of alternative predictors of consumer behaviour. They assessed social class, life-stage, lifestyle and disposable income across 20 items by four methods of discrimination. They concluded that:

> — social grade *does* discriminate
> — no alternative classification provides *consistently* better discriminatory powers
> — no *one* classification works best across all product fields,
>
> *but*, . . .—sometimes other classifications discriminate *more*, and frequently they are *just as powerful* as Social Class (O'Brien and Ford, 1988: 309—italics are original authors' emphasis).

In the case of holidays, the scores achieved by the "predictors" were life-stage,

83, lifestyle, 88 and social class, 87 (O'Brien and Ford, 1988: 297). As a caveat, however, it must be noted that the holiday behaviour analysed was simply the purchase of a "main holiday". It can be contended that lifestyle categories can be more important when seeking to assess the *type* of holiday that is undertaken.

Given therefore the findings that conventional motivation factors such as the need to escape from daily pressures (Krippendorf, 1987; Ryan, 1993), and the role of conventional socio-economic variables appearing to retain some validity as a general predictor of consumer behaviour in holiday-taking, the findings of a recent sample of 1127 British holiday-takers are of interest. The sample was selected from data derived from the British Market Research Bureau's characteristics of above-average spenders on holidays, matched with a geo-demographic coding (Mosaic), with names and addresses selected on a disproportionate random sample from the East Midlands in the UK in 1992. After tests on British samples, the questionnaire was based on holiday-motivation items selected from the Beard and Ragheb Leisure Motivation Scale (1980, 1983). The purpose of the research was an attempt to replicate the factors of the Leisure Motivation Scale, derive clusters of holiday-takers and assess their satisfaction with the holiday experience (Ryan, 1993). Although the derived lifestyle clusters did carry some predictive ability for the choice of attributes of holiday destinations and activities, life-stage factors continually emerged as important determinants. (In the following summary of results a seven-point Likert-type scale was used, where seven represented the maximum score.)

As might be thought obvious, the need to consider a spouse and children did in fact emerge as an important factor in determining holiday choice—more important than the past experience of a given type of holiday, whether the destination had been previously visited, the time of year, the brochure or the price of the holiday.

Marital status also affected the motivations for taking holidays. Married couples ($n = 456$) tended to score higher on relaxation needs than single people (*$n = 329$; mean of 5.73 against 5.44, $t = 2.31$, $p = 0.02$*), but lower on items relating to social needs. Those with children under the age of 16 rated relaxation needs even more highly than those without children.

Age also had a significant impact upon holiday motivations. Those between 36 and 65 ($n = 905$) are significantly different from other age groups in emphasizing a need to get away from the daily hustle and bustle of life (*mean for those aged 35 to 65 = 5.8, F-ratio = 11.3, $p = 0.000$*). Table 7.1 details some of the results.

With reference to the desired attributes of the holiday destination, again social aspects such as age, the presence of children and marital status have significant impacts upon holiday destination choice. As might be expected single people rate an active nightlife and nightclubs more highly (*mean for single people = 4.6, F-ratio = 27.30, $p = 0.000$*), while those who are married rate the accommodation and facilities for children more highly (*mean for this group = 5.8, F-ratio = 373.7, $p = 0.000$*)[1].

Hence, from UK studies, social class and life-stage appear to retain some useful predictive power for holiday expenditure. What of other countries and questions of

Table 7.1. Life-stage and scores on selected holiday attributes

Item	Bachelor	Full nest	Empty nest	Survivor	F-ratio	Prob.
Holiday-taking motives						
Sport	3.5	2.8	2.4	1.5	18.55	0.000
A calm atmosphere	4.5	5.6	5.6	5.5	11.40	0.000
Avoid daily hustle	5.1	5.8	5.8	5.0	11.30	0.000
Relax mentally	5.5	6.1	6.1	5.3	11.20	0.000
Physical relaxation	5.1	5.7	5.4	5.2	4.80	0.002
Holiday destination attributes						
Children's facilities	1.2	5.8	1.6	1.1	373.7	0.000
Nightlife	4.6	2.5	2.2	1.8	27.30	0.000
Scenic location	5.5	6.0	6.3	6.4	14.21	0.000
Historic location	4.2	4.9	5.2	4.9	10.80	0.000
Comfortable accommodation	5.4	6.0	6.1	6.4	9.61	0.000
Interesting culture	4.8	5.2	5.4	4.9	3.83	0.009
Number	329	343	93	82		

Note: a seven-point scale is used where:
7 = very important
1 = of no importance

actual tourist behaviour? Bojanic (1992), on the basis of a sample of 2000 US citizens who travelled to Europe, found significant differences between stages as to their likes and dislikes. Gibson and Yiannakis (1993) found evidence of the importance of life-stage in tourist roles, while Lawson (1991), in a study of New Zealand tourists, has also found changes in choice of activity and destination at varying stages of the life cycle.

THE IMPACT OF FAMILY LIFE-STAGE ON CHOICE OF HOLIDAY DESTINATION AND ACTIVITY

It is not difficult to develop a simple relationship between life-cycle stage and holiday activity. Using the work of Lawson (1991) and Bojanic (1992), and adapting a schema of the former, Table 7.2 can be suggested. This simplified model also indicates how, to some extent, the trends of self-actualization and the importance of experience noted above might be emerging. It can be contended that of the above groupings, it is those without children who are the most likely to show some of the behaviour patterns noted by Forbes and Pearce; and perhaps where it is demonstrated by others it might be a function of high discretionary income, and perhaps associated higher levels of education. As the childless become a larger grouping within the traditional tourist-generating societies, their motivations

Table 7.2. Life-stage preferences

Life-stage	Preferences
Bachelor	Beaches, nightlife, not concerned about children, socially orientated to peers.
Newly married	Still liking beach resorts—more concern about accommodation and restaurants, still wanting "adventure". Continuing to a modified degree past holiday patterns but changing accommodation.
Full nest I	Children important in vacation decision taking, special amenities/facilities for children important, still like beaches, types and availability of shops important.
Full nest II	Children less important because more able to take care of themselves—beaches, accommodation, shopping still important.
Empty nest	Accommodation, shopping still important but more interest in travel around destination, quality of provision more important. Higher interest in culture as an observer and to a lesser degree as a potential "participant". Nostalgia emerging as a holiday motivation.
Solitary survivor	Safety, comfort, price/quality relationship important.
Single parent	Price considerations, beaches, accommodation—attitude towards children varies dependent upon age of child and ability to leave child with others. Nature of other holiday takers can be important.
Middle-aged couples	Interested in local customs, history, culture. Without children. Good accommodation; quality is important. High disposable income and prepared to spend.

assume a greater importance; but such motivation becomes but an *additional* theme within the explanation of holiday-taking, not necessarily a *replacement*.

IMPLICATIONS FOR ISLAND TOURISM

What does this research indicate? First, it must be made clear that it is not being argued that market segmentation by lifestyle is unnecessary—it is only being pointed out that the more conventional categorization of life-stage is still an important marketing segmentation tool, albeit perhaps in an amended form as described above. This actually poses a series of advantages for many of the smaller islands concerned with marketing themselves as tourist destinations. A number of such islands are heavily dependent upon tourism but equally have a small-scale economy and are unable to afford the costs of undertaking marketing-segmentation exercises based on the lifestyle of each of its target markets or buying such information. Using size of population as a proxy for the size of the economy or the ability to obtain the necessary expertise (not a satisfactory measure it is recognized but one which will suffice for this argument), many of the island destinations are quite small; and thus would have difficulty in buying detailed psychographic profiles of their tourist markets. For example the populations of Martinique, Dominica, Bonaire and Saba, to take but a random list, are 330 000, 81 000, 10 000 and 1000 respectively. Life-stage data also has the advantage of not only being more accessible but also of being more easily understood in terms of defining the needs of clients; and unlike the categorizations of tourists based upon small samples generated by academics for their cluster analysis, any findings can be more easily monitored and perhaps even replicated.

In both the author's current research, and that of Bojanic (1992), one obvious finding is that for many the presence of beaches is an attracting factor—and, again to labour the obvious, islands have beaches! But how do these market groups use beaches? From responses to both open-ended and Likert-type questions in the author's current research, it seems that for families with young children the beach is a social facility where children can play with other children, where parents can meet with other parents and share the duties of overseeing children. Young adults will use the beach for play, but with their peers, and might also require water sports facilities. Backman *et al.* (1986) in a study of Texas beaches concluded from factor analysis that beaches fell into three main categories—first, those comprised of opportunities to be active, to be social and to be seen; second, the benefits of safety and being there for children; and third, those relating to scenic and seasonal factors. Each tended to attract different groupings of tourists based, not surprisingly, on life-stage segments.

From this, one marketing implication is that island tourist authorities could note that the conventional life-stage factors are important; that beaches are also important but also that beaches should not compete for all age and family-type groupings. Market segmentation implies product segmentation. Just as manufacturers of fast-moving consumer goods create product and packaging differences to appeal to different consumers, so, too, tourist authorities could conduct tourist audits of beaches to manage and plan them to meet specific market segment needs based on life-stage family activities. This has very real implications for the development of access to beaches (by road, by paths, the need for car parking); for the type of beach development (hotels, toilet provision, types of catering facility) and for the level of coastal development. For example, the middle-aged without children would prefer beaches accessed by longer walks from car parks through a coastal landscape, whereas those with young children might require car parks located by the beach itself.

This discussion also presupposes that islands are large enough to cater for a wide range of market segments and are equally accessible to all. Patently, this is not always true, and some smaller islands with more limited resources or more distant locations need to develop appropriate marketing strategies. What is viable for the Balearics is not true for, say, Madagascar. But what might be true is that, given a lack of other information about the market segments within the tourist-generating areas, it is valid to base product design and publicity upon life-stage market segments. Thus, at a simple level, beach design and planning, allied with publicity material about an island's beaches, can be an effective marketing ploy in attracting tourists. It might also be essential. From a marketing perspective, given the increased competition from all manner of tourist attractions, islands need increasingly to examine what, if anything, is specific and unique to them. Other destinations can compete in terms of climate and diversity of culture. Hotels, entertainment, water sports and, yes, even beaches, are not the prerogative of islands. Dependent upon their size, what most islands can offer is accessibility to a wider range of seascape and beaches than might be the norm on larger land masses. The relationship between land and sea, that contrast between restless motion and stable rock, is generally perpetual in the case of islands. If anything is unique about most islands when compared to continents it is this, and hence the more important is the need to examine carefully the role of beaches and their appeal in developing tourism strategies and subsequent marketing.

CONCLUSIONS

In the above literature and research review, much of what emerges might be felt to be "obvious". But sometimes the obvious needs to be stated. There is a tendency today in some quarters to feel that market research must be "sophisticated" and engage in exercises such as the creation of psychographic or lifestyle profiles, and certainly the academic literature is replete with overlapping but different typologies. Even allowing for the social changes referred to above, life-stage still carries significant validity as a predictor of tourist motivation and behaviour. Perhaps researchers, academics and consultants are drawn instinctively to the new rather than the norm and, in their interest in new family structures, overlook the validity that is still left in the old concepts. Many European, Caribbean and other islands do have a strong appeal for the young and those with children, and for those seeking the more contemplative experience; especially those islands with a variety of beaches. These demands are likely to continue for some time, in spite of new fears about over-exposure to the sun. The marketing implications noted above are consistent with demands for more environmentally sensitive tourism planning and, if anything, reinforce the need for a proactive planning and monitoring by those involved in tourism policy creation.

This is not to argue that newer methods of segmentation are without value—very far from it. However, smaller island tourist authorities seeking to understand their markets more fully, but without the resources to undertake more sophisticated reviews of their clients, surveys that establish life-stage can still reveal data that can be interpreted and acted upon as a means of undertaking tourist promotion, planning and development. The lack of access to more sophisticated databanks becomes no reason to avoid the costs and disciplines of market research!

NOTE

1 t = t-test, a test comparing two mean (average) scores to assess whether the difference between the two is significant. The actual value of the t-test can depend upon sample size, and hence the associated 'p' (probability) is important in interpreting the t-test. If $p < 0.05$ it means the result can only have occurred five in a hundred times by chance, and is thus significant. If $p < 0.01$, then the result would only occur one in a hundred times by chance, and if $p < 0.001$, then the result could only occur by chance one in a thousand times. Since, under these circumstances the chance of the event happening is so rare, then any difference that does occur is likely to be significant and is occurring because of real differences between the groups being examined. The *F-ratio* is similar to the t-test, but here more than two groups of mean scores are being compared. Again the value of the F-ratio can depend upon sample sizes, and hence the associated probability level aids in interpretation.

REFERENCES

De Albuquerque, K. and McElroy, J.L. (1992) "Caribbean Small-Island Tourism Styles and Sustainable Strategies". *Environmental Management*, **16**(5), 619–632.

Backman, S.J., Ditton, R.B., Kaiser, R. and Fletcher, J. (1986) "An Investigation of Benefits Sought at Texas Beaches". *Proceedings, Tourism Services Marketing, Advances in Theory and Practice*, W. Benoy Joseph, L. Moutinho and I.R. Vernon (eds). Cleveland, Academy of Marketing Science and Cleveland State University, 53–62.

BARB Bulletin (1987a), BARB, London, March.

BARB Bulletin (1987b), BARB, London, August.

Beard, J.G. and Ragheb, M.G. (1980) "Measuring Leisure Satisfaction". *Journal of Leisure Research*, **12**(1), 20–33.

Beard, J.G. and Ragheb, M.G. (1983) "Measuring Leisure Motivation". *Journal of Leisure Research*, **15**(3), 219–228.

Bitner, M.J., Boons, B.H. and Tetrault, M.S. (1990) "The Service Encounter: Diagnosing Favourable and Unfavourable Incidents". *Journal of Marketing*, **54** (Jan), 74–84.

Bojanic, D. (1992) "A look at a modernised Family Life Cycle and Overseas Travel". *Journal of Travel and Tourism Marketing*, **1**(1), 61–80.

Cohen, E. (1974) "Who is a tourist? A conceptual clarification". *The Sociological Review*, **22**, 527–555.

Cohen, E. (1979) "Rethinking the Sociology of Tourism". *Annals of Tourism Research* **6**(1), 18–35.

Cornish, P. and Denny, M. (1989) "Demographics are Dead—Long Live Demographics". *Journal of the Market Research Society*, **31**(3), 363–374.

Crompton, J.L. (1979) "Motivations for Pleasure Vacations". *Annals of Tourism Research*, October/December, **6**(4), 408–424.

Diener, E., Colvin, C.R., Pavot, W. and Allman, A. (1991) "The Psychic Costs of Intense Positive Emotions". *Journal of Personality and Social Psychology*, **61**, 492–503.

Economist Intelligence Unit (1985) *Tourism Forecasts to 1990*. EIU, London.

Edgell, D.L. (1993) *World Tourism at the Millennium—an Agenda for Industry, Government and Education*. US Department of Commerce, April.

Edgell, D.L. (1993) "Trends in World Tourism". In M. Conlin and D. Hawkins (eds), *Proceedings of The 2nd International Island Tourism Forum*, 16–19 May, Centre for Tourism Research, Bermuda College, Bermuda.

Emery, R. (1981) "Alternative Futures in Tourism". *International Journal of Tourism Management*, March, 241–255.

Fielding, K., Pearce, P.L. and Hughes, K. (1992) "Climbing Ayres Rock: Relating Visitor Motivation, Time Perception and Enjoyment". *Journal of Tourism Studies*, December, **3**(2), 49–57.

Forbes, R.J. and Forbes, M.S. (1992) "Special Interest Travel". In J.R. Brent Ritchie and D.E. Hawkins (eds), *World Travel and Tourism Review*. vol 2. Wallingford, CAB International, 141–144.

Forbes, R.J. and Forbes, M.S. (1993) "Special Interest Travel—Creating Today's Market Driven Experiences". In M. Conlin and D. Hawkins (eds), *Proceedings of The 2nd International Island Tourism Forum*, 16–19 May, Centre for Tourism Research, Bermuda College, Bermuda.

Gibson, H. and Yiannakis, A. (1993) "Patterns of Tourist Role Preference Across Life Course". In S. Glyptis (ed), *Proceedings of The 3rd International Leisure Studies Conference*. Loughborough University, England.

Independent (1993) "Britain is Top of the EC Divorce League". *The Independent*, London, 6, 10 July.

Jefferson, A. (1993) "Cross Channel Opportunities for Britain—1994 and beyond". *Tourism Management*, **14**(6), 424–430.

Kotler, P. (1967) *Marketing Management Analysis: Planning and Control*. Englewood Cliffs, Prentice Hall.

Krippendorf, J. (1989) *The Holidaymakers*. Oxford, Heinemann.

Laing, A. (1987) *The Package Holiday Participant: Choice and Behaviour*, unpublished Ph.D thesis, Hull University, England.

Lawson, R. (1991) "Patterns of Tourist Expenditure and Types of Vacation across the Family Life Cycle". *Journal of Travel Research*, **29**(4), Spring, 12–18.

Mazanec, J.A. (1992) "Classifying Tourists into Market Segments: a Neural Network Approach". *Journal of Travel and Tourism Marketing*, **1**(1), 39–60.

O'Brien, S. and Ford, R. (1988) "Can We at Last Say Goodbye to Social Class?" *Journal of the Market Research Society*, July, **30**(3), 289–332.

Pearce, P. (1988) *The Ulysses Factor—Evaluating Visitors in Tourist Settings*. New York, Springer-Verlag.

Ragheb, M.G. and Beard, J.G. (1982) "Measuring Leisure Attitudes". *Journal of Leisure Research*, **14**, 155–162.

Ryan, C.A. (1991) *Recreational Tourism: A Social Science Perspective*. London and New York, Routledge.

Ryan, C.A. (1993) "Correlations between Clusters Based on the Ragheb and Beard Leisure Motivations Scale and Attributes of Desired Holiday Locations". In S. Glyptis (ed), *Proceedings of The 3rd International Leisure Studies Conference*. Loughborough University, England.

Ryan, C.A. (1995) "Learning about Tourists from Conversations— the over 55s in Majorca". *Tourism Management*, in press.

Urry, J. (1991) *The Tourist Gaze*. London, Sage.

Yiannakis, A. and Gibson, H. (1992) "Roles Tourists Play". *Annals of Tourism Research*, **19**(2), 287–304.

Yiannakis, A. and Gibson, H. (1993) "Patterns of Tourist Role Preference across the Life Course", paper presented at *Leisure in Different Words*, Third International Conference of the Leisure Studies Association, July 1993, Loughborough University, England.

8 Development and Marketing of International Tourism in Small Island States

PHILIPPE WING
University of Ulster, UK

Confronted with a limited number of development options, many small island states regard tourism as a panacea for their mounting economic difficulties. There is a misguided belief among the policy makers of these countries that the existence of sea, sand and sun can act as catalysts for the development of an international tourist industry. However, apart from the need for a sound infrastructure (e.g. good network, water and electricity supply) and superstructure (e.g. different types of accommodation, catering facilities), the marketing of the tourist product is equally important as the international tourist market is highly competitive and there is a high level of substitutability.

DEVELOPMENT ISSUES

Small economic and geographic size often militates against the development and marketing of international tourism in small island economies. Their isolation and remoteness may further exacerbate tourism development. If an island is not accessible to the outside world, especially in the main tourist-trigger countries by air and sea transport, then the development of tourism can only take place on a small scale. Most island states are relatively remote and isolated, even if they are linked to other countries, because of the limited and infrequent sea and air service since there is normally insufficient demand for regular services. However, there is a high level of commitment to develop and market tourism with a view to developing and diversifying their narrow economic base.

It must be acknowledged that an island state may face one or a combination of socioeconomic problems (see Table 8.1). These cannot be resolved unless sound economic solutions can be found. One of the prescribed remedies advocated by powerful multilateral organizations (e.g. The World Bank) and key donor countries (e.g. European Union member states) is to develop a tourist industry which is generally accepted by governments of these islands since tourism

Island Tourism: Management Principles and Practice
Edited by Michael V. Conlin and Tom Baum

Table 8.1. Socioeconomic problems in small island states

Factor	Degree	Problem	Example
1. Population density	High	Small physical size	Mauritius
2. Resources (natural, physical, technological and financial)	Low	Poor land quality, weak private sector, lack of savings and inward investment	St. Lucia
3. Agricultural productivity	Low	Small holdings and failure to modernize	Papua New Guinea
4. Land distribution	Uneven	Colonial legacy	Fiji
5. Political stability	Poor	Dualism in society	Madagascar
6. Employment	Low	Narrow economic base	Sri Lanka
7. Unemployment	High	Dependency on one or two crops for export	Jamaica
8. Production costs	High	Economics of scale	Seychelles
9. Economic growth	Low	Too remote from their international export markets	Comoros
10. Foreign debt	High	Mismanagement, overmanning and and corruption	Cuba

development can be initiated without a high level of investment as compared to the other economic sectors (e.g. manufacturing).

Can the development of international tourism become the panacea to their mounting economic problems? As a major earner of foreign exchange and an important creator of employment, tourism is expected to alleviate some of these economic problems, to reduce the islands' substantial dependence in a small range of export commodities and to broaden their narrow economic base. It is clear that the main rationale for tourism development is purely economic, not to foster friendship. However, there is a dilemma between the marketing of these places as exotic destinations but not promoting them as poor, remote, albeit idyllic tourist destinations.

On many island states such as Maldives and the Seychelles in the Indian Ocean, Bahamas and Jamaica in the Caribbean and Fiji and Tonga in the Pacific, tourism has become the dominant economic sector while in others it has not been possible to develop tourism on a commercial scale because either the facilities needed are not available or their problem of remoteness and accessibility has not been resolved. This is the case of the Malagasy Republic whose potentials are immense in terms of touristic assets, but the low level of economic development compounded with a high degree of political and social instability have made tourism an unattractive proposition to the transnational tourist corporations. The latter are reluctant to invest in "high-risk" countries as their investments can earn a higher rate of return in other, safer island states.

Unlike the small island states' traditional agricultural exports, which have been affected by lower demand, declining prices, intense competition and protectionist measures, tourism has relatively few restrictions since tourists from the developed countries are allowed to move freely for holidays to the small island states. Most developed, rich countries have few constraints on the outflow of foreign currency for touristic purposes. Such freedom of movement is irrelevant unless the tourist product is properly promoted and marketed. But marketing is an expensive exercise which very few small island states can undertake because of their scarce financial resources. In this instance, will it be more beneficial for neighbouring small island states to pool their limited financial resources to make their marketing more effective?

THE MARKETING OF TOURISM

The marketing of tourism is a challenging and daunting exercise since small and unfocused promotional budgets cannot make any significant impact in the highly competitive international tourism market. Most small island states do not market their tourist product in the main tourist-generating countries because of lack of financial resources. Instead, they rely upon the international private sector for promotion. Those islands which do have the financial power to embark on an international promotional and marketing campaign must take into account the complex segmentation of the total market. Jefferson and Lickorish (1988) categorise these segments as specialist markets, mass markets and mini-mass markets. Most island states can be considered as belonging to the specialist markets. But it is difficult to put all island states into the same category as the quality of the tourism product and the degree of accessibility varies from island to island.

Policy makers and National Tourist Offices (NTOs) must formulate the appropriate marketing policies and strategies conducive to tourism growth. In theory, since tourism is an amorphous industry consisting of many diverse businesses, it will be sensible for the promotion of an island to be undertaken by the government. In practice, most small island states lack the heavy funding of the developed countries and therefore are unable to set up representatives' offices in their main trigger markets. For example, a small island state like Kiribati, located in the South Pacific, is not in a position to open offices in many countries even though tourism is an important element of its economic strategy. In essence, there must be close collaboration with all those involved with the tourist industry so that the marketing efforts of the private and public sector may become more productive.

THE PROBLEMS OF LOCATION

Location plays a decisive role in the development of small-island tourism and in the type of tourism development that can take place. Those islands close to large tourist markets, e.g. Bahamas and Bermuda close to the USA and Canada have a distinct advantage in transport costs, while those scattered and out of the way of principal shipping and airline routes, e.g. Samoa and Vanuata distant from New Zealand and Australia, are in a disadvantageous position. Some of these remote islands are even a long distance from each other, implying that multi-destination holidays can only be organized with difficulty. If those remote islands remain inaccessible because of the difficulty in establishing viable transport links, it will not be easy to develop tourism on a scale which will make it viable. The main problem facing such small islands is not their remoteness, which can be overcome by easy accessibility, but their isolation. Bermuda is a typical example of a small island which has been able to develop tourism as the major sector in its economy.

With the possible exception of the Caribbean islands which are located near their North American markets, most islands do not have the same advantage. Because of their location, islands in the South Pacific have found that the cost of transport acts as a barrier to the movement of tourists. Since precisely their expensiveness does not make it feasible for them to compete against cheaper island destinations, when marketing their tourist product they must emphasize their isolation and their consequent uniqueness because isolation is becoming a scarce commodity. Thus, a degree of isolation can be regarded as an asset if these islands are able to develop an exclusive type of tourism.

Isolation becomes functional only if islands become more easily accessible. Since all island tourism destinations are to some extent in competition with one another, there is a need to differentiate their product in terms of price, quality and scarcity. Islands which are remote must appeal to a different type of clientele than those which are close to tourist-generating countries. For example, islands in the Caribbean region have a more established tourist industry and their advanced stage of tourism development means that they already have a captive market. "New" island tourist destinations are products which need a far more intensive and specialized marketing support to win acceptance, market share and sustained demand.

As demand for international tourism is concentrated geographically, in theory it looks easy to tap all the markets. But, in practice, it is not possible to achieve this goal because of two inhibiting factors. First, insufficient promotional expenditures are available to penetrate all the developed countries' markets. It will be more pragmatic to market the tourist product in a few selected countries. Second, there is intense competition because most island destinations seem to offer the same "exotic tropical destination".

Although a degree of competition between the islands is inevitable, small-island destinations within the same region must co-operate in joint marketing efforts, especially when an "island-hopping" circuit involving two or more island states is being promoted. The differentiation of their product in the marketing process must emphasise their complementarity. Furthermore, most small islands must regard multi-destination holidays as necessary to their tourism development because some of the islands are so small that they have only limited tourist capacity. Once saturation levels have been reached, then there is a need to market this type of tourism to increase average spending per visitor-day.

Ability to influence demand through their own marketing and promotional activities is severely limited, although the NTOs can promoted image-building. But the distribution system of an international tourism industry is such that they cannot market their tourist products directly to the market place because of the high costs involved. The distribution channel is dominated by transnational corporations with interests in airlines, tour operation and retailing. For instance, tour operators and travel agents can "make or break" any destination because tourists may not have a clear idea of their holiday destination. These intermediaries become important marketing agents as they act as go-betweens for the countries.

ASPECTS OF MARKETING

The marketing of small-island tourism must emphasize the quality of the product in relation to others because there is a multitude of destinations selling an undifferentiated product. Small islands must concentrate their efforts on creating positive aspects in the minds of potential tourists. The high quality usually identified with island tourism must be preserved and enhanced since it represents an important asset in the marketing process. Islands with an advanced stage of tourism development will adopt different marketing strategies from those whose tourist industry has just begun. The former can diversify their markets by marketing and promoting their tourist product in other potential tourist-generating countries, while the latter must start by concentrating on a few markets.

Small islands whose tourism development is still at an embryonic stage must concentrate their marketing efforts on a relatively select up-market clientele, who can be expected to bring in the maximum net economic and employment benefits per bed-space because this segment of the market has a high level of disposable income. More-established destinations are more concerned to attract larger numbers of tourists because their aim is to improve the utilization of existing facilities and hence, this is the cheapest way to gain additional benefits from tourism.

The need to maintain a good image is acknowledged as being vital in the marketing of small-island tourism. Since tourists do not have prior knowledge of the product they are buying, they normally take into account the image projected by NTOs, tour operators and the media. Because of the prevailing intense competition in the international market place, image becomes a critical factor in directing tourist flows. High holiday costs exclude a large section of the potential tourists and in marketing small-island tourism, the images of these destinations must be projected with care in a few specialized publications with a view to tapping the targeted segment.

Pricing is itself another important element in the marketing of small-island tourism. The high price of a holiday to these destinations might be based on their distance and on the high quality of the product. If the marketing efforts are directed towards attracting the up-market tourist, then the standard of accommodation and other facilities must be equally high. In principle, there is nothing wrong with the high price of island tourism but tourists, like any consumers, are primarily concerned with value for money. This is true whether the holiday is in the luxury-priced category or at some modest level. Some island destinations have been criticized for failing to match the expectations of their consumers. Tour operators, who are powerful marketing agents, and tourists alike will not accept a product of lower quality. If high quality is not maintained, this will result in a fall in demand.

A drop in demand which might be caused by recession or any other economic problem in the trigger markets must not be reacted to by excessive price reduction because that will only attract a different type of clientele. Once an island destination becomes known as a mass-tourism package destination it will be difficult to regain an up-market image. Small islands can lose control over the type of tourism product they want to promote and market unless the authorities in such destinations take care to preserve their exclusive "paradise" and exotic image.

There may be conflicts of interest between the tour operators and the small islands. The former are more influenced by profit-maximization through high-volume, high-turnover and lower-cost product if there is a drop in demand. On the other hand, the islands because of their limited tourism capacity, want to maximize tourism benefits by attracting high-income clientele. However, the small islands must offer a high-quality product in order to satisfy their customers. In marketing small-island tourism, the local authorities must be aware that a tourist product may be easily replaced by both tourists and foreign-tour operators with an alternative destination.

The operators' marketing policies are based on creating a "mix" market for their tourist industry as they are able to provide different types of accommodation. In the long-haul markets (Europe) and in the medium-haul markets (South Africa) their aim is to stress their exclusive image. Unlike most of the Caribbean islands where charters are permitted, Mauritius and Seychelles do not permit charter flight operations from Europe and South Africa because of the need to preserve a high-quality image. Their ability to attract high-spending tourists is indicative of their intention to go for mass tourism although in their short-haul market (Reunion), they have promoted their destinations as being cheap and affordable.

Demand for selective tourism poses major difficulties to most small-island economies. The Seychelles and Mauritius prefer to concentrate their marketing efforts in South Africa and Europe because these tourists have a higher propensity to spend in relation to the short-haul market. This implies that the supply of superstructure, more particularly accommodation and entertainment, should be of international standard. Access to this market requires expensive facilities which the local entrepreneurs are unable to develop and finance. Therefore, small-island economies must adopt a cautious approach towards the development and marketing of selective tourism.

No island should depend on one type of tourism, especially where local participation might be excluded on the grounds of cost. Even though there is a definite tendency to favour selective tourism because of its income and price inelasticity, policy makers must rationally adopt policies which will bring more benefits to the economy. The presence of a market-mix is important for the development of this industry because the market for selective tourism remains the virtual monopoly of foreign enterprises. This type of exclusive tourism is not appropriate for small-island economies as this will result in increased dependency.

The market for low- and middle-income tourism is normally dominated by local entrepreneurs who will be able to operate and manage the small-to-medium sized hotels. These will not require the high level of service demanded from luxurious hotels. One major advantage is that such establishments will make more use of local supplies. However, the governments have failed to encourage the establishment of small hotels because there is a feeling that the low-income tourists do not have the same impact as the up-market visitors.

Tourism marketing policies will depend upon the type of tourism development available in the small-island economies. The policy makers must adopt a balanced approach towards the promotion of tourism. Total reliance upon an expensive tourist product is not conducive to market diversification and to national interests if local people cannot participate in the development of their islands. A "mix" product ranging from low- to high-income tourism will be beneficial to their developing economies.

Tourism offers the small-island economies the opportunity to diversify their narrow economic base. Since islands have an undifferentiated product, they can try a "co-operative" marketing agreement which will allow them not only to complement each other but also to break into other markets. However, political instability in one of the islands might lead to the collapse of such an agreement. Islands which want to develop their industry exclusively by appealing to up-market tourists are also under threat because of the volatility of the tourist industry and because tourist demand is controlled by foreign tourist operators over which small islands do not have any control. It would be more appropriate to implement a "mix" tourism marketing strategy. The proper management of their fragile environmental and cultural assets must be ensured so that the tourist product will retain its high quality and its exclusivity.

FURTHER READING

Archer, B.H. and Wanhill, S. (1981) *The Economic Impact of Tourism in Mauritius*. University of Surrey.

Baldachino, G. (1993) "Bursting the Bubble: the Pseudo-development Strategies of Micro-states". *Development and Change*, **22**, 29–51.

Beekhis, J.V. (1981) "Tourism in the Caribbean". *Ambio*, **10**(6), 325–333.

Betram, C. (1986) "Sustainable Development in Pacific Micro-economies". *World Development*, **14**(7), 802–822.

Britton, R. (1979) "The Image of the Third World in Tourism Marketing". *Annals of Tourism Research*, **6**(3), 318–329.

Bryden, J.M. (1973) *Tourism and Development: a Case Study of the Commonwealth Caribbean*. Cambridge University Press.
Burkart, A.J. (1985) "Small island phenomena". *Tourism Management*, **6**(1), 2–3.
Butler, A. (1985) *An Introduction to Mini-economies*. Grumer.
Cheung Young, P. (1981) "Tourism in the Development of Small States: Jamaica's Experience". Conference on Small Economies.
Cohen, R. (1983) *African Islands and Enclaves*. Sage.
Commonwealth Secretariat (1985) *Vulnerability: Small states in the Society*. Commonwealth Secretariat.
Damas, W.G. (1965) *The Economies of Development in Small Islands with Special Reference to the Caribbean*. Montreal, Montreal University Press.
Dilley, R.S. (1986) "Tourist Brochures and Tourist Images". *Canadian Geographer*, **30**(1), 59–65.
Dommen, E.C. and Hein, P. (1985) *States, Microstates and Islands*. Croom Helm.
Economic Commission for Africa (1981) *Study of Tourism in the Indian Ocean*. ECA.
Faber, M. (1984) "Island Microstates: Problems of Viability". *The Round Table*, (4), 372–376.
Gayle, D.J. and Gandrich, T.N. (1993) *Tourism Marketing and Management in the Caribbean*. London, Routledge.
Harden, S. (1985) *Small is Dangerous: Microstates in a Macroworld*. London, Frances Pinter.
International Bank for Reconstruction and Development (1975) *A Study of the Contribution of Tourism to the Antiguan Economy*.
Jalan, B. (1982) *Problems and Policies in Small Economies*. IRBD. Croom Helm.
Jefferson, A. and Lickorish, L. (1988) *Marketing Tourism*, Longman, Harlow.
Latimer, H. (1985) "Developing-island Economies—Tourism and Agriculture". *Tourism Management*, **6**(1).
Legarda, B. (1984) "Small Island Economies". *Finance and Development*, **21**, 42–43.
Lickorish, L.J., Bodlender, J. and Jenkins, C. (1991) *Developing Tourism Destination*. Longman.
MacNaught, T.J. (1982) "Mass Tourism and the Dilemma of Modernisation in Pacific Island Communities". *Annals of Tourism Research*, **9**(3), 359–381.
McEachern, J. and Towley, E.L. (1974) *Ecological Guidelines for Island Development*. International Union for Conservation of Nature and Natural Resource.
Naya, S. (1983) "Asian and Pacific Developing Countries: Development Issues and Challenge". *Asian Development Bank*, **1**(1), 1–40.
Oglethorpe, M. (1985) "Tourism in a Small Island Economy: the Case of Malta". *Tourism Management*, **6**(1), 23–31.
Rajotte, F. and Crocombe, R. (1980) *Pacific Tourism as Islanders See It*, University of the South Pacific. This book outlines the dangers of tourism development as perceived by the small tourist-receiving island states.
Rawat, R. (1985) "Product marketing". Tourism and Air Transport Conference, Manila.
Shand, R.T. (ed.) (1980) *The Island States of the Pacific and Indian Oceans: Anatomy of Development*, the Australian National University.
Selwyn, P. (ed.) (1975) *Development Policy in Small Countries*. Croom Helm.
Tata, R.J. (1978) "Poor and Small Too: Caribbean Mini-states". *Focus*, **29**(2), 1–12.
Treaster, J.B. (1987) "Finding the Right Caribbean Island". *International Herald Tribune*, 20 November, 7–9.
Tsusaka, A. (1984) "South Pacific Developing Countries: Development Issues and Challenge". *Asian Development Review*, **2**(1), 65–81.
United Nations Committee on Trade and Development (1974) *Developing Island Economies*. United Nations.
United Nations Development Advisory Team (1979) *South Pacific: Guidelines for the Development of Tourism*. United Nations.
Virahsawmy, R. (1975) *The Characteristics of Island Economies, Seminar Papers*. University

of Mauritius.

Waters, S.R. (1994) *Travel Industry World Year Book: The Big Picture vol. 37*. Child & Waters. This publication reviews the annual performance of the tourism industry world-wide although the emphasis is in favour of the United States.

Williamson, P.F. (1987) "Tourism in Small Island Nations: a fragile dependence". *Leisure Studies*, 6(2), 117–146.

Wing, P.C.L. (1981) *Tourism in Mauritius*. MSc Dissertation, University of Strathclyde. Discusses the importance of formulating and implementing the right policies for the development of tourism.

Wing, P.C.L. (1994) "Marketing in Small Island States". In S.F. Wilt and L. Moutiaho (eds), *Tourism Marketing and Management Handbook*. Prentice Hall, 467–477.

Wing, P.C.L. (1994) "Multi-nation Promotion". In S.F. Wilt and L. Moutiaho (eds), *Tourism Marketing and Management Handbook*. Prentice Hall, 395–398.

World Development(1980) Special issue on islands, 8(12). This collection of articles discusses the development policies that are needed to make them more viable.

9 Redeveloping Mature Resorts for New Markets

LARRY E. HELBER
Helber Hastert & Fee, Planners, Inc., Hawaii, USA

INTRODUCTION

Most mature resorts, and in particular those that have not benefited from comprehensive planning from the outset, follow a development cycle in which popularity ultimately leads to decline. This can also occur with master-planned resorts when their layouts lack the flexibility to adapt to changing markets or when progressive development deviates substantially from the initial vision and concept. In attempts to reverse a resort's decline, most redevelopment solutions centre on infrastructure improvements, environmental cleanup and "cosmetic" upgrades to enhance the built form. Less attention is given to establishing new products which cater to emerging growth markets. This chapter examines the latter alternative and provides examples in which the identification of new markets forms a key strategy in revitalizing mature resorts.

THE LIFE CYCLE OF TRADITIONAL RESORTS

The evolution of most traditional tourist and resort destinations is characterized by a life cycle with five distinct phases: discovery, "in spot", maturity, decline and redevelopment. The first three stages are often a result of unrestrained growth. As the destination matures, the early adventurous and independent visitors are replaced by the mass-market tour and convention travellers, and hotel and tourist facility development increases accordingly. The resort becomes overly commercialized and begins to lose its original qualities and character. This signals a downward trend to decline characterized by the need to discount prices which in turn appeals to budget tourists and bargain hunters and the eventual conversion of tourist accommodations to facilities catering to local residents. At this point, the once popular resort or tourist destination can only be revived through massive redevelopment and marketing if it is to come back to life.

Island Tourism: Management Principles and Practice
Edited by Michael V. Conlin and Tom Baum

There are two primary factors contributing to the life cycle of resorts as described above: lack of comprehensive planning and lack of government leadership.

Lack of planning

Most traditional resort destinations did not have the benefit of an initial master plan or development blueprint. Instead, the areas were shaped more by the collective interests and profit motives of small parcel owners seeking to maximize the development potential of their lands. Little regard was given to surrounding uses or to the needs of the resort community at large. Some individual land owners considered market trends prior to the development of their projects but most based their projects on gut instincts and presumptions that once built, people would flock to patronize them.

Lack of government leadership

In the past, many local governments accommodated the support needs and requirements of private-sector resort developers through the provision of roads, utilities and public services in newly emerging resort destinations. There was little planning on the part of governments with respect to establishing area carrying capacities, sizing utilities and services based on such capacities, establishing environmental protection measures and providing major public open spaces and recreation areas to counterbalance high-density resort developments. Likewise, many zoning ordinances and other land development controls were put into effect after substandard development patterns were set. The absence of government leadership and control has contributed to the decline of many once-popular resort destinations through overbuilding, overcrowding and destruction of the natural resources that attracted tourists in the first place.

COMPREHENSIVE PLANNING FOR SUSTAINABILITY

Two significant concepts were introduced in the 1960s and 1970s to counter the life cycle of maturing destinations and establish sustainability in them. The first focused on national and regional *tourism master planning*—a process which, among other things, inventoried tourist attractions and resources, matched potential niche markets with these resources, designated areas appropriate for tourist and resort development and established their carrying capacities and infrastructure requirements. Developing countries such as Sri Lanka, Turkey, Taiwan, Fiji, India and Malaysia quickly embraced national tourism planning and established development programmes as a means of broadening foreign exchange. More advanced tourist destinations such as Hawaii, Australia and Mexico focused on regional planning and development to spread the benefits of tourism from capital cities to other areas within the country or state.

The second concept was the *integrated destination resort*, first pioneered in

Hawaii in the late 1950s by several large land owners. This innovative development approach centred on the preparation of a master plan for a total site that integrated resort accommodations and facilities to form a self-contained visitor destination.

Tourism planners, government officials and visitor industry leaders hailed the integrated resort concept as a viable alternative to unplanned coastal tourist/resort strips characterized by a hodgepodge of facilities with little regard to appropriate building densities, heights or design continuity. Private investors also favoured the concept and, as a result, integrated resort developments flourished in the 1970s and 1980s and are now found throughout the world.

REDEVELOPMENT CONSTRAINTS

While comprehensive tourism and resort master-planning efforts have been effective in positioning newly emerging tourist/resort destinations for sustainable development, they have had marginal to detrimental affects in curbing the decline of older, mature resorts. In Hawaii, as an example, the 1960 Visitor Destination Development Plan promoted the development of integrated resorts on the outer or "Neighbor Islands" as a means of diversifying tourism within the state. This strategy has proved to be highly successful in stimulating tourism development on the Neighbor Islands (Kauai, Maui, Hawaii) but it has been at the expense of the state's oldest resort—Waikiki—where its share of total visitors has steadily decreased over the last two decades.

Likewise in Thailand, the once famous Pattaya Beach Resort, located some 120 kilometres southeast of Bangkok, has steadily been in decline as visitors are attracted to the country's new resort destinations such as Phuket Island. These new destinations are a product of the national government's regional tourism planning efforts and implementation policies related to infrastructure development, environmental protection and investment incentives.

Mature resorts are also handicapped by numerous physical constraints which limit their ability to adapt to changing market demands. These often include a land-tenure pattern dominated by numerous small privately owned parcels, a fixed pattern of roads and public utilities, high-density and high-rise development, traffic congestion, pollution problems, minimal shoreline setbacks and lack of sizeable public open spaces. As a result, redevelopment efforts to retain or broaden market share tend to be more cosmetic in nature, such as street landscaping, modernizing building façades, pedestrian malls and shoreline promenades. While such efforts enhance the aesthetic aspects of the resort, they often fall short of providing a new focus of attractions and activities that are capable of sustaining growth and attracting new markets.

Master-planned resorts are not immune to decline and the need for redevelopment. While the planning process is geared to establishing long-term sustainability, actual implementation often strays from the original plans. Hawaii's first master-planned resort—Ka'anapali Beach Resort on Maui—was originally conceived as a low- to mid-rise complex with a relaxed, rural Hawaiian character as an alternative to Waikiki's high density. The initial hotel and condominium projects were subject to the resort's self-imposed design standards and architectural review process. These were subsequently shelved as escalating land values and other factors brought pressure for increased density and high-rise development. Today, in its mature state, Ka'anapali's once scenic beachfront is lined with large hotels and condominiums rising to 12 storeys in height.

Ill-conceived master plans can also hinder a resort's long-term viability. Plans that spread and intersperse low-rise development with major open spaces to preserve a natural, rural character run the risk of producing lifeless resort settings. Concentration is important in site planning to produce social nodes or "positive congestion", and placement of activities/attractions that enhance user convenience. Master plans that favour a predominant mix of residential components over tourist facilities can become real-estate developments where cash flow and profit motives sacrifice visitor satisfaction.

EXPANDING MARKET SHARE

A key to maintaining or enhancing a mature resort's viability is the attraction of new niche markets through redevelopment. These markets may represent seasoned travellers seeking traditional products such as gaming, conferences and conventions, golf and cultural experiences. Or they may be travellers in search of new experiences as defined by emerging demographic trends, expanded special interests and time/value patterns.

The ageing of the baby boomers is creating a new demand for health and wellness centres, gourmet food and beverage experiences, soft adventure travel and boutique/retreat resorts which emphasize personal attention and a strong sense of place. The growth and increasing affluence of minority populations and the expanding middle class of rapidly developing countries in regions such as Southeast Asia will bring renewed interest in luxury facilities and amenities which equate to self-fulfilment, status, image-building and quality of life. Elderly populations are broadening their interests through travel to destinations that combine learning experiences with leisure and recreational activities.

Changing leisure patterns are placing increased value on localized travel—frequent nearby short-duration trips—in lieu of long-haul, extended vacations. Mature resorts located near or adjacent to major urban centres can benefit from this trend; however, inner cities are increasingly vying for their share of the proximate leisure markets.

NEW PRODUCTS

As mature resorts struggle to identify new market opportunities, much attention will be directed to technological innovations stemming from new entertainment media and the integration of computers, television and telecommunications. Virtual reality and other high-tech attractions will bring a new generation of entertainment through advanced simulation of actual adventures, sporting and cultural events coupled with three-dimensional visual and acoustical effects. However, the substantial costs associated with this technology and the related need for mass patronage may limit the use of these products as a strategy for redevelopment.

Beyond the boundless possibilities associated with media technology, most mature resorts will focus on refinements of more traditional products and forms of leisure to attract new markets. These will include conference and convention centres, themed attractions, festival market places, casinos, holistic health centres, golf academies, exercise and fitness centres and youth activity facilities. There will also be a renewed interest in recapturing a sense of place and the special qualities which first drew visitors to the resort area.

As previously noted, physical and land-tenure constraints and the development character may limit a mature resort's ability to incorporate major redevelopment projects. Such a resort can, however, attract new markets by being positioned as a "base-camp" or staging point for a broad range of special-interest day or extended-stay excursions in nearby areas. These include golfing outings, sailing, scuba diving, eco-tourism adventures, hiking, wine tasting and the like. Orientation and learning centres would be located within the resort where visitors broaden their knowledge and skills prior to pursuing special-interest excursions.

REDEVELOPMENT STRATEGIES

The significant growth in world tourism and corresponding surge in new tourist/resort destinations, coupled with expanding market interests, has heightened the challenges for mature resorts to remain competitive. The following examples illustrate the redevelopment strategies which have been or are currently being considered in mature resorts to expand market share by attracting new markets.

Palmas del Mar

Palmas del Mar is a 2750-acre integrated resort/residential community situated on Puerto Rico's Caribbean coast near Humacao, approximately one hour's drive from San Juan. The picturesque site, characterized by rolling hills, palm groves and white sand beaches, was acquired by the Sea Pines Company in 1969. The company subsequently prepared a master development plan which included several smaller-scale hotel sites, three 18-hole golf courses, numerous beachfront and hillside condominium sites and house lots, a Port Grimaud-style harbour/marina development and support recreation and leisure activities. In total, the plan incorporated 11 600 resort and non-resort units. Initial development focused on the harbour and its adjoining condominiums, the 40-unit Palmas Inn and Villas, several beachfront condominium developments, an 18-hole golf course and the subdivision of nearby house lots. The residential products were marketed principally to US East Coast buyers. A second 102-room hotel was later added through conversion of a beachfront condominium complex.

In the 1970s and 1980s, ownership of Palmas del Mar changed several times, and each new owner amended the master plan to meet its financial objectives. In each instance, emphasis was placed on residential condominium and lot sales at the expense of new tourist facility development. As a result, the resort's two hotels and numerous condominiums enjoyed favourable occupancies during school holidays and the summer period but typically experienced low occupancies during the remainder of the year.

In 1991, the resort's present owner, MAXXAM Properties, Inc., initiated a master-plan update study. A principal aim was to identify specific projects that would enhance the resort's market position and bring life to the project. An in-depth study of the resort identified numerous weaknesses:

- Emphasis had been placed on holiday/second home (condominium) development. As a result, the resort was a virtual ghost town during most of the year as condominiums historically have much lower annual occupancy rates than full-service hotels. Additional hotels were essential to draw people to the resort and justify a full range of recreational, retail and entertainment facilities.
- Beyond the natural site features and an 18-hole golf course, the resort had very few visitor activities and facilities. Those recreational, retail and entertainment facilities available to resort guests were scattered throughout the resort, rendering them inconvenient to potential users.
- The attractive harbour and marina was not a tourist amenity but was lined with waterfront condominiums enclosed by gates. There were no public promenades or activity nodes to make the marina/harbour a true visitor attraction.
- Over the years, the sales of Palmas' substantial residential products shifted from predominantly overseas to local buyers, with the resort becoming more a bedroom community to San Juan. The indiscriminate mixing of permanent resident families with transit holiday visitors was also the cause of numerous operational and social problems.

Fortuitously, MAXXAM Properties still had control of a number of prime undeveloped parcels which enabled the development of new tourist facilities as a strategy for revitalization. As a part of the update study, four principal holiday markets were considered important to reposition the resort:

- US (Atlantic seaboard)/international high-end/family-holiday guests
- International/regional incentive, conference and convention attendees
- Puerto Rican day visitors
- International day visitors staying elsewhere on the island.

To attract these markets, the revised master plan and implementation programme focused on the delineation of resort and residential precincts, concentration of tourist facilities/activities and the creation of a strong Caribbean flavour. Within the resort precinct, emphasis was placed on new resort accommodation, meeting facilities and a broad range of shopping, entertainment and recreational activities that would significantly increase both overnight and day visitors. These included:

- The clustering of three major hotels with a total of 1500 rooms at Candelero Point;
- A Caribbean Marketplace centrally located to the three hotels to include a cultural centre, casino, day/evening entertainment venues and conference centre;
- Beach club/sports centre central to the major hotels;
- Redevelopment of the outer marina area into a small harbour village with specialty shops, food/beverage outlets, waterfront entertainment and a staging point for cruises, excursions and water sports;
- Expanded golf facilities and the redevelopment of the old golf clubhouse area into a resort recreation centre with emphasis on activities for teenagers and younger children;
- Provision of a Creative Learning Centre to serve as an orientation and staging point for nearby eco- and adventure-tourism excursions.

These and other projects were deemed essential to reverse the trend where increased real-estate interest had, over time, diluted the resort's character and market appeal. Expanded tourist volume and activities at Palmas also enhance future holiday residential sales, which remains one of MAXXAM's principal businesses.

Waikiki

In many respects, Waikiki, located on Hawaii's Island of Oahu, is a classic example of a major resort which has matured without the benefits of early comprehensive planning. Instead, the once swampy 618-acre area adjoining Honolulu was reclaimed in the late 1920s and subsequently subdivided by different interests into numerous small lots for residential and tourist facility development. Over the years, Waikiki has been transformed from a relaxed "country" retreat to a bustling high-density urban resort. Waikiki now contains 32 600 visitor and 14 500 residential units and accommodates a daily population of over 130 000 people.

With Waikiki's increased popularity as a prime tourist destination and its corresponding development have come growing problems ranging from crime, prostitution, drug dealing to over-commercialism, congestion and loss of Hawaiian character. These and other situations have resulted in sporadic renovations and improvements but without an underlying theme or overall concept to bring them together. Hawaii's tourism industry leaders have long been concerned with Waikiki's decline. Over the years, the resort has lost market share to new resort development on the Neighbor Islands, and now stands to lose additional visitors to new integrated resorts being constructed on Oahu.

Previous studies have examined Waikiki's problems and have resulted in one-way traffic patterns, beach widening and other infrastructure improvements. However, recent events, including the Gulf War and the subsequent reduction in world tourism, have triggered a new, critical look at the resort's role in sustaining Hawaii's tourism and economic growth. In 1989, a high-level conference was held which addressed Waikiki's future. This was followed by the sponsoring of five recognized design teams by one of Waikiki's major land owners to provide planning recommendations for the resort. Concurrently, the City–County government undertook a master-plan study to address policies and public-area improvements to facilitate Waikiki's redevelopment.

Most of the recommendations and subsequent physical action programmes have centred on the improvement of existing tourist activities/resources and on measures to regain the resort's Hawaiian setting. The private sector has also recently initiated the redevelopment and upgrading of many hotels and other facilities to meet changing market demands. These efforts range from complete restoration of historic properties to hotel modernization programmes emphasizing expanded outdoor recreation facilities and extensive public-area amenities.

By far the most significant recommendation stemming from the recent planning efforts is the development of a convention centre directed at new markets to bring renewed life to Waikiki. This proposal has strong endorsement by industry leaders, and the state legislature is currently considering appropriate sites both within and adjacent to Waikiki. Of the many studies over the years which have addressed Waikiki's future, the convention centre proposal is the first which provides a new product aimed at attracting new markets.

Bali

The Indonesian island of Bali is one of the world's most exotic and fabled resort destinations. Its beaches, culture and profound scenery have long been favourite attractions to Western European, Australian and North American holiday travellers. The upgrading of Bali's international airport in the late 1960s to receive commercial jet aircraft greatly facilitated access and stimulated tourist facility development at the island's two popular beach destinations—Sanur and Kuta. Both places have evolved into substantial resorts but without the benefit of any comprehensive planning and systematic infrastructure development.

In 1972, to counter the growing problems of uncontrolled tourism/resort development, the Indonesian government undertook a tourism master-plan study for the island overall. A key development strategy was the designation of the Bukit Peninsula, and specifically Nusa Dua at Bali's southern tip, for integrated resort development to accommodate future tourism growth. A resort master plan for Nusa Dua was then prepared in 1975 which featured ten hotel sites, a major convention centre, a cultural centre, a shopping village, an 18-hole golf course and other recreational amenities.

Although Nusa Dua was actively promoted in the traditional European, Australian and North American markets, the resort languished with little investor or visitor interest for over a decade. Development did not progress beyond an initial 400-room, five-star hotel. Kuta and Sanur remained the favoured spots despite all the problems associated with over-development. The traditional markets favoured a more relaxed Balinese atmosphere over a modern, five-star integrated resort.

During this same period, the economies of Japan, Singapore, Malaysia and other Asian countries expanded rapidly. This resulted in emerging new markets of increasingly affluent people with a pent-up demand for out-of-country travel. Of particular significance is their compelling interest in enjoying a Western lifestyle characterized by luxurious accommodations, elegant shopping, sophisticated meeting venues and golf.

In the mid- to late 1980s, Nusa Dua redirected its product and marketing to cater to these new regional travellers. Eight new major hotels reflecting the grandeur of five-star international properties were built. Priority was also placed on the construction of the golf course and a state-of-the-art convention centre—both now in operation. And recently, a master plan was completed for a nearby major resort development which includes additional golf courses, a marina (Indonesia's first) and canal residential house lots principally for regional holiday and second-home buyers. These new regional markets are expected to give Bali a much needed boost in renewing tourism growth.

CONCLUSION

As new markets are created through changing patterns of leisure and emerging demographic trends, they will present both competitive threats and redevelopment opportunities to mature resorts. The challenge will lie in a destination's ability to adapt to these market changes. It will need to go well beyond beautification campaigns, infrastructure improvements and aggressive marketing to retain its competitiveness. Sustainability will be achieved by attracting new markets through on-going product development similar to the need to offer new attractions at theme parks. Strategic alliances between resort hoteliers and operators of attractions and excursions outside the resort will also be essential, especially where land tenure, high-density development and other constraints preclude opportunities for major internal redevelopment.

10 Managing Demand Fluctuations in the Context of Island Tourism

TOM BAUM AND RAM MUDAMBI
University of Buckingham, UK

ISLAND TOURISM AND DEMAND FORECASTING

Demand for tourism products fluctuates greatly in most resort locations and this has major consequences for the operation and management of tourism facilities, notably hotels. In some extreme locations, such as the Falkland Islands (Baum, 1993), the Aran Islands off the west coast of Ireland (Keane *et al.*, 1992) and in parts of Scotland, the impact of seasonality results in an operating season of as little as three to four months for hotels and other tourism businesses and even within those time frames demand is not constant. Within rather more stable tourism environments, demand can also exhibit considerable volatility, between peak and trough months of the year and, at a micro level, between different days of the week and even within a 24-hour business cycle, for example with respect to food and beverage outlets in a hotel.

Thus, forecasting demand is an essential function within tourism and, especially, hotel businesses. Failure to understand the major market parameters within which a company is operating and, consequently, failure to forecast demand with reasonable accuracy can have drastic business consequences, as EuroDisney's first-year operating experience readily demonstrates. Failure to anticipate and cater for growth in demand likewise can result in financial underachievement through pricing at a level that is lower than the market can take and a substantial number of potential customers who are both disappointed and frustrated and, even more seriously, take their custom elsewhere.

Within the normal tourism context, excess demand in a specific location may result in both short-term and long-term localized dispersement policies by individual hotels and by resorts on a collective basis, supported by special transportation arrangements and, possibly, new infrastructure in the form of roads and railways. Thus, the prospect of very high occupancy levels during a "honeypot" event, such as the 1992 Olympic Games in Barcelona, resulted in accommodation and facilities' managers utilizing hotel stock in resorts and cities some considerable distance from the main venues and transporting visitors to Barcelona on a daily basis. At a micro level, off-loading of guests to alternative local

Island Tourism: Management Principles and Practice
Edited by Michael V. Conlin and Tom Baum © 1995 John Wiley & Sons Ltd

establishments, at a time of over-booking, is common practice in the hotel industry. Longer-term high occupancies may stimulate local building but, if development costs are excessively high for the target market, location of such developments may be rather further afield than the existing main hotel sites. Hong Kong has witnessed this process, with the cost of real estate on Hong Kong Island and in Kowloon forcing mid-market and budget developments to consider more remote locations such as the New Territories and potentially even outside of the Territory, in China. Likewise, the considerable growth in hotel-bed provision in Jahore Bahru, in the past few years, has the potential to act as a "safety valve", during periods of excess demand in Singapore. At the micro level, real-estate costs influence companies such as Campanile in their hotel location policies, with the result that properties are frequently sited in less-favoured areas such as industrial parks.

In the context of true island tourism, responses to excess demand, of the kind illustrated above, are not feasible, especially where geographical remoteness is a major problem as in the case of locations such as Bermuda, Mauritius, the Seychelles and Tahiti. If local facilities cannot accommodate excess demand, in most cases tourists and tour operators will seek alternative destinations, not necessarily even proximate to that location, and business will be lost entirely to the original island. This scenario, if sustained over a period of time, has, potentially, very serious consequences for the industry as a whole in that destination island.

Remote island tourist destinations may also suffer greater disadvantage, to that faced elsewhere, during times of excess supply. Destinations and their individual businesses, primarily hotels, can only compete internally for business, on the basis of price, value or quality. In other respects, competition, as in the case of excess demand, may be with far-removed alternative destinations, where the purchaser is choosing generic product attributes (sun, sea and sand) in making the decision. However, the same does not apply when the purchaser's interest is in location-specific attributes such as historic monuments or features of a destination's culture. Thus, for example, the Maldives may be able to entice visitors away from Mauritius or Fiji at a time of excess supply, on the basis of their common generic product profile, but cannot compete with Easter Island's unique historic artefacts to compensate for business downturns.

There appear to be fundamental differences in the way that competition operates in island destinations compared to equivalent resort locations or properties in non-island locations. Here, competitiveness can operate on a far wider geographical scale. For example, hotels in locations such as Brighton, Oxford and Canterbury can readily compete for a share of the London tourist market, when their own business is slack—of course, this process can also operate in reverse—but this facility offers opportunities which are not available to island destinations.

Because of the restrictions placed on marketing and competitive alternatives by geographical factors, island destinations need to give particular focus to forecasting levels of tourist arrivals and, through this, to manage pricing policy in a way that maximizes revenue in times of both excess supply and excess demand. Various techniques do exist for this process at both the macro and micro level. Immediate historic data is, generally speaking, used by national tourist authorities to predict performance, with respect to tourist arrivals within the short- to medium-term time frame. The World Tourism Organization (undated) have summarized techniques of this nature in the form of general guidelines. A similarly useful source for forecasting models at the macro level is Bar-On (1989).

At a micro level, the widely used forecasting techniques to maximize revenue yield within short time frames broadly fall under the generic heading of yield management. These techniques are especially favoured by larger hotel businesses. The technique, which originated in the airline industry and gained ground in the hospitality sector from the mid-1980s onwards, is designed to assist hotels to go beyond traditional occupancy objectives and to achieve maximum revenue from each room available for sale. The literature on yield management is relatively extensive and good illustrations include Orkin (1988); Relihan (1989); Lockwood and Jones (1990); Russo (1991); Jones and Hamilton (1992); Shaw (1992); and Lieberman (1993).

In this chapter, we present a technique for analysing forecasts, based on the Ricardian model, that offers hotel businesses a methodology that falls between the direct use of simple projections from historic arrivals and occupancy data and the very specific and short-term results obtained from yield management. The technique is of particular value in the context of relatively isolated island tourism destinations in that its analysis benefits greatly from the completeness and "purity" of arrivals data which island status guarantees. Furthermore, the analysis focuses on internal competitive pricing strategies between hotels and other facilities within the destination and, therefore, loses much of its power in an environment where tourists have the option to utilize hotel accommodation or other facilities in a wide geographical area.

In this chapter, we present the principles that underpin Ricardian analysis, with particular reference to hotel markets and illustrate its application through work undertaken in Bermuda, focusing on major resort hotels on the island. The objective is to present the technique in a way that may stimulate replication of the analysis undertaken here and its practical application, collectively, by hoteliers and tourist authorities in island tourism destinations.

A BERMUDIAN CASE STUDY

Background

We have described the detailed application of this forecasting methodology elsewhere, both in the context of UK outbound fully inclusive tourism (Baum and Mudambi, 1994) and in the specific context of one island, Bermuda (Baum and Mudambi, forthcoming). These sources give full details of the computation involved in utilizing Ricardian analysis. What we propose to do here is focus on the data generated in the latter study, namely that based on Bermuda, and to describe, in general terms, how the methodology can be applied in the island context.

Bermuda provides an excellent location by which to demonstrate the application of Ricardian forecasting techniques within the island hotel and tourism context. Particular features that relate to Bermuda and that are especially conducive to the use of the technique include:

- The island's remote location in the west Atlantic, which means that it is very unlikely to act as a "shared" destination with any other location, in that it is not a likely participant in dual- or multiple-destination packaging.
- Its size and location mean that data collection is likely to be much more complete than is the case with other destinations.
- Bermuda's dependence on one relatively homogeneous market (the United States).
- The small number of major competing hotels on the island creates an environment in which hotels have market power and a large degree of oligopolistic interdependence.

In addition to benefiting from the above (in the sense of their support for the techniques of Ricardian analysis), a number of further and more general assumptions are made with respect to this forecasting approach. These are that:

- the quality of hotels varies and this places restrictions on prices which may be charged;
- hotel quality can be measured and ranked in terms of revenue-generating capacity; and
- hotel room rentals are completely unstorable: thus, an empty room represents revenue lost forever.

These principles are applicable to Bermuda as they are elsewhere.

Data utilized

In order to utilize the Ricardian technique for forecasting purposes, it is necessary to obtain comprehensive, reliable and complete data with respect to tourist arrivals, hotel rates (see below), hotel occupancies and to control these against a standard and recognized index for the full period in question.

In this study we analysed data with respect to the large resort hotels in Bermuda for the period 1980 to 1992. Published peak rates (Spring and Summer) and off-peak rates (Fall and Winter) were obtained from various issues of the *Bermuda Hotel and Guest House Rates*, available from the Department of Tourism. The deficiencies inherent in the use of published rate sources are recognized but these provided the only consistent and comparable data for the purposes of the study. Reliable data on actual, achieved rates are not available in published form. A total of seven resort hotels provided the sample for the study, all of which operated for the full period in question. In 1992, these seven hotels controlled 2527 rooms out of a total of 4237 rooms in 81 establishments registered under the Hotels (Licensing and Control) Act of 1969. This represents a control of 60% of all available rooms on the island. This figure, high as it is, probably understates the market power exercised by the large resort hotels, since many of the rooms which they do not control are of relatively lower quality and would not be considered suitable by resort hotel patrons. (By quality we refer both to the room itself, as well as the allied services—restaurants, pool, entertainment etc.—provided by the establishment.)

Further, it is important to note that fears of the erosion of market power through new competition are non-existent, since the period in question is one where virtually all new hotel building was prohibited in Bermuda. Thus, the only changes to the overall island hotel stock have been through removal or closure.

Monthly tourist arrivals and the consumer price index were obtained from the *Bermuda Digest of Statistics 1992*, published by the Ministry of Finance. In addition, an alternative deflator was constructed using the wages of hotel staff, reported in the digest. The most recent arrivals' information was obtained direct from the Department of Tourism; and hotel occupancy figures were provided by the Bermuda Hotel Association.

Estimation and results

Analysis of this data, utilizing the methodology outlined above, provided results which conform to the predictions of the Ricardian model. The application of Ricardian analysis was carried out using a three-step procedure. In the first step, traditional time-series trend analysis was used to generate forecasts of occupancy (the main indicator) and tourist arrivals (a subsidiary indicator). In the second step, forecasts were subtracted from actual outcomes to create error terms. Positive errors reflect excess demand, whereas negative errors reflect excess supply. In the third step, hotel rates sorted by the level of excess demand (or supply) in the period to which they relate.

The Ricardian analysis predicts that hotel rates should react asymmetrically to the state of the market. When there is excess demand, hotel rates should reflect the level of demand. However, when there is excess supply, hotel rates should behave erratically and be unrepresentative of the level of demand.

The predictions of the Ricardian model are supported by the data. During periods of excess demand, rates behave systematically: they fall as the level of excess demand falls. However, during periods of excess supply, the rates behave erratically, without any discernible pattern. In fact, some of the highest rates are registered when excess supply is greatest.

CONCLUDING REMARKS

The fundamental prediction of the Ricardian model is that oligopolistic competition in a market with large seasonal fluctuations, and hence periods of considerable unused or underutilized capacity, is likely to see systematic demand-driven pricing during periods of excess demand but unsystematic pricing during periods of excess supply. Recognition of this framework will allow island destinations, especially their collective hotel associations, to formulate policies to minimize the deleterious effects of rivalrous behaviour, both in the short and long run.

Thus, in the short run, it is critical for each operator to recognize whether a period is one of excess demand or supply. Periods of excess supply will inevitably see considerable non-price competition and market-share realignment. Implementation of market-share strategies during a period of excess demand will, in all probability, be wasted effort.

In the long run, for tourist boards and hotel associations, the Ricardian analysis provides a means of analysing past pricing decisions and hence computing the present and future effects of changes in the hotel stock.

REFERENCES

Bar-On, Raymond (1989) *Travel and Tourism Data*. London, Euromonitor Publications.

Baum, Tom (1993) "The Falkland Islands". *Proceedings of the Second Island Tourism International Forum*, Bermuda College, Bermuda.

Baum, Tom and Mudambi, Ram (1994) "A Ricardian Analysis of the Fully Inclusive Tour Industry". *The Service Industries Journal*, **14**(1), 85–93.

Baum, Tom and Mudambi, Ram (1995) "An Empirical Analysis of Oligopolistic Hotel Pricing: the Case of Bermuda Resort Hotels". *Annals of Tourism Research*, **22**(1).

Jones, P. and Hamilton, D. (1992) "Yield Management: Putting People in the Big Picture". *The Cornell Hotel and Restaurant Administration Quarterly*, **33**(1), 89–95.

Keane, M.J., Brophy, B. and Cuddy, M.P. (1992) "Strategic Management of Island Tourism". *Tourism Management*, **13**(4), 406–414.

Lieberman, W.H. (1993) "Debunking the Myths of Yield Management". *The Cornell Hotel and Restaurant Administration Quarterly*, **34**(1), 34–41.

Lockwood, Andrew and Jones, Peter (1990) "Applying Value Engineering to Rooms Management". *International Journal of Contemporary Hospitality Management*, **2**(1), 27–32.

Orkin, E.B. (1988) "Boosting Your Bottom Line With Yield Management". *The Cornell Hotel and Restaurant Administration Quarterly*, **28**(1), 52–56.

Relihan, W.J. (1989) "The Yield-management Approach to Hotel Room Pricing". *The Cornell Hotel and Restaurant Adminstration Quarterly*, **29**(2), 40–45.

Russo, J.A. (1991) "Variance Analysis: Evaluating Hotel Room Sales". *The Cornell Hotel and Restaurant Administration Quarterly*, **32**(1), 60–65.

Shaw, M. (1992) "Positioning and Pricing: Merging Theory, Strategy and Tactics". *Hospitality Research Journal*, **15**(2), 31–40.

World Tourism Organization (undated) *Guidelines on the Methodology Applicable for Making Annual and Medium-term Forecasts (relating to tourism development and promotional plans)* Madrid, WTO.

Part II

ISLAND TOURISM MANAGEMENT PRACTICE

11 A Framework for Tourism Development on Fragile Island Destinations: the Case of Bonaire

RONNIE PIETERS AND DIANA GEVERS
Tourism Corporation, Bonaire, NA

INTRODUCTION

Bonaire is endowed with a variety of natural and cultural assets which, taken as a whole, provide the basis for the attraction of visitors from abroad and the development of tourism. These assets include outstanding marine resources, unspoiled natural scenery, a pleasant year-round climate, an uncrowded environment and a friendly, welcoming population. These assets should be preserved and nurtured not only because they are appreciated by visitors from other lands but because they are valued by the present population and will be by generations yet to come.

The development and promotion of tourism is in the interest of the people of Bonaire and will be encouraged in so far as it contributes to economic and social well-being by creating job opportunities for local people, generates receipts for local businesses, increases foreign-exchange earnings and does not exceed the island's carrying capacity. Development which does not take careful account of environmental and human resource concerns could deplete or eliminate the very assets which makes Bonaire attractive to visitors and local residents alike.

Tourism in Bonaire should develop in a planned and orderly manner so as to provide the maximum benefit to the island and its residents and to ensure that any adverse effects on the social, economic, cultural and general quality of life of the people of Bonaire and the environment are minimized. The objective should be to achieve a managed growth path and a sustainable level of tourism development. This necessitates finding and striking the fine balance between the facilitation of tourism growth and the control of associated developments, bearing in mind that without careful conservation of Bonaire's primary tourism resources, it may cease to have a viable tourism product. A comprehensive national tourism policy is therefore essential if tourism is to grow in an orderly way.

Island Tourism: Management Principles and Practice
Edited by Michael V. Conlin and Tom Baum

MISSION STATEMENT

The overall objective for the development of tourism in Bonaire is to enable the people of Bonaire to benefit from the promotion and development of tourism by providing an optimum level of economic contribution consistent with the overall protection of Bonaire's environmental assets, cultural heritage, human resources and lifestyle.

GENERAL POLICY GUIDELINES

While this objective has to be adhered to by all those involved in the tourism sector, whether private sector or public sector, it is for the public sector to enact policies and to carry out programmes to reach the stated objective.

To this end, the government will:

1. Encourage the orderly, fair and reasonable development of tourism resources within the context of a carefully planned and executed Tourism Development Plan.
2. Give full active support to the development of tourism activities which raise the wealth of Bonaire and its inhabitants.
3. Ensure a pattern of tourism development consistent with the protection and conservation of the island's natural resources and attractions, particularly its off-shore reefs and which also guarantees public access to the coastal zones. This ensures locals' and visitors' access to diving sites, beaches and fishing areas.
4. Strive continuously to improve and upgrade the product which Bonaire has to offer to international and domestic tourism in order to consolidate a strong and competitive position in targeted overseas markets.
5. Encourage a balanced and diversified growth in the number, types, place of origin and travel motivations of visitors to Bonaire by stimulating well-researched and financed marketing and promotion campaigns and, while encouraging further expansion of the diving market, actively explore other leisure-oriented markets compatible with Bonaire's character and image.
6. Encourage a tourism development that caters to high-quality—and specialty, non-mainstream tourists: i.e. boutique tourism.
7. Encourage the modernization and competitiveness of the accommodation sector.
8. Grant licences and leases for new development only to bona fide investors, with a demonstrated planning and delivery capability, who are willing to follow the guidelines set out in this policy statement.
9. Maximize job opportunities for Bonaireans and other qualified Antilleans at all levels of skill and responsibilities in the tourism sector by expanding training opportunities for nationals already working in or potentially interested in entering the tourism industry and by limiting the validity of work permits of expatriates in cases where suitable qualified Antilleans are not available to such

reasonable periods of time as are required for the training of local counterparts. Bonaire's labour policies should seek to encourage Bonaireans and other qualified Antilleans living elsewhere to consider taking up job positions in Bonaire.

10. Encourage Bonairean and Antillean ownership and management of tourism facilities and services, utilizing locally available capital resources and seek foreign capital only for those investments for which local funds and/or management capabilities are limited or not available.
11. Encourage a more intensive exploitation of the scope for linkages between tourism and other sectors of the local economy, particularly agriculture, livestock, fisheries, handicraft and services.
12. Encourage the Antillean Air Company, as well as other airlines which currently service Bonaire, or which may service Bonaire in the future, to provide on a year-round basis a reliable and convenient air service at a competitive price.
13. Facilitate the entry and exit of visitors at all ports of entry and strive to ensure that facilities are improved to keep pace with the demands of visitors and other passengers.
14. Exploit the positive effects of tourism on the socio-cultural fabric of Bonaire, while minimizing those aspects which may create potential conflicts or loss of cultural identity.
15. Create a better understanding among residents and public officials of the importance of tourism to the island's economy; and foster a spirit of continued hospitality and friendliness toward visitors.
16. Promote tourism in a manner that fosters visitors' understanding and respect for the culture, customs and ethnic traditions of local residents and for the delicate and varied ecology of the island.
17. Continue to work closely with the Caribbean Tourism Organization, the Caribbean Hotel Association and strengthen ties with other regional and international organizations involved in the areas of tourism, economic development and conservation.
18. Establish and implement the necessary institutional changes and legislation necessary for the attainment of the above policies and goals.
19. Consonant with the above, strive to strengthen the functions, capabilities and resources of Tourism Corporation Bonaire, which is the agency of the Bonaire tourism sector.

SPECIFIC POLICIES

New hotel development

The projected growth in tourist accommodation is far in excess of the development goals of the Tourism Strategic Master Plan and the Bonaire Tourism Structure Plan. From the first quarter of 1991, the government has imposed an official moratorium on all new hotel and related tourist accommodation developments, including condominium and time-sharing projects, for an initial period of seven years during which no new permits for such development will be issued. In addition, all existing permits for new lodging developments and extensions to existing properties will be reviewed and, where appropriate, renegotiated so as to ensure that the total number of lodging units is kept below 1600 units.

It is expected that this policy will result in a re-focusing from an emphasis on attracting large new projects to facilitating the upgrading of the existing tourism product and stimulating small business growth. Investment in other viable tourism-related facilities, both by Bonaireans and overseas investors, will be encouraged provided such projects conform to the guidelines set out in this policy statement.

Physical planning

The Bonaire Structure Plan (1990) presents a zoning plan for guiding land-use development, including the designation of areas reserved for tourism and tourism-related facilities. All proposals for development require planning approval and must be submitted in the first instance to the Legal Department to verify their conformance with the stipulated requirements of the structure plan.

Final approval is given by the Executive Council on the advice of the inter-departmental Planning Committee of which the tourist office needs to form part. Building permits are issued by the Public Works Department and will not be granted unless the project has been approved by the Executive Council (or Planning Committee). Project developers have the right to appeal with the Parliament of Bonaire within 30 days after notice.

Protection of the environment

All major development proposals must be accompanied by a thorough environmental impact study conducted by an independent, qualified expert. The government or Tourism Corporation can submit a developer's plan to an outside independent appraisal at the developer's expense.

Effective 1994, coastal zone development will be stopped for a period of at least five years and only projects already underway and with valid permits will be allowed to be completed. This is pending the findings of a baseline study of Bonaire Marine Park on the subject of marine environmental impacts on coastal areas.

The maximum permitted building height for tourist lodging projects is 11 metres (three-storey) and eight metres (two-storey) in environmentally sensitive areas. No building development is permitted in the following conservation areas: Washington-Slagbaai Park, the Lac area, Klein Bonaire; and the designated linear beach park areas as defined in the Structure Plan.

A permit is required for the erection of all advertising signs and billboards which must conform to certain specified standards. The operation of jet skis and similar high-powered marine craft is totally prohibited.

Bonaire Marine Park (BMP)

The number of divers and other persons using the Marine Park will be monitored and limited if necessary for the conservation of the coral reefs and the protection of the island's tourism industry. To preserve marine life, especially on Bonaire's reefs, existing fishing laws regulating fishing in the proximity of the coastal area's must be strictly enforced.

Further research will be undertaken by the BMP to determine the precise carrying capacity of the park, whether in terms of the maximum number of users or the intensity of use by various categories of user. The annual admission fee payable by any person diving in the Marine Park will be increased to $25 per diver per year as a direct contribution to the operation and maintenance of the park. At the same time, there will be an intensified marketing effort to attract visitors to Bonaire for reasons other than diving.

Diving shops

A permit is required by all operators of diving shops and similar establishments who must comply with the conditions governing the operation of such establishments as stipulated in the Marine Environment Ordinance. The government will carefully monitor, and, where necessary, control the number of diving shops permitted to operate in Bonaire, bearing in mind the finite carrying capacity of the Marine Park and the possible need to limit the number of diving visitors, or the number of dives per diver, or both, at some future date.

The government intends to establish a comprehensive legislation framework to govern the use Bonaire's marine resources for all other users. This legislation includes set charges for the various categories of users. Local users of marine

Figure 11.1. Reef diving off the coast of Bonaire

resources are charged for the dollar amount in Antillean guilders ("local" is defined as all persons who register Bonaire as their island residence).

Product development

The Tourism Corporation and government will continue to pursue a "dive-plus" marketing strategy that will make Bonaire more competitive in existing and new diving-markets while at the same time reaching out to new potential "niche" markets in the general leisure markets in existing and new geographical markets. The government intends to welcome and actively support proposals to upgrade and expand the current tourism product to appeal and cater to identified up-market segments such as birdwatching, windsurfing, fishing, snorkelling, cycling, the family market, sailing, etc.

Investment

Investment in viable tourism projects, other than those pertaining to the accommodation sector, will be welcome, both from Bonaireans and overseas investors, although quite naturally the government will seek to stimulate and foster local investment. The government will actively encourage Bonaireans to invest in tourist-related facilities such as restaurants, bars, entertainment facilities, watersports and other sports facilities and attractions, transportation and communications facilities, tour and travel operations, retail outlets, handicraft, etc. through the provision of small capital loans and technical advice from the Development Bank of the Netherlands Antilles and other agencies.

In addition, Bonairean investors in approved projects can receive a tax holiday consisting of:

- full exemption from import duties for all construction materials including furniture, fixtures and equipment;
- exemption from property taxes for up to eleven years;
- a reduction of all income taxes to 2% for up to 11 years.

For Bonaireans, the minimum capital investment needed to qualify for the above tax incentives will be reduced to Naf. 250 000 for approved projects in the tourism sector (excluding the accommodation sector). Foreign-owned companies that wish to qualify for tax incentives are required to establish Bonaire subsidiaries which include Bonairean citizens as directors and/or include a government nominee on their boards. Tax incentives will no longer be offered to foreign investors for hotels on land-development projects. They will continue to be offered for the renovation of existing hotel properties, whether owned by Bonaireans or overseas investors. In this way, it is hoped to redirect financial mechanisms and an incentives policy away from large new accommodation projects in favour of the promotion of small, locally owned and managed tourism-related businesses and the upgrading of existing accommodation establishments.

Tourism linkages

It is intended that tourism will increasingly be utilized as a catalyst for the development of other economic activities in Bonaire, particularly agriculture, fisheries, handicrafts and other services, and Bonaireans will be encouraged to invest in such projects.

Condominium and time-sharing developments

No permits for new condominiums or time-sharing projects will be issued before 2000 AD. Existing permits for such developments will be reviewed and renegotiated where appropriate. In the intervening period, the government will make provision for the regulation of future condominium and time-sharing developments. The government will need to be satisfied at the planning-application stage as to the experience and competence of the proposed management company before approval is given. Profits from the re-sale of condominium units will henceforth be subject to tax, and owners of condominium units will be obliged to allocate a minimum number of weeks each year for renting.

Casinos and gaming establishments

The government does not intend to issue any new additional licences for casino operations in Bonaire, whether stand alone or part of a hotel establishment. The government's policy is to have one "low-key type" casino for the whole island. The operation of coin-operated gaming machines other than in casinos is totally prohibited.

Fast-food restaurants

No permits will be issued for high-profile American-style fast-food restaurants. Priority will be given to the establishment of high-quality international, gourmet, ethnic and local restaurants.

Cruise tourism

Priority will be given to the development of land-based as opposed to cruise tourism. In that respect, the government will not actively seek to promote cruise tourism or allocate funds for that purpose. Not more than one cruise ship will be permitted to dock at the port of Bonaire at any one time. At the same time, every effort will be made to maximize on-shore spending by cruise passengers and to seek to convert cruise visitors into future stay-over tourists. Cruise ships will be required to remain for a whole day and passengers are not allowed to take food and beverages off the ships.

In order to increase the revenue benefits from cruise tourism, the government has

Figure 11.2. An aerial view of Kralendijk

imposed a passenger head tax of US$5 per manifested passenger on board all cruise ships calling at Bonaire from 1 April 1994. The head tax will be increased to US$10 at the beginning of 1995, in accordance with CTO guidelines.

Cruise companies and/or their agents will be responsible for disposing of garbage generated by cruise ships visiting Bonaire and will not be permitted to leave any garbage on the island. They will also be responsible for dealing with any pollution, accidental or otherwise, caused by cruise vessels. The government of Bonaire will impose a fine of up to $500 000 for those ships found guilty of polluting.

Yachts

A mooring fee of US$15 per day has been charged from the beginning of 1994 for all anchoring yachts visiting Bonaire and not using the (private) Marina. The government will ensure that in due course adequate moorings are available and that suitable arrangements are made for the removal and disposal of garbage for a reasonable charge.

Charter boats

All operators of charter boats must have a licence. Licences are only issued for boats taking visitors for day or evening cruises. Operators are not permitted to take hotel visitors on overnight cruises unless this is done by prior agreement with the hotels. No licences will be issued for the operation of live-aboard diving boats.

Manpower training

The government will ensure that the necessary "on-the-job" training is provided for Bonaireans wishing to work, or who are already working, in the tourism industry. Assistance will be sought from national and international donor agencies in the fields of instruction and student training. Developers will be required, as part of their project proposal, to introduce on an ongoing basis a programme of "in-house" training and induction training for their employees. The government intends to institute a national certification programme for all persons employed in the tourism industry in both the public and private sectors, so that eventually all posts are filled by qualified personnel.

Work permits

Application for work permits for expatriates will not be entertained in cases where suitably qualified Bonaireans or Antilleans are available to fill the vacant positions. Where applications for work permits are granted, they will be limited to the periods or time required to train locals. The charges for work permits for expatriates were raised to Nafls 1000 from July 1994 and for renewals of permits to Nafls 400.

Tourism education

The government will ensure that tourism-related subjects are introduced into the curricula of all island primary and secondary schools so that school leavers are fully aware of the importance of tourism to the island economy and of career opportunities in tourism, both as employees and as owner/managers of tourism-related enterprises.

Public awareness

The government will mount an ongoing programme to increase public awareness of the role that the community at large is expected to play in the development of the tourism sector, including the reception of visitors and the maintenance of an unspoiled environment. The government will continue to support the "Tene Boneiru Limpi" campaign and other community programmes geared towards preservation and enhancement of Bonaire's cultural heritage and natural beauty. It will also give top priority to the realization and implementation of environment protection legislation, including an effective control mechanism and apparatus.

CONCLUSION

Tourism can, if carefully planned, managed and promoted, become the mainstay of the economy of Bonaire. The hospitality industry affects and embraces people from all walks of life, and the increasing economic benefits which it can bring will reach everyone. However, it is necessary to strike a balance between the economic benefits that may be brought by an ever-increasing number of visitors and the possible negative impacts of this growth in tourism on the natural and cultural environment of Bonaire. The purpose of the National Tourism Policy is to ensure that this balance is achieved and that the island's unique natural and cultural assets are preserved for the enjoyment of future generations of Bonaireans and visitors.

APPENDIX: BONAIRE

Location: 50 miles north of Venezuela, 30 miles east of Curaçao, 86 miles east of Aruba and 1720 miles from New York. At 12 5′ north latitude, 68 25′ west longitude. Outside the hurricane belt.

Size: 24 miles long by 3–7 miles wide, 112 sq. miles. Highest elevation is Brandaris Hill, 784 feet.

Language: Papiamentu and Dutch. English and Spanish widely spoken.

Government: With a population of 11 500 Bonaire is the second largest in size of the five Netherlands Antilles islands: Bonaire, Curaçao, St. Maarten, Saba and St. Eustatius. Since January 1986, Aruba no longer forms part of the Netherlands Antilles. The Netherlands Antilles is an autonomous part of the Kingdom of the Netherlands. Its form of administration is a parliamentary democracy. The Queen of the Netherlands represents the Crown. Bonaire has a lieutenant governor, F. Goedgedrag, residing in Kralendijk, the island's capital. There is a Legislative Council, called "*Staten*": (Parliament), an Executive Council and an Advisory Council. The seat of the central government is in Willemstad, Curaçao. Each island territory has its own legislative and executive body called an Island Council.

12 The Competitiveness of the Maltese Islands in Mediterranean International Tourism

LINO BRIGUGLIO AND LESLIE VELLA
University of Malta, Malta

INTRODUCTION

This chapter will discuss Malta's position in terms of price competitiveness as an international tourist resort compared with other Mediterranean countries. It will also consider non-price factors which influence tourism demand. Tourist expenditure has a relatively large direct impact on the Maltese economy, contributing around 15% to the Gross Domestic Product. Multiplier analysis related to Maltese incoming tourism indicates that tourism expenditure tends to have a higher multiplier effect than the bulk of merchandise exports, since the value-added content of production associated with tourism tends to be relatively high (Briguglio, 1992). Moreover, demand analysis related to Maltese incoming tourism would seem to suggest that the tourist inflow to Malta is very price elastic. Some studies have indicated that with a 1% change in the real exchange rate of the Maltese lira, tourism to Malta changes by 3% in the opposite direction, everything else remaining constant (Gatt, 1984). For these reasons, changes in the competitive position of Malta as a tourist resort would have major repercussions on the Maltese economy.

The method used in this chapter to compare Malta's competitive position in a Mediterranean context is based on tour-operator brochure analysis. It compares prices of package holidays from the UK, Germany and the Netherlands to Malta and a number of other Mediterranean tourist destinations. The computations are classified by hotel types and duration of stay.

The chapter is organized as follows. The next section briefly describes the Maltese economy and the contribution of tourism to the Maltese and the Mediterranean economies. The section after that summarizes the results of an analysis of prices in different Mediterranean resorts and assesses Malta's competitive position in the summer of 1993. The last section discusses some non-price factors which also influence tourism demand and the choice of one resort over another; it also comments on the overall conclusions of the chapter.

Island Tourism: Management Principles and Practice
Edited by Michael V. Conlin and Tom Baum

TOURISM IN MALTA AND IN THE MEDITERRANEAN

Malta is a small Mediterranean island with a population of around 355 thousand and a land area of 316 sq. km. The Maltese GDP at factor cost amounted to approximately US$2,000 million in 1992. About 27% of the Maltese GDP is contributed by the manufacturing sector, about 33% by the services sector and 25% by the public sector. The public sector in Malta as defined in production statistics excludes limited liability companies with government majority shareholding. If these are included, the share of the public sector would rise to around 40%. The remaining 17% is contributed by the agriculture, fishing, construction and quarrying sectors, and by domestic property income.

The labour force in Malta amounted to around 137 thousand in 1992, with an unemployment rate of just under 4%. Around 25% of those gainfully occupied are employed in government departments, 8% in public corporations and another 8% in companies with government majority shareholding. Thus just over 40% of the employment in Malta is in the public sector. The remaining 60% are divided almost equally between private direct production and private market services.

As stated, tourism has a major impact on the Maltese economy. In 1992, tourist consumption expenditure in Malta (including accommodation) directly contributed around 15% of the Maltese GDP, and around 25% of foreign-exchange earnings from exports of goods and services. Tourism also contributed to the domestic economy through international transportation. In 1992, transportation expenditure amounted to an estimated 2% to the Maltese GDP and around 5% of earnings from exports of goods and services. These are estimated by the authors, on the basis of percentages applicable for 1990, since data for 1992 is not available.

As regards employment, the tourist industry directly employs around 6.5% of the total gainfully occupied population. It should be noted here that tourist expenditure generates employment in the transportation, banking, retail, agricultural, fishing, construction and other industries which are not classified as forming part of the tourist industry.

Maltese tourism statistics

In 1992, the number of visitors to Malta amounted to 1 054 711, of which 95% were tourists and 5% were cruise passengers. The number of incoming tourists has increased rapidly in recent years, with an average rate of growth of 20% per annum between 1982 and 1992. More detailed statistics appear in the appendix to this chapter.

Nationality

In 1992, just over 52% of tourists came from the United Kingdom, 15% from Germany, 8% from Italy, 5% from France, 4% from Libya and 3% from the Netherlands. The remaining 13% came mostly from Western Europe and North America. The percentage share of British tourists has tended to decline in recent years, whereas the German, Italian and French sectors have tended to increase their percentage shares.

Seasonal pattern

During the same year, around 36% of tourists came during the July–September period, 44% came during the shoulder months of March to June and October and the remaining 19% came during the winter months. In recent years there has been a tendency for the winter months to take a larger proportion of the total tourist inflows.

Average duration of stay

In 1992, the last year for which we have complete annual statistics for duration of stay, the average stay per tourist was of 12 days. In recent years the average stay per tourist has tended to decline.

Tourist accommodation

The number of tourist beds in 1992 was 42 898, of which 48% were in hotels, 31% in apartment hotels and 17% in holiday flats; the remaining 4% were in guest houses. Hotel accommodation consisted mostly of the four-star and three-star categories, with a 84% share of the total; five-star hotel accommodation accounted for only 5% of total hotel accommodation.

In 1991, the average occupancy rate in all establishments was around 55%. The rate rises to 61% if only hotels are considered. A more detailed analysis of occupancy rates indicates that in the three- and four-star hotels, the rates increase to 65% and in the five-star category they reach 75%. If the summer months are considered in isolation, occupancy rates would of course be much higher (see Table 12.G in the Appendix).

Mediterranean tourism

In this study, "Mediterranean Region" refers to all countries bordering the Mediterranean Sea, and one country, Portugal, which has a Mediterranean character but does not border the Mediterranean Sea. The Mediterranean region is the most popular tourist destination in the world. The countries bordering the Mediterranean have diverse attractions to offer to the tourist—not just sun, sea and sand. The Mediterranean is renowned for its archaeological, historical and artistic heritage. The reliable summer weather and the food and wines of the region are also important attractions.

In 1990, the number of tourists to the Mediterranean amounted to 155 million (see Table 12.1). Italy, Spain and France together attracted around 70% of Mediterranean tourists. The remaining 30% were shared among Greece, Portugal, the former Yugoslavia, Turkey, Morocco, Egypt, Tunisia, Cyprus, Algeria, Israel and Malta.

Table 12.1. Mediterranean tourism (1990)

Country	Tourists' expenditure as: % exports goods and services	% exports of services	Number of tourists
Algeria	1	13	1 137
Cyprus	42	60	1 561
Egypt	11	17	2 411
France	7	25	51 542
Greece	20	38	8 873
Israel	8	30	1 063
Italy	9	48	27 260*
Malta	26	60	872
Morocco	21	63	4 024
Portugal	16	68	8 020
Spain	22	63	34 432*
Tunisia	20	60	3 204
Turkey	15	50	4 799
Yugoslavia (former)	13	44	7 880

*Spain includes Gibraltar and Italy includes San Marino.
Sources: Tourist arrivals are taken from the *Yearbook of Tourism Statistics*, WTO (Annexes, 1992). Foreign-exchange inflows are taken from *International Trade and Development Statistics*, UNCTAD (1992).

Income from tourism in this region (with the exception of Algeria and Libya) constituted an important share of total income from exports of goods and services of those countries which can be regarded as developing, as can be seen from Table 12.1. The table shows that the Mediterranean developing countries which seem to rely most on tourism expenditure for foreign-exchange earnings are Cyprus, Malta, Morocco and Tunisia, with Cyprus being the most dependent.

MALTA'S COMPETITIVE POSITION IN 1993

In this section we report on the results of an exercise which attempts to measure and assess Malta's competitive position in the Mediterranean region in Summer, 1993. The study was carried out under the auspices of the National Tourism Organization of Malta by L. Vella with assistance from A. den Broeder and J. Vlek for the German and Dutch analysis. The method is based on a tour-operator brochure analysis. The approach is a simple one and consists of comparing the prices charged by different tour operators for similar package holidays in different Mediterranean countries.

The study covers tourists originating from three countries: the UK, Germany and the Netherlands. Together, tourists from these countries account for about 70% of all incoming tourists to Malta accommodated in hotels and complexes. The prices of the package tours from the different countries are in the currency of the country of origin and cover accommodation on a half-board basis. The hotels sampled were those featured in the Thomson Summer Sun 1993 brochure for the UK, the Neckermann Summer 1993 brochures for Germany and Neckermann and Hotelplan Summer 1993 brochures for the Netherlands. The number and the categories of hotels sampled are given in Table 12.2.

This approach has a number of limitations. First, it does not relate to all types of tourism, since it only covers those who visit Malta on package tours on a half-board basis in hotels and complexes. This amounts to around 60% of all incoming tourists in Malta. Second, it only covers tourists originating from three countries. Had we been able to include Italy as well, the number of "package" tourists covered would have been nearer to 80%. However the Italian market is very fragmented and it was not possible to produce meaningful results from this segment since there was no brochure which could be regarded as representative of the market. Furthermore, share of package-tour travel among Italian tourists is very small. Third, it was not possible for us to compare prices with all Mediterranean countries. However the countries chosen are the most direct competitors with Malta because they offer a product which is similar to the Maltese one. Fourth, in the country of origin, only one major tour operator was used. The reason for this restriction was to permit annual comparisons of prices on an ongoing basis. It should be noted however that the tour operators chosen were the market leaders in their respective countries. Fifth, there is no homogenous price for a package holiday in a given category of hotels in a given country. For this purpose an averaging exercise had to be carried out, and the competitiveness comparisons apply to such averages.

The UK segment

Table 12.3 summarizes the competitiveness scores and ranking of Mediterranean resorts according to prices derived from the Thomson Summer Sun 1993 brochure.

Table 12.2. Number and categories of sampled hotels

	UK	Germany	Netherlands	
	Thomson	Neckermann	Hotelplan	Neckermann
Spain	59	58	12	25
Greece	26	94	27	—
Portugal	10	14	7	5
Cyprus	30	15	20	12
Malta	18	17	18	11
Tunisia	—	41	5	16
Turkey	—	40	19	5
	143	279	108	74

UK: Thomson analysis covers 2-, 3-, 4- and 5-star hotels.
Germany: Neckermann analysis covers 3- and 4-star hotels.
Netherlands: Hotelplan analysis covers 3-, 4- and 5-star hotels; Neckermann analysis covers 3- and 4-star hotels.

Table 12.3. Malta's competitive scores and rank in UK segment for summer 1993

	7-Day package		14-Day package			
	4-star	3-star	4-star	3-star	WAV*	Rank
Malta	100	100	100	100	100	4
Spain	93	92	94	96	94	1
Majorca	92	96	93	102	96	2
Greece	99	99	99	99	99	3
Portugal	119	121	132	138	128	5
Cyprus	125	128	129	137	130	6

*WAV means weighted average of all scores.

Malta is given a score of 100 and prices of other countries are indexed in proportional terms. The last column of the table is a weighted average, where the weights are according to the number of tourists in the four categories of the table.

According to Table 12.3, Malta does not feature among the highest-priced package-holiday destinations. Portugal and Cyprus are more expensive. On the other hand, mainland Spain and Greece offer cheaper prices than Malta. Majorca is also cheaper than Malta, with the exception of the 14-day package in a three-star hotel. It appears also that the lack of competitiveness with Greece and mainland Spain is more marked in the seven-day package tours. In the 14-day package tours, especially in the three-star-hotel category, the lack of competitiveness with Greece and mainland Spain is not so marked. In the case of Majorca, Malta actually is cheaper in the 14-day, three-star-hotel category. At the same time, price competitiveness with Portugal and Cyprus is more marked in the 14-day package, especially in the three-star category. These results would seem to suggest that for British package holidays, the most competitively priced in Malta for Summer 1993 were those in three-star hotels for a 14-day holiday.

The German segment

The competitiveness scores and rank pertaining to tours from Germany are summarized in Table 12.4. It can be seen that Tunisia, Greece and Turkey are cheaper than Malta, whereas Cyprus and Portugal are more expensive. Prices charged in Greece and mainland Spain are more competitive in the 15-day package tours in four-star hotels and more expensive in the eight-day package tours. In the case of Majorca, the eight-day package tours appear to be more competitive than those offered by Malta. In the eight-day package category, Malta ranks fourth. In the four-star category, Malta's lack of competitiveness with the better-priced resorts is not as marked as in the three-star category. On the other hand, the three-star category shows a higher degree of price competitiveness with Cyprus, which, like Malta, is an island resort and directly competes with Malta.

With regard to the 15-day package tours, Malta ranks fifth, but in the three-star-hotel category, its prices are very close to those of Greece and Majorca, so that to all

Table 12.4. Malta's competitive scores and rank in German segment for summer 1993

	8-Day package		15-Day package			
	4-star	3-star	4-star	3-star	WAV	Rank
Malta	100	100	100	100	100	4
Tunisia	90	87	92	87	89	1
Turkey	98	97	96	92	96	2
Majorca	99	94	105	99	99	3
Greece	102	105	96	99	101	5
Spain	103	114	95	112	106	6
Portugal	120	107	127	107	115	7
Cyprus	133	137	135	141	137	8

intents and purposes Malta can be classified as almost, but not quite, third. Moreover, in this same category there appears to be a higher degree of price competitiveness with Cyprus, which, as stated, directly competes with Malta for tourism. For these reasons, it may be concluded that for German package tourists, the most competitively priced tours in Malta may be those in three-star hotels for a 14-day holiday.

The Dutch segment

Table 12.5 pertains to tourism from the Netherlands which only constitutes a small share of incoming tourism to Malta. Here again the table confirms the overall tendencies that Cyprus and Portugal are more expensive package-tour destinations and that Tunisia is a cheaper one. Malta appears to be less competitive than Greece and mainland Spain and in the same range as Turkey. In Table 12.5 there is some evidence that the three-star-hotel category is the most competitive because in this category Malta ranks fourth, whereas in the other categories Malta ranks fifth. Considering the eight-day and 15-day tours in the three-star category, it appears that the 15-day tours are more price competitive *vis-à-vis* Cyprus, which, as stated above, is a close competitor with Malta.

Table 12.5. Malta's competitive scores and rank in Dutch segment for summer 1993

	8-Day package		15-Day package			
	4-star	3-star	4-star	3-star	WAV	Rank
Malta	100	100	100	100	100	5
Tunisia	93	88	97	93	93	1
Spain	94	94	95	96	96	2
Majorca	94	90	100	94	95	3
Greece	94	100	90	100	96	4
Turkey	100	103	97	100	100	6
Portugal	115	112	125	123	119	7
Cyprus	125	129	128	134	129	8

NON-PRICE FACTORS AFFECTING TOURISM DEMAND

Although price competitiveness probably has a very important influence on tourism demand, other factors have to be considered in this regard (Crouch and Shaw, 1992; Calantone *et al.* 1987). In studies on tourism demand, many non-price factors have been found to have a significant impact on tourism inflows, and a strategy for promoting tourism should not therefore focus exclusively on price competitiveness.

The following is a brief discussion of some non-price factors affecting tourism—a non-exhaustive list, but one which we consider to be of direct relevance to the Maltese tourist trade. As we shall show, some of these factors are not within the control of the Maltese operators or the Maltese tourism authorities, but others are and can therefore form part of a tourism strategy for enhancing the tourism product in Malta.

Income of tourists

Economic conditions in the country from which tourism originates are a very important factor affecting tourism trade (Truet and Truet, 1987). This is a factor over which the host country has no control whatsoever. If the country from where tourism originates experiences economic growth, demand for tourism is likely to grow. Thus, for example, the Mediterranean region would probably experience an increase in tourism following an increase in real personal incomes in Britain and Germany.

Transport connections

Improvements in the quality and the frequency of air and sea connections between the country from which tourism originates and the host country improve the attractiveness of the host country. In Malta, Air Malta has been an important factor in promoting tourism from Europe, and further developments of this airline will have a direct bearing on the Maltese tourist industry. The same is true with regard to sea transport between Malta and Sicily.

Political factors

Political factors in the host country itself and in its region, have important effects on tourism inflows. This is only too evident in the former Yugoslavia, where tourism has to all intents and purposes been wiped out in the areas hit by the civil war. Conditions in neighbouring countries are also likely to affect tourist trade in a given country. For example, if the Lockerbie case were to flare up into warfare between Libya and the US, tourism to Malta would be very negatively affected because of Malta's proximity to Libya. Political conditions in competing resorts are, of course, also important. The civil war in the former Yugoslavia has to an extent boosted tourism in other Mediterranean resorts, including Malta.

The role of tour operators

The tour-operator factor cannot be overemphasized, particularly where package tours are very popular. Tour operators commit themselves to send tourists to a destination through advance agreements with hoteliers, airlines and ground handlers and therefore have a vested interest in promoting tourism to the resorts which feature in their brochures. For this reason, they invest a substantial amount of time, effort and money in actively publicizing these resorts. Such publicity is very different from "tourist office" advertising in that it is actually selling something tangible rather than creating an awareness of the attractions of a destination.

As is well known, tour operators produce attractive full-colour brochures which are distributed free to all enquirers through travel agencies, where a person-to-person contact is made with prospective tourists. In general, a destination which has been successful in attracting the attention of a wide-range of operators is likely to achieve good tourism results.

Exchange rates

This variable influences price competitiveness, but it may be arbitrarily determined in the host country, irrespective of efficiency within the tourist industry itself (Gerakis, 1965). In Malta, for example, the government operates a system of effective devaluation for British tourists called "the Forward Buying Rate", which enhances the price competitiveness in this segment.

Development of new products

The type of product demanded by tourism is complex and not easy to define (Goodall, 1991). Although there are some constants in its make-up, such as good hotels, its total composition is ever-changing because tourists are becoming less passive and more demanding, and their choices are becoming increasingly sophisticated. It is therefore not enough for a country to rest on its sea, sun and sand endowments for attracting tourists. This is especially so with regard to competition in the Mediterranean, where most countries offer these three "Ss".

Mediterranean destinations have to identify other attractions and selling-points and seek to project themselves in those areas in which they have or can develop the greatest comparative advantage. Malta has, in fact, been very busy identifying such areas to the extent that a sizeable proportion of the National Tourism Organization's promotional funds and activities are specifically directed towards the development of new segments. Catering for niche markets is particularly important in this regard, especially in the case of off-season tourism.

One area that Malta can exploit further is its archaeological and historical heritage. Other products that can be further developed include winter activities, conference and incentive travel and language instruction.

Marketing and advertising campaigns

It is a well-known fact that producing a product is not enough for success. It must be marketed, and this is especially so in tourism where intense competition exists. Marketing makes more sense where the product is differentiated, and advertising campaigns need to highlight the special products that are likely to have better results. Very often the best form of publicity is made by the visitors themselves. It appears, from sample surveys carried out by the National Tourism Organization of Malta, that previous visits and recommendation by friends and relatives are important considerations on which many tourists base their decision to choose Malta.

Human-resource development

The availability of adequately and professionally trained staff is an essential component of today's tourist business without which the product on offer would be at a disadvantage. Well-trained personnel are not only required in hotels and restaurants but also in the various other service establishments such as agencies, airports, passport control and other places where contact with tourists is made. Malta has invested heavily in this sector and the Institute for Tourism Studies, established in 1988, is now providing trained employees for all sectors of the industry on an ongoing basis.

Hygiene and environmental factors

Hygiene, safe food, overall cleanliness and good water supply are factors which enhance or denigrate the reputation of a host country more than anything else. The hygienic and environmental aspects of tourism are becoming increasingly important as a factor affecting the choice between one country and another as tourists are becoming more health conscious and more aware of the dangers associated with pollution.

Improving tourists' services

The facility with which tourists can book their airline and hotel accommodation is a consideration which is not always given adequate attention. However, in an era where time is money, and where decisions to travel are sometimes taken at short notice, this factor may have an important bearing on the choice of one destination as against others.

Avoiding wasting time and queuing for booking for and utilizing facilities within the host country are also very important factors that render a tourist destination attractive. The increased use of electronic processing devices is conducive towards these ends, and their increased implementation would enhance the image of the host country as an efficient tourist destination.

CONCLUSIONS

In this study we have attempted to shed some light on Malta's competitive position for Summer 1993 as a Mediterranean tourist destination. We have compared prices from tour-operator brochures in the UK, Germany and the Netherlands. The main results that emerged from the exercise are as follows:

1. In general, Malta ranks somewhere in the middle in terms of price competitiveness among Mediterranean tourist destinations.
2. As regards package tourism from the UK, Portugal and Cyprus are more expensive, whereas mainland Spain and Greece are cheaper than Malta. Majorca is also cheaper than Malta, with the exception of the 14-day package in a three-star hotel.
3. As regards package tourism from Germany, it appears that Tunisia, Greece and Turkey are cheaper than Malta whereas Cyprus and Portugal are more expensive. Prices charged in Greece and mainland Spain are more competitive in the 15-day package tours in four-star hotels and more expensive in the eight-day package tours.
4. That Cyprus and Portugal are more expensive package-tour destinations than Malta, and that Tunisia is a cheaper one also applied in the case of tourism from the Netherlands. Malta appears to be less competitive than Greece and mainland Spain and in the same range as Turkey.
5. The results would seem to suggest that the most competitive package Malta can offer is a two-week holiday in a three-star hotel.

It is important to note again that these results have to be interpreted with caution. The main reason for this is that the averaging exercise carried out in this study conceals a degree of variation in prices of similar categories of package holidays in the host countries. However there are at least three important tendencies that appear to be consistent enough to be considered reliable. These are (1) that Malta is more competitive than Cyprus in all categories of package tours; (2) that Malta is by and large within the same price range as Greece in the case of UK tours and (3) that Malta is less competitive than mainland Spain in the case of UK tours.

The finding that Malta tends to be more competitive than Cyprus is important for the Maltese tourist industry. Cyprus, like Malta, is a small island with a small population, and is probably Malta's most direct competitor. An important reason for Cyprus's lack of competitiveness is probably due to more expensive airfares from Western Europe. The finding that Malta is almost on a par with Greece with regard to competitiveness with respect to UK package tours is also encouraging for the Maltese tourist trade.

An important conclusion that can be derived from the study is that mainland Spain is more competitive than Malta for British tourists. This is possibly due to cheaper air fares and economies of scale. In a way, this may not constitute a serious disadvantage to Malta because it discourages the very low spenders among British tourists from choosing Malta for their holidays. As a matter of fact, the Maltese tourism authorities do not seem to be extremely bothered about this, primarily because low-spending British tourists do not enjoy a good reputation in Spain and second because the value added of such a tourist segment is probably very low in relative terms.

The conclusion that Malta tends to be more competitive for the two-week holiday may be explained by the possibility that in Malta the daily accommodation rate is very competitively priced, and in a relatively longer stay this takes a larger proportion of the package cost. It needs to be stressed again that price competitiveness is not the only factor that affects tourist demand. We have listed a number of factors which may make Malta an attractive destination despite being uncompetitive in price or which, on the contrary, may work against any price advantage that Malta may have.

In the case of Malta, larger outlays on marketing and promotional campaigns, more attention to human-resource development, increased use of electronic processing devices, improvements in overall cleanliness and in water supply would seem to be the most important non-price considerations to enhance the island's image as a tourist destination.

REFERENCES

Briguglio, L. (1992) "Tourism Multipliers in the Maltese Economy". In P. Johnson and B. Thomas (eds) *Perspectives on Tourism Policy*. London, Mansell.

Calantone R.J., di Benedetto, C.A. and Bojanic, D. (1987) "A Comprehensive Review of the Tourism Forecasting Literature". *Journal of Travel Research*, **26**, 13–17.

Crouch and Shaw (1992) "International Tourism Demand: A Meta-analytical Integration of Research Findings". In P. Johnson and B. Thomas (eds) *Choice and Demand In Tourism*. London, Mansell.

Gatt, J. (1984) *Decline in Tourism—Causes and Effects*. Unpublished BA (Hons) dissertation. University of Malta.

Gerakis, A.S. (1965) "Effects of Exchange Rate Devaluations and Revaluations on Receipts from Tourism". *International Monetary Fund Staff Papers*, **12**, 365–384.

Goodall, B. (1991) "Understanding Holiday Choice". In C. Cooper (ed.) *Progress in Tourism, Recreation and Hospitality Management*. London, Belhaven, 58–77.

Truet, D.B. and Truet, L.J. (1987) "The Response of Tourism to International Economic Conditions: Greece, Mexico and Spain". *Journal of Developing Areas*, **21**, 177–190.

APPENDIX

Table 12.A. Mode of travel (000s)

	1988	1989	1990	1991	1992	Average (%)
Air	747.4	790.2	827.0	848.3	930.1	89
Sea	93.9	92.6	101.4	87.0	124.7	11
Total	841.3	882.8	928.4	935.3	1054.7	100

Source: National Tourism Organization, Malta.

Table 12.B. Visitor category (000s)

	1988	1989	1990	1991	1992	Average (%)
Tourists	783.8	828.3	871.8	895.0	1002.4	94
Cruises	57.4	54.5	56.6	40.3	52.3	6
Total	841.3	882.8	928.4	935.3	1054.7	100

Source: National Tourism Organization, Malta.

Table 12.C. Annual tourist arrivals (000s)

	1988	1989	1990	1991	1992	Average (%)
Winter*	138.1	151.0	160.1	167.0	191.5	18
Shoulder**	339.5	368.0	388.3	386.4	446.7	44
Summer***	306.2	309.3	323.4	341.7	364.2	38
Total	783.8	828.3	871.8	895.0	1002.4	100

*Winter months: Jan., Feb., Nov., Dec.
**Shoulder months: Mar., Apr., May, Jun., Oct.
***Summer months: Jul., Aug., Sept.
Source: National Tourism Organization, Malta.

Table 12.D. Tourist expenditure (million Maltese lira)

	1988	1989	1990	1991	1992	Average (%)
Travel	138.2	143.8	157.4	175.3	180.5*	78
Transport	45.0*	44.0*	40.0*	41.2*	49.1*	22
Total	183.2	187.8	197.4	216.5*	229.6*	100

Source: National Accounts of the Maltese Islands.
The Maltese lira approximately averaged US$3 during the 1988–1992 period.
*Estimated by the author.

Table 12.E. Tourist arrivals by nationality (%)

	1988	1989	1990	1991	1992
UK	60.8	59.5	51.6	51.2	52.4
Germany	9.9	11.1	14.9	15.2	15.3
Italy	6.5	6.4	7.3	7.2	7.6
Libya	4.7	3.8	4.1	5.2	3.8
France	3.1	3.4	3.9	3.8	4.5
Netherlands	2.3	2.1	2.5	2.6	2.9
Others	12.7	13.7	13.7	14.8	13.5
Total	100.0	100.0	100.0	100.0	100.0

Source: National Organization, Malta.

Table 12.F. Tourist accommodation: number of beds

	1989	1990	1991	1992	Average
Hotels	19 712	19 669	19 079	20 611	47.6%
Complexes	11 799	12 801	13499	14 085	31.3%
Guest houses	1 703	1 765	1 697	1 473	4.0%
Holiday flats	7 626	7 404	6 619	6 729	17.1%
Total	40 840	41 639	40 894	42 898	100.0%

Hotels: of hotel accommodation 84% is 4-star and 3-star and 5% are 5-star hotels.
Complexes: class I is 49% and classes II and III are 45%.
Occupancy: In 1991 average occupancy in hotels was just under 62% and in all establishments around 56%.
Source: National Tourism Organization, Malta.

Table 12.G. Occupancy rates and length of stay in 1991

	Occupancy rates (%) Hotels	Complexes	Total	Length of stay (days)
Winter*	42.2	27.8	37.0	12.4
Shoulder**	61.3	46.4	52.6	9.8
Summer***	82.6	77.1	78.1	10.6
Year	61.5	47.3	54.1	10.5

*Winter months: Jan., Feb., Nov., Dec.
**Shoulder months: Mar., Apr., May, Jun., Oct.
***Summer months: Jul., Aug., Sep.
Source: National Tourism Organization, Malta.

Table 12.H. Dutch market: Neckermann and Hotelplan

	Average prices scores							
	8-Day package				15-Day package			
	4-star		3-star		4-star		3-star	
Malta	100	100	100	100	100	100	100	100
Greece	94	—	100	—	90	—	98	—
Tunisia	94	89	93	83	100	93	101	85
Spain	94	—	97	90	95	—	101	92
Turkey	105	95	100	105	105	88	98	103
Portugal	117	113	116	109	126	123	126	120
Cyprus	123	127	128	130	127	129	135	133
Majorca	—	94	94	85	—	100	103	85

13 Island Competitiveness Through Festivals and Special Events: the Case of Newfoundland

DONALD GETZ
University of Calgary, Canada

INTRODUCTION

Cities, regions and countries have found that competitiveness in the global tourism market can be enhanced through event tourism: the systematic planning, development and marketing of festivals and special events as tourist attractions, image-makers and catalysts for infrastructure and other desired developments. As well, events can be considered as an alternative to capital-intensive developments and can be highly sustainable when based on the host community's support.

In this chapter the unique challenges and opportunities facing event tourism for island destinations are discussed within a framework of strategic planning and management. Following a brief review of the tourism literature on events and islands, a summary is presented of the general roles of festivals and events in tourism development and marketing. Unique elements of event tourism for island destinations are highlighted, then a strategic planning and management framework is utilized to shape the remainder of the chapter. An example from the island of Newfoundland illustrates many of the points. Practical advice is given on possible strategies for enhancing island competitiveness through event tourism.

Literature review

Little has been written on the subject of event tourism in island destinations. The subject of cultural commercialization has been debated, such as the analysis of ceremonies as attractions in Sulawesi, Indonesia (Crystal, 1989; Adams, 1990). Noronha (1979) observed a loss of traditions in Bali—where rituals became tourist attractions—but McKean (1989) argued that tourism in Bali revitalized traditions and helped shape the identity of young Balinese. Andronicou (1979) commented on how the government in Cyprus encouraged cultural events through educational programmes, with tourism providing the impetus for such cultural enhancement.

Economic impacts of event tourism on islands have been mentioned, such as the TT motorcycle races being the major tourist attraction (up to 50 000 visitors) on the Isle of Man (Nixon, 1990). Bermuda has for many years employed special events

Island Tourism: Management Principles and Practice
Edited by Michael V. Conlin and Tom Baum

and themes to attract tourists. Lewis and Beggs (1988) reported on the creation of Rendezvous Time in 1960 as a way to attract off-season visitors, with the Festival of Performing Arts added in 1975. Blum (1989) said that after 23 years Rendezvous Time did have a significant effect on improving winter occupancy rates. However, some Bermudians have noted that most tickets to performances are sold to residents, making it difficult for tourists to participate.

In the Caribbean, O'Reilly (1987) assessed the tourism potential of festivals and events, like Trinidad and Tobago's Carnival. He was unhappy with the way in which West Indian celebrations were reduced to mere entertainment in tourism enclaves and argued instead for bringing tourists into the community to experience festivals on equal grounds with residents.

ROLES OF FESTIVALS AND EVENTS IN TOURISM

As attractions, events can appeal both to special interest travellers who seek very targeted benefits, and to the mass tourist market. Research has shown that while most events, including the biggest, rely on mainly local and regional audiences, many do attract substantial numbers of tourists or help justify a trip. They can be particularly useful in generating travel to out of the way places and in the off-season.

Given the difficulty of hosting mega-events like World's Fairs or Olympics on islands, other strategies can be pursued—particularly the creation of "Hallmark Events". They should be of cultural significance to the resident population and have strong, communicable imagery. To the extent possible, they should tie in with broader destination themes. In this way, the image of event and destination become inseparable and mutually reinforcing.

Smaller events can also contribute significantly to international tourism competitiveness—the Australian Tourist Commission in its development of five theme years (1993–1997), noted that special events, regardless of whether they directly motivate a trip, add value to the visitor's experience. This is especially true when they facilitate host–guest contacts and reveal the local culture and way of life. Small events also provide spending outlets for tourists and can put money directly into the hands of local people.

Mega-events and Hallmark events, through high media coverage, help shape positive destination images. Community events and related imagery should be major elements in promotional campaigns, as increasing numbers of tourists are searching for authentic cultural experiences and ways to interact with their hosts. Holding high-profile events has also been used to help re-create a destination's image following bad publicity.

Major events can lead to new infrastructure, urban renewal projects and increased tourism investments. But large events can generate problems, so caution is required. Generally, small-scale and short-duration events, using existing infrastructure and involving the community, will generate few negative impacts.

Even small communities can create major benefits. Several villages in Canada have experienced their own financial legacies from annual, one-day festivals, leading to better community facilities and healthier local charities. These villages also found that popular annual events put them on the tourist map, led to upgrading of local businesses and created an overall positive image of a place that is good for living and investment.

Festivals and events bring life to otherwise static built attractions, shopping areas and parks. They are particularly useful for heritage interpretation areas, such as old towns, forts and harbours—resources found on many islands. Events can be held with minimal physical impact, lead to better host–guest relations, foster nature and heritage conservation and generate community-based tourist developments. In this way they are an alternative to mass tourism and can be sustained through community support.

Unique aspects of event tourism in island destinations

It appears that few island destinations have stressed festivals and special events in their tourism strategies, even though many islands have successful events. As the necessity increases to develop distinct competencies for competitive advantage, it is inevitable that island destinations will look more to their natural and/or cultural resources, including festivals and events (Haywood, 1993). At present, a number of obstacles and challenges exist.

Many of the issues and potentials facing islands are similar to mainland destinations, but with regard to event tourism several unique aspects can be identified. These factors are shown in Figure 13.1 in relation to possible strategies for achieving competitive advantage.

Island attractiveness

It is usually more difficult and expensive to travel to islands, so special effort is needed to create a positive image and provide added value. Events can give a particular boost to islands needing image enhancement, especially by stressing unique resources and themes that make an island experience worth the cost and effort. Authenticity of cultural and environmental attractions can be highlighted through special events where hosts meet guests on an equal basis.

Capacity

As well as accessibility and transport limitations, island often lack the physical space, services and basic resources necessary to host large events. Accordingly, small events with strong image-enhancement potential might have to substitute for mega-events. This is reinforced by the fear of negative impacts of large events (or events likely to generate behavioural problems) on sensitive environments and communities. In other words, because carrying capacity is a particularly important issue on many islands, carefully planned and managed events are a desirable product.

The references cited earlier show that island cultures can be especially

Factors affecting competitiveness	Possible strategies
Attractiveness Accessibility Image Security Hospitality	Stress positive aspects of remoteness (smaller, more intimate events) Develop all-inclusive event packages Piggyback events on other packages Capitalize on unique island resources for water and environmental-based events Capitalize on unique cultural resources to stress authenticity of the "island experience" Maximize positive image-making roles of events through mega-events or Hallmark events Maximize perceived friendliness and security through events which facilitate host–guest relations
Capacity	Stress small events or those with fixed limits Utilize existing infrastructure Match events to resource limits and the community's ability to absorb
Organization and leadership	Capitalize on existing organizations and their leadership to produce events Maximize partnerships and collaboration Recruit and train volunteers
Marketing management	Maximize corporate sponsorship with an international audience Promote add-on events to the mass market Develop events for niche markets Sell event packages internationally through agents and tour companies Attract high-yield event tourists Free and inexpensive events provide added value
Quality	Training is necessary Stress authentic experiences and spontaneity, not high service levels or sophisticated product Cultivate at least one international-quality Hallmark event Bid on high-quality, one-time events (e.g., tournaments) Package events with other island products such as shopping, beach experience, eco-tours, culture
Support services	Focused research is required to identify target markets, evaluate satisfaction and test new event products Form research consortiums

Figure 13.1. Event tourism is island destinations—possible strategies for competitive advantage

susceptible to cultural commoditization or the demonstration effect. Islands must therefore consider all possible impacts of events and develop those which best suit the indigenous culture. Haywood (1993) advocates development of a portfolio of attractions and events which reflect national values, cultures, institutions and history, with dignity and authenticity preserved when developing the island's distinctive competency.

Organization and leadership

The leadership necessary for producing indigenous events or developing and bidding on new ones might be a weakness for island destinations. Management training will be necessary, with emphasis on building from existing groups. A volunteer recruitment and training programme is likely to be essential.

The possibility exists for developing multi-island events and attracting those which tour, thereby reducing local organization. But bidding on one-time events can be especially difficult, so thought should be given to establishment of an event development corporation or strategic bidding partnerships.

Marketing management

Many island destinations are over-reliant on beach tourism and should diversify. It can be difficult to get the typical beach tourist interested in cultural or sporting events, so an effort to have these included in pre-sold packages should be made. Taking events to the beach resorts is an alternative. More important will be target marketing to segments who will travel specifically for events.

The high cost of many island trips is a limiting factor. To combat this limitation requires niche marketing and an emphasis on high-yield tourists, rather than mass tourism (Holder, 1993). Event tourists can be one of those valuable niches, while events in general provide added value to all visitor experiences. High costs of island visits can be compensated partially through free and inexpensive events which provide significant value-added to the experience. A two-price system can be established for higher-priced events, setting aside a proportion of tickets for residents and the rest for pre-selling with tourist packages.

Quality

Providing services and events to the standards required by tourists is a global challenge but can be exacerbated where there is little experience with special-event production. Training will be necessary, as will careful planning of the event/attraction portfolio and evaluation research.

Stressing authentic experiences and spontaneity, rather than high structured and sophisticated events, could be an effective strategy for creating quality tourist experiences. Small events can also be packaged with high-quality products such as shopping, dining and sports. On the other hand, developing at least one high-quality Hallmark event should be a goal of every destination.

Support services

Island destinations may have a problem doing the research and evaluations necessary to capitalize successfully on event tourism. Intelligence and marketing support systems might therefore have to be shared with other destinations. Very small destinations will have to overcome these limitations through marketing partnerships (Holder, 1993).

STRATEGIC MANAGEMENT OF EVENT TOURISM IN ISLAND DESTINATIONS

Strategic destination management involves the following interrelated components: situation analysis (resource analysis and environmental and future scanning); goals and objectives; strategy formulation; target marketing strategy; positioning strategy; marketing-mix strategy; organization and management support systems (Heath and Wall, 1992). Ongoing evaluation, feedback and planned innovation are also necessary.

Situation analysis

An evaluation of the current situation involves a resource assessment and environmental/future scanning. Resources for events are as diverse as the destination's physical environment, heritage, culture and economy: all elements can be used as themes. Indeed, authenticity and event attractiveness can be maximized by making certain that festivals and events fit the destination and are supported by the host population. Unique events and themes should be highlighted, especially if they have potential to attract niche markets or generate a strong image. In addition to existing and potential events, resource analysis must also examine labour (many volunteers will be needed), organizational and leadership capabilities. Strengths and weaknesses of the event sector should be evaluated in the context of overall tourism resource potential.

The environmental scan should examine the factors and trends affecting the destination, its marketing/planning organizations and the individual events. As well as identifying the destination's strengths and weaknesses, with respect to the competition and the market-place, threats and opportunities should also be examined carefully. To do this requires a scanning of current conditions, trends and the factors shaping the future. Key points related to event tourism are listed below.

As the number and variety of festivals and special events continues to grow, increasing partnerships are developing among arts, culture, leisure, environment agencies and event organizations. This often requires acknowledgement of new goals, such as the conscious planning for tourism by heritage agencies, or the struggle to obtain community input and commitment by tourist-oriented groups. For tourist destinations, these questions must be addressed:

- Who are the key groups/agencies that should be forging partnerships and policies for events?
- What is the role of the national tourist organization or other groups in developing and supporting festivals?

- Is there a risk of too many events overall, or of one type?
- Should festivals be regulated and the numbers and activities controlled? Or is free enterprise the guiding principle?

More and more destinations are striving for advantage by developing and promoting events aggressively. The key is to convey the image of a destination that is alive with events, a culture which celebrates itself and a destination attractive and hospitable to visitors all year round. Some questions to answer:

- What slogan(s) or theme(s) are most suitable?
- What is needed to make it happen?
- Who should play the lead role?

A number of cities and destination areas have set up event offices or corporations charged with the attraction (through bidding) and fostering of major tourist-oriented and/or resident-oriented events. Should all destinations form an event development corporation? Perhaps existing organizations could do the same job.

Attractions, convention centres, hotels, historic properties and resorts are very active in creating special events to attract publicity, generate repeat visits and utilize surplus capacity in low seasons.

- What is the potential for increased private-sector events?
- And for public/private/non-profit partnerships?

Event sponsorship has grown dramatically, with arts and community festivals gaining ground on sports; few events can survive without it. Now sponsors are much more demanding in the benefits they expect, so events must carefully assemble and sell sponsorship benefit packages. There is a risk of goal displacement to satisfy sponsors, inappropriate sponsorships and over-dependence. There is also intensifying competition for sponsorship dollars.

- Would it be better to have festival sponsorship generated by a central festival/event agency acting on behalf of all its members?
- Is there a need for policies or ethical guidelines to regulate sponsorship?

There is increased professionalism in the field of festival management and event tourism. College programmes have been established; the International Special Events Society has recently established a certification process, while the International Festivals Association has had for some time its own Certified Festival Executive programme. Destination perusing event tourism must identify their needs for event-related education and training.

Many cities have constructed sports complexes for events and special-purpose festival places: settings in parks, downtown areas or waterfronts, which facilitate a variety of indoor/outdoor performances and assemblies. These are typically programmed by a special-event group but may also provide rentable space for other event organizers.

- What are the area's festival places?
- Are they adequate?
- What would be the ideal festival/event venue, suited to the destination?

There has been an unfortunate pre-occupation with mega-events which is often accompanied by irrational politics, a lack of cost–benefit evaluations and disproportionate resource allocation. The value of annual festivals and smaller special events can be greater, certainly in the long run. Collectively, there is little cost and considerable gain to be realized from an integrated approach to festivals and events when compared to the costs and risks associated with bidding for mega-events.

"Hallmark Events" are desired by every destination; they create a positive image, attract visitors both to the event and to the area, and provide a vehicle for promoting smaller events. Existing events can be elevated to this status or new ones invented. They will require special resources and promotions to get established.

- What existing events have potential to achieve "Hallmark" status? Can one be invented?
- What are organizers of other successful events doing that should be emulated?

Unfortunately, most events are not produced or promoted with tourists in mind. The events are lacking in attractiveness for tourists and tour operators as they contain no targeted benefits. Pricing is non-existent or fails to recognize that some segments will pay more for certain opportunities. Ticketing is impossible, owing to the nature of the event or lack of advertising and distribution systems. No arrangements are made linking transport, accommodation or other attractions and services. Nothing special is done for tourists and tour operators to provide added value. Successful events and destinations are reversing these patterns through event tourism strategies.

- Identify and promote existing event packages.
- Created new packages for event tourists and as add-ons for other visitors.

There have been too few comprehensive impact studies done to help evaluate events. Of the studies undertaken to date, most have exaggerated the intended or real benefits of events through inappropriate assumptions and the use of economic tools not intended for evaluating events. Specifically, income and employment multipliers have frequently been abused to create exaggerated estimates of benefits (for a complete discussion, see Getz, 1993).

Better analytical tools are required, notably cost–benefit assessments. We have to be told what it costs to produce an event, and what is the return on investment.

However, even events that lose money or break even can generate worthwhile benefits to the community. On the other hand, profitable events might generate unacceptable impacts. We also want to know how economic costs and benefits stack up against social, cultural and environmental impacts.

- Are costs and benefits evaluated by event managers?
- Overall, what are the main benefits and costs of festivals and special events to the destination?

Consider how much controversy was generated by the 500th anniversary of Columbus's "discovery" of America. Was it worth the bother? And many communities have found to their horror that events can go wrong, leading to vandalism or even rioting. Events are becoming more controversial, and security is a headache (see, for example, British Columbia Task Force on Public Order, 1993).

Because festivals are celebrations, with some group proudly displaying their cultural values, they are always going to be risky. And because mega-events are always political in nature, given their appetite for resources, they will always be scrutinized with care. The essence of all festivity and celebration is commitment—by organizers, volunteers and supporters who believe in something.

Mission, goals and objectives

What roles are events to play in the overall destination strategy? Event tourism can be either a major or supporting sector, and its linkages with other tourism, economic, social/cultural and environmental policy fields should not be forgotten. Sample event tourism goals and objectives are provided in Getz (1991), and they should encompass the following:

- the extent to which existing events are to be developed and promoted as tourist attractions;
- planned development of new event attractions;
- support to be given to events;
- benefits expected from events, and how to evaluate them;
- negative impact avoidance and amelioration;
- acceptable costs and who is to pay for them.

Getz and Frisby (1991) have developed a framework and guidelines which can assist municipalities and other agencies in developing appropriate policies and assistance programmes for events.

Strategy formulation

An event tourism strategy will follow from the general goals and strategy of the destination. The event tourism component should include overall directions for the sector on product expansion and diversification and market penetration or expansion, as well as guidance for individual events and related organizations. A method of co-ordinating activities or forming partnerships should figure prominently in an event tourism strategy.

A target marketing strategy will be a part of, or evolve from, the general event strategy. Identifying specific event tourist segments (i.e. niche marketing) is required, but the strategy should also determine how to attract the mass market to events. Although event tourism has been scantily researched, some studies have shed light on international demand patterns and market segments. A series of surveys has been conducted jointly by Canada and the US to evaluate foreign markets, and these yield insights on event tourism that could also be valuable to other countries (for example, Tourism Canada, 1987). The studies reveal several distinct but potentially inter-related preference groups: sports; arts and culture; nature and outdoors; touring; and those looking for city action and comfort. It is important to understand that event tourism is a segmented market, and specific benefits and modes of packaging are required to attract different segments.

Positioning strategy

Based on distinctive competencies (that is, unique, high-quality event themes and products) and on overall tourism goals, a positioning strategy can be completed. Positioning will be achieved through the marketing mix and will differentiate the island from its competitors. Events can provide a central or supporting role in positioning. For example, an island destination could position itself as being unique and world class with respect to a particular theme; events can provide the tangible products by which visitors experience the theme. Alternatively, the destination could position itself as a "festival island", with events as the main attractions.

Developing the marketing mix

Of the normal marketing-mix components (product, price, place and promotion), the element requiring most attention is that of packaging (which can be viewed as being both a product and a means of distribution). Packaging events is a weak point for many destinations, so a detailed discussion follows.

Figure 13.2 shows two models, the first pertaining to events as the core or focus of a package, and the second treating events as add-ons to other products. Where events are the core, they will be closely linked to shopping, food and beverages—partly at the events, and partly external. Accommodation is a vital component for the international visitor and it must be suited to their preferences and the nature of the package. Adding other recreational, touring, shopping and dining opportunities to the package provides an augmented product and generates higher, more dispersed income for the destination.

The add-on event provides extra value to the independent traveller and the convention or incentive visitor. Events can be produced at hotels or be a lure for

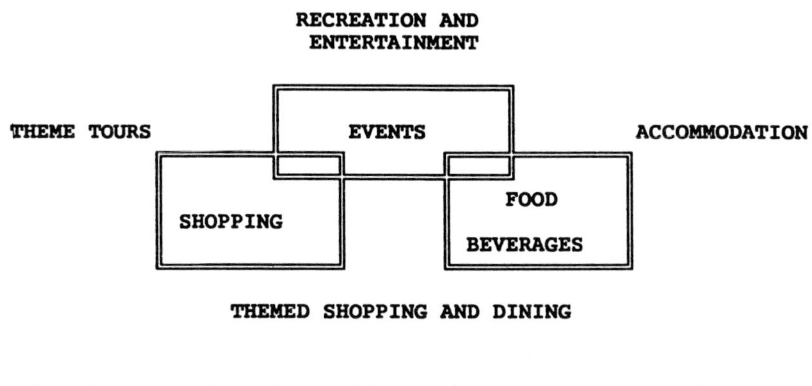

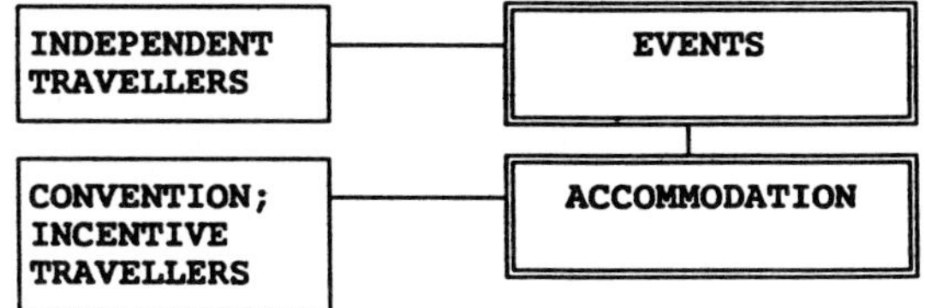

Figure 13.2. Event tourism packaging

getting visitors into the destination area and away from their hotels or resorts, thereby leading to additional spending.

Related to this concept are specific packaging implications, as indicated in Figure 13.3. Competitive advantage can be gained by finding new and better combinations and promoting them more effectively. Partnerships between events and tour companies are needed to make some of these packages work. Most festivals and special events have a variety of elements. They are packages of sports, participatory recreation, dining, drinking, entertainment and spectacle. Accordingly, each event must be analysed for its various target markets. One specific package is illustrated in Figure 13.4, in which events and eco-tourism are combined with a beach holiday.

Organization and management-support systems

Developing and implementing an event tourism strategy will require a lead player and alliances among industry, cultural, and other groups. In many destinations a facilitating policy and financial assistance will be required to initiate and sustain the strategy, particularly with respect to training leaders and volunteers and to

Event types	Accommodation	Dining	Other activities	Shopping
Sports	All types; urban and resorts	Basic eating	Nightlife; adventure; amusements	Sports souvenirs
Ethnic	All types; urban and small town	Ethnic food; themed restaurants	Ethnic areas	Authentic crafts
Lifestyle; food festivals	All types; urban; small towns	Themed, specialty dining; wines	Nightlife; wineries; countryside tours	Wines; special products
Performing arts	Mostly urban; upscale hotels	Fine restaurants	Theatre; museums; galleries	Art; crafts; fashion
Small-town festivals and fairs	B&B; inns; farms; motels	Festival food; modest restaurants	Sightsee; historic sites	Local produce; crafts
Eco-events	Camping; budget	Festival food	Wilderness; adventure	Eco-friendly products

Figure 13.3. Event tourism packaging

marketing. A separate organization might be necessary to make bids on events or actually to produce events.

In addition to market research, the strategy must include systematic evaluation of product and service quality, visitor experiences and the effects of events on the island's economy, environment and culture. The main purposes of evaluation are to improve events, increase positive impacts and to avoid or ameliorate negative effects. Constant innovation will be necessary to keep event products fresh and to enhance their quality.

CASE STUDY: CORNER BROOK WINTER CARNIVAL, NEWFOUNDLAND

This case study highlights a number of the issues and potential strategies available to island destinations. Corner Brook is a city of approximately 23 000, located on the west coast of the island of Newfoundland, Canada. Its location is remote from other cities, the regional population is small and access is restricted. Most off-island visitors to Corner Brook arrive by private automobile, having taken the ferry from mainland Canada. There is also a regional airport nearby which provides scheduled air service, and this is an important asset. A few cruise ships also visit, as Corner Brook lies at the end of scenic Humber Bay. Existing tourism is dominated by

Accommodation: beachfront resort	
Nature attractions:	Wildlife observation and interpretation Guided hikes, boat rides, flights, scuba Photography Sightseeing travel in remote areas, including archaeological sites Environmental fair (exhibits, performances, seminars)
Cultural attractions	Entertainment at resort receptions, nights 1 and 6 Stops at one or more village festivals (at least three hours—evenings preferable; shopping for local art and crafts, souvenirs; meals arranged in advance; beverages extra) Half day to participate in a festival or major sporting event
Services to be supplied by tour company:	Guide/interpreter; nature and photographic information or seminars All ground transport Passes for access to parks etc. Tickets to events Information or seminars about events and local culture Welcome and farewell receptions with traditional entertainment; theme party Advice/information on shopping (prices, quality, authenticity)
Services to be supplied by the event:	Hosts and guides to the activities Access to performers and organizers Meeting residents as equals Theme parties

Figure 13.4. A beach–ecotourism–events package (1 week)

friends and relatives, independent automobile touring (scenery based), bus tours and outdoor recreation enthusiasts. Intra-provincial travellers are important, but the Newfoundland population offers a very small, dispersed domestic market.

Tourism is highly seasonal, peaking in summer, and a combination of problems with the island ferry service, high costs and economic recession resulted in falling occupancy rates in the early 1990s. Other weaknesses include: limited accommodation and services; low awareness levels; lack of major built attractions (especially for poor weather); lack of packaged tours and fragmented marketing. The area has considerable potential for adventure and eco-tourism, including the appeal of nearby Gros Morne National Park. With considerable provincial financial assistance, a skiing facility has been developed near Corner Brook and is intended to become a four-season resort. Culture has been identified as a strength, as Newfoundlanders remain distinct from the rest of Canada, especially in terms of lifestyle and the arts.

In this context, festivals and special events were determined to have a major role to play in both the city's and region's tourism development strategies. Existing events would have to be strengthened and marketed more aggressively, and new events were recommended. The consultants assessed potential events for the region in terms of their ability to attract visitors, within the themes and goals of the broad strategy. For example, consideration was given to a series of festivals and sporting events to capitalize on the region's association with the explorer James Cook and with the earliest visitors—the Vikings.

Corner Brook's Winter Carnival was the subject of a separate but related development and marketing plan. It is the region's largest and best-established annual event and has the advantage of being closely linked to the skiing facility (it is timed to coincide with the peak skiing period in February). In addition to organizational, management and funding recommendations, the proposed development plan for the Carnival evaluated marketing opportunities and proposed a full marketing mix.

Product development for Corner Brook Winter Carnival

A major need was development of a central venue with indoor/outdoor facilities and the kind of programming which could attract both residents and tourists. A new civic centre could be designed to be a suitable festival place, and it would also have the advantage of being able to foster other events. A partnership with the nearby ski facility at Marble Mountain would strengthen the Carnival, but event managers had to work harder to attract skiers—who tended to fly to the area but spend most of their time at the hill—into city-based activities. Figure 13.5 illustrates target market and product ideas generated by consultants.

Programme planning advice was also given. Definition of the core programme concept was thought to be a key, so that thematic continuity and quality improvements could be realized; in addition the Carnival organizers could refer to the core concept when evaluating the programme and new product ideas. More systematic and visible theming of all activities was suggested.

Marketing goals

Some of the key goals formulated were: engage in permanent image-building and pre-event communications; target residents (the majority of customers) to become repeat visitors; careful target marketing to promote the Carnival as a tourist attraction, including development of suitable packages; a hospitality and quality-control strategy; internal marketing to foster a customer orientation; cultivate intermediaries and sponsors to maximize marketing effectiveness; provide a mix of free and paid activities; create a truly festive atmosphere throughout the city and at a recommended central venue.

Team sports	Jointly develop and promote competitions in and around the Carnival Produce trophy ceremonies featuring Viking Games motif Provide official Carnival souvenirs to teams
Ski and Carnival package	Jointly market packages with Marble Mountain ski resort Target existing and potential off-island skiers Sponsor ski races/competitions
Homecoming	Target Newfoundland club across Canada Develop Carnival packages especially for expatriates Produce official Homecoming events
Adventure tour package	Work with adventure tour companies Include the Carnival in a Western Newfoundland adventure tour
Meeting add-on	Target meetings, conventions and trade shows Add Carnival activities or Carnival theme party to other activities
Theme parties	Produce theme parties available all year to promote the Carnival
Day trips	Market within the region Target affinity groups such as seniors' clubs Hire buses or develop packages with tour companies Provide hosts and guides, tickets to events

Figure 13.5. Suggested target markets and product ideas for the Corner Brook Winter Carnival
Source: Marshal Macklin Monaghan and D. Getz, 1993

Target markets

These were established with reference to accessibility, proximity, special interests and desired benefits. In addition to targeting several key cities on and off the island, other segments were:

- alpine skiers: inclusive packages for weekends and weeks would combine skiing with accommodation and ticketed Carnival activities;
- sports teams: they would be attracted to new and improved competitions involving sponsorship, prizes and media coverage;
- friends and relatives: fostering a homecoming atmosphere and series of events to attract expatriates;
- other winter sports: considerable potential exists for snowmobiling, ice fishing, cross-country skiing and other winter packages that could include the Carnival;
- business travellers: people already in the province could be lured to attend the event; new trade shows and meetings could be fostered and attracted to coincide with the Carnival.

Communications/promotions

Of the recommended communications actions, several key items can be noted:

- the need for a more attractive, informative, revenue-generating souvenir programme/calendar of events;
- intensive use of the Viking mascot and logo;
- full-time public-relations efforts;
- a publicity strategy to obtain free, favourable exposure on and off the island;
- sales promotions, in partnership with corporate sponsors;
- targeted paid advertising;
- developing a line of merchandise for direct sales and licensing.

The Corner Brook Winter Carnival is an example of the special challenges facing events in remote, island locations. To elevate the annual event from a mostly local experience to a tourist attraction with high levels of economic benefits will require an effective organization, partnerships and investment. Particular attention to strengths and weaknesses of the city and region revealed opportunities and constraints. These were important in shaping marketing goals and actions. Perhaps the key point was identification of target markets and the actions necessary to cultivate appropriate market segments. Equally important was the conclusion that the product must be oriented specifically to the target segments—what is popular with residents must not be weakened, but new features are necessary to attract and hold visitors.

CONCLUSIONS

Event tourism is taking its place alongside other special interests as a major tourism planning and marketing tool. Festivals and special events are powerful attractions and they provide "value added" to international tourists; they can attract highly desirable market segments and at the same time contribute to authentic and sustainable development. It is not a stand-alone sector but complements other forms of tourism—especially those related to sports, culture and lifestyle.

Much more research is needed to understand event tourism in island destinations, and more packaging initiatives are required to take advantage of event tourism potential. There are a number of potential obstacles when developing event tourism in islands that must be considered, most notably the difficulty of hosting mega-events which depend on high accessibility and require considerable infrastructure and space. But through community-based events, cultivation of high-profile Hallmark Events and creative marketing using the image-enhancing power of events, even the smallest island can employ event tourism successfully.

REFERENCES

Adams, K. (1990) "Cultural Commoditisation in Tana Toraja, Indonesia". *Cultural Survival Quarterly*, **14**(1), 31–34.

Andronicou, A. (1979) "Tourism in Cyprus". In E. deKadt (ed.), *Tourism: Passport to development?* Oxford, Oxford University Press, 237–264.

Blum, E. (1989) "Tourism Officials Cite Growing Appeal of Culture-related Travel". *Travel Weekly*, 18 May.

British Columbia Task Force on Public Order (1993) Excerpts from "Report of the task force on public order". *Festival Management and Event Tourism: An International Journal*, **1**(2).

Crystal, E. (1989) "Tourism in Toraja (Sulawesi, Indonesia)". In V. Smith (ed.), *Hosts and Guests: the Anthropology of Tourism*. Philadelphia: University of Pennsylvania Press, 139–168.

Getz, D. (1991) *Festivals, Special Events and Tourism*. New York, Van Nostrand Reinhold.

Getz, D. (1993) "Event Tourism: Evaluating the Impacts". In B. Ritchie and C. Goeldner (eds), *Travel, Tourism and Hospitality Research: a Handbook for Managers and Researchers* (second edition). New York, Wiley.

Getz, D. and Frisby, W. (1991) "Developing a Municipal Policy for Festivals and Special Events". *Recreation Canada*, **19**(4), 38–44.

Haywood, M. (1993) "Attractions and Events: Price–value Considerations". In B. Ritchie, D. Hawkins *et al.* (eds), *World Travel and Tourism Review 1993*. Wallingford, CAB International, 245–248.

Heath, E. and Wall, G. (1992) *Marketing Tourism Destinations*. New York, Wiley.

Holder, J. (1993) "Island Tourism and the Price–value relationship: a Global Perspective". In B. Ritchie, D. Hawkins *et al.* (eds), *World Travel and Tourism Review 1993*. Wallingford, CAB International, 223–230.

Lewis, R. and Beggs, T. (1988) "Selling Bermuda in the Off Season". In A. Vladimir (ed.), *The Complete Travel Marketing Handbook*. Lincolnwood, NTC Business Books.

Marshall Macklin Monaghan and Atlantic Engineering Consultants (with Donald Getz) (1992) *Regional Tourism Plan for Corner Brook, Bay of Islands, Humber Valley and White Bay, Newfoundland*. Toronto.

Marshall Macklin Monaghan and Getz, Donald (1992) *Corner Brook Winter Carnival Development Plan*. Toronto.

McKean, P. (1989) "Towards a Theoretical Analysis of Tourism: Economic Dualism and Cultural Involution in Bali". In V. Smith (ed.), *Hosts and Guests: the Anthropology of Tourism*. Philadelphia, University of Pennsylvania Press, 119–138.

Nixon, D. (1990) "Cats, Kippers, and TT Races: Tourism and Culture in the Isle of Man". *Cultural Survival Quarterly*, **14**(2), 43–45.

Noronha, R. (1979) "Paradise Reviewed: Tourism in Bali". In E. deKadt (ed.), *Tourism: Passport to Development?* Oxford, Oxford University Press, 117–204.

O'Reilly, A. (1987) "The Impact of Cultural Hallmark/Mega-events on National Tourism Development in Selected West Indian Countries". *Revue de Tourisme*, **4**, 26–29.

Tourism Canada (1987) *Pleasure Travel Markets to North America: Japan, United Kingdom, West Germany, Highlights Report*. Ottawa.

14 Island-based Urban Tourism: the Case of Victoria

PETER E. MURPHY
University of Victoria, Canada

INTRODUCTION

To many people the combination of island and urban tourism may appear to be yet another oxymoron, but in reality the two do go together in terms of practical tourism management. The link between island urban locations and visitors can be traced to the early settlements, where invaders or colonists established the first toehold in their new environment. Such settlements were often based on the presence of safe harbours, good water supplies and arable land that would support a growing population. Not only did such locational determinants influence the urban settlement pattern of the islands, in turn they created the very attractions and infrastructure necessary for the tourism that followed. Evidence of this pattern can be seen in all oceans and on all scales. In Australia the dominance of Sidney as the major city and entry point, based on its historical significance, has contributed to its position as the major tourism centre of that island continent. In the Atlantic, the island of Bermuda's tourism activity is dominated by the two towns of Hamilton and St. George's.

The purpose of this chapter is to illustrate the important links that exist between urban and island tourism, using my home island of Vancouver Island as an example. While many of the general features of urban tourism are applicable in an island context, this chapter will highlight some which have increased significance in an island situation. These features include the sense of place and scale commonly associated with smaller islands, the increased significance of gateway centres and the overall sense of value involved with island vacations.

Urban tourism is a simple concept at first glance, signifying tourism that is taking place in an urban (village, town or city) context. However, closer examination reveals it to be a complex and highly significant aspect of tourism. Even where the declared purpose of a pleasure trip may be far removed from any urban reference, as in the case of resort or outdoor recreation tourism, these trips very often depend on urban tourism facilities for complementary activities or outright functional support such as transportation, accommodation and meals.

Despite the fact that much tourism takes place in an urban context, most of the literature until recently has ignored this setting and its implications for the industry. Ashworth (1989: 33) maintains there has been a "double neglect". He contends that not only has tourism neglected the urban context but that urban studies have also failed to observe the importance of tourism activity to the life of the city. Possible reasons for this include the difficulty of isolating tourism activity from residential activity and spending, as well as the variety of motives visitors have for visiting centres of commerce and learning where they may be a tourist one moment and a business person or student the next. However, this situation is beginning to change as the service economy continues to grow at the expense of the manufacturing sector and as the population ages. Both trends have exhibited the importance of developing a leisure–cultural component into the urban fabric for the benefit of business and the local quality of life. Such trends are beginning to stimulate research activity on both sides of the Atlantic—as in the case of Jansen-Verbeke's (1988) study of leisure and tourism patterns in select Netherlands cities and Broadway's (1993) analysis of Montreal's changing tourism landscape—and have led to a call for more urban tourism research and development (Murphy, 1992).

Vancouver Island off the west coast of Canada is approximately 250 miles long and 50 miles wide, with a land area of 12 519 square miles (32 100 square kilometres). "It is the largest of North America's offshore islands" (Foster, 1979: 51), and it is second only to Vancouver as the major tourist region destination in British Columbia. It traditionally receives approximately 20% of the province's person trips and tourism expenditures (British Columbia, 1981–1989). Its popularity is due in part to its proximity to the mainland, being separated by 20–30 miles of sheltered and island-studded water, and its diversity of attractions.

At the southern tip is the metropolitan region of the provincial capital, Victoria. In 1991 its census population was 287 897 and it received an estimated 3.15 million visitors who spent an estimated Cdn.$750 million. This city offers the full range of urban attractions and due to its historical links and political position is the main gateway to the island (Figure 14.1). To the north of this capital city lies an island containing a variety of small towns, each with its own distinctive character based on some local resource-based industry such as fishing, lumber or mining. Further north lies a wilderness not accessible by road, and maintaining this wilderness experience are the Pacific Rim National Park and the Strathcona Provincial Park. Set among some prime fishing and sailing waters, with a climate that permits golf twelve months in the year, Vancouver Island's tourism industry continues to expand as its more traditional resource-extractive industries decline.

SENSE OF PLACE AND SCALE

Islands hold a special place in people's minds. Smith (1987) in his dissertation on *The Imaginative and Experiential Significance of the Island* observes "although a strait may be narrow and relatively easily traversed, the sea acts to confirm isolation in a manner which is disproportionate to the ease of travel or distance factors"

Figure 14.1. Inner harbour of Victoria, with Provincial Legislative Assembly in background

(Smith, 1987: 223). Consequently, islands have developed distinctive characters and an unusual fascination for many mainlanders. In his search of the extensive fictional and non-fictional literature devoted to islands, Smith has noted they frequently possess opposing characteristics emerging from common roots. For example, an island's insularity can encourage both the freedom to develop a robust independence and the capacity to become inward-looking and backward. Similarly, their isolation can lead to either utopian aspirations of an idealistic society (an ideal vacation) or to dystopian functions which dehumanize the site and limit personal liberty through military and penal servitude (a restrictive vacation). Finally, there is a clear distinction between insiders, residents who have a meaningful attachment to the place, and outsiders who come from different backgrounds and with personal short-term objectives.

In terms of island tourism this means we can expect islands to offer a special opportunity and challenge. Their insularity and distinctiveness are becoming even more prized as the global economy homogenizes world societies. Thanks to the advances in air travel and reasonable prices of cruiseship vacations, more people can reach these fabled shores. However, due to their relatively small size and insular populations these "priceless microcosms" (Islands Protection Society, 1984: 11) are particularly vulnerable when the condition of separateness is broken and the resource base over-extended.

For Vancouver Island tourists, the short flight over or ferry trip through the intervening straits represents a distinctive break with the hurly-burly of the mainland or their more distant homelands. The immediate perception is of a slower pace of life, in a smaller and less-developed environment that offers a more human-scale setting and fulfilling experience. These are some of the constant comments collected in a series of visitor surveys conducted by Tourism Victoria over the past few years. Table 14.1 indicates the top seven features of a Victoria vacation which have been constant over the years and over the seasons. In the Summer 1989 survey, 96% of Victoria's visitors either strongly agreed or agreed that the city had attractive scenery and this was the number-one feature until this past summer when it was edged into second place by Victoria's beautiful gardens. Likewise the friendliness of the small city and its more relaxing pace are constantly appreciated by 75–85% of the visitors.

This sense of place is continued throughout the island via the promotional literature and the types of tourism development that have taken place. For example, in the Cowichan and Chemainus Valleys to the north of Victoria, the recent emphasis has been on the development of an eco-museum (Wood, 1993). Here several communities are striving to preserve the best of the past, the best of the present and to develop a more diversified and secure future. Tourism is an active part of this renewed community spirit, as visitor interest in the forest industry's past and present practices is encouraged through the development of local museums and the provision of visitor tours of local forest and mill operations. This is perhaps best exemplified by the spirit of Chemainus, a small town that temporarily lost its only significant employer when the lumber mill was closed and torn down. Rather than become a commuter or ghost town while a new and smaller mill was built, the town turned to its heritage and developed a series of murals reflecting its forestry heritage and its sense of place (Figure 14.2). Not only did this project bring in thousands of tourists and thus diversify its local economy, it provided the community with a renewed sense of pride. Likewise the town of Port Alberni and villages of Ucluelet and Tofino on the west coast of the island are preparing for the inevitable shrinkage in their traditional lumber and fishing industries by investing in their heritage and environment for the benefit of local residents and tourists. In Port Alberni they have

Table 14.1. Visitor satisfaction levels in Victoria

	% (rank)			
	Summer 1989	Fall 1990	Winter 1992	Summer 1993
Attractive scenery	96(1)	96(1)	97(1)	96(2)
Beautiful gardens	95(2)	91(3)	96(2)	96(1)
Clean	94(3)	94(2)	94(3)	90(3)
Pleasant climate	90(4)	70(7)	88(4)	80(6)
Friendly	85(5)	84(5)	86(7)	83(5)
Interesting attractions	84(6)	84(4)	87(5)	85(4)
Relaxing and restful	77(7)	81(6)	87(6)	76(7)

Sources: Exit surveys published by Tourism Victoria.

Figure 14.2. Chemainus mural

built a new fishing pier, Ucluelet emphasizes the recreational value of the nearby national park and Tofino promotes the local whale-watching opportunities. In all these cases local communities are redefining their relationships with their heritage and surrounding environment, embracing those aspects which create their sense of place and make them distinctive and attractive destinations.

Since islands are microcosm environments they are particularly sensitive to external encroachment and development, including the impact of tourism. British Columbia and Vancouver Island are aware of the delicate balance within island ecosystems and have started to address the situation. An early proposed tourism development strategy for the province (Marshall, Macklin, Monaghan Ltd, 1979) recommended a diverse strategy for Vancouver Island. This included a conservation emphasis around Victoria, because it was approaching capacity levels in the summer, and an economic development and diversification emphasis in the northern areas where there were underutilized resources and tourism opportunities. Since then, many of the consultants' recommendations have come to pass through either government planning or industry action. For example, Tourism Victoria, the capital city's destination-marketing association has been emphasizing shoulder season and winter development and promotions to spread the business load more evenly and more effectively. As a result the high season has now stretched from its traditional three summer months into a six-month period. Up-island more resorts have been developed to take advantage of the outdoor recreation and scenic resources, such as the recent First Nations' Tsa.Kwa.Luten Lodge near Campbell River (Figure 14.3). In this way the tourism activity is being spread throughout the island, reducing the pressure on prime sites and diversifying the economy for the

Figure 14.3. Tsa.Kwa.Luten Lodge on Quadra Island, near Campbell River

residents, and providing visitors with more varied attractions and more reason to come and stay.

A major feature of the Marshal, Macklin, Monaghan (1979) recommendations was the need to develop quality attractions and destinations, linked together by nodal-corridor transport systems. This feature is especially relevant to a large closed system like Vancouver Island, where there are basically four major entry points into its world—Victoria, Nanaimo, Courtenay/Comox and Port Hardy. For the island's tourism to develop throughout all its regions, it needs to draw visitors from these four entry points into the hinterland.

GATEWAYS AND LINKAGES

Pearce (1987) outlined the significance of gateways and routes to tourism in his book *Tourism Today*. He discusses the need to understand the flow of tourists in order to meet their needs better and develop more sustainable tourism businesses. He describes the four basic types of routes identified in a British Columbia study of visitor travel patterns (Pollock *et al.*, 1975) which were:

1. *the direct route*, whereby visitors entered and left through the same zone or gateway;
2. *the long traverse*, whereby visitors entered at one end of the region and departed at the opposite end;
3. *the short traverse*, where visitors followed diagonal-type routes across the edge of a region;
4. *the loop*, where visitors returned to their point of entry via a different route.

These different types of visitor routings are very significant to islands, such as Vancouver Island, which want to draw visitors away from the gateway sites and spread the benefits of tourism throughout the whole island economy.

Pearce applied this typology to the visitor patterns occurring in New Zealand and found that the three international airline gateways of Auckland, Wellington and Christchurch received the bulk of the visitors, with Auckland receiving two-thirds of all arrivals. Wellington, the capital, had the largest proportion of direct-route visitors reflecting its large business and official travel component; whereas the other two gateways had more of the other travel types because of their dominance of the north and south islands which have a variety of tourist attractions. From Auckland and Christchurch there were both short (within an island) and long (both islands) traverses, with Pearce noting "many vacationers thus arrive at one gateway, tour the country, and leave via a second gateway" (Pearce, 1987: 64): an ideal tourism situation and one probably encouraged by the parameters of a "once in a lifetime" trip.

This form of analysis has been conducted on Vancouver Island by Murphy and Keller (1990) using 1987 summer travel data from both residents (insiders) and visitors (outsiders). Vancouver Island and the neighbouring Gulf Islands were divided into seven subregions (Figure 14.4). Each has a known number of entry/exit points, and using travel questionnaires it was possible to track the routes used by both visitors and residents during their vacation trips. Sometimes the respondent failed to report on all the subregions visited, but since their origin and entry/exit were known it was possible to fill in the gaps and develop a complete data set.

A simple examination of the total reported travel patterns by both island visitors and island resident tourists showed there was a hierarchical visitation pattern similar to that noted by Pearce in New Zealand. More than 80% of the respondents reported having visited the Greater Victoria district and 45% visited Nanaimo—the island's principal gateways (Table 14.2). In terms of the districts adjacent to these two gateways, there was a steady decline in the reported visitation rate. The

Table 14.2. Reported and actual visitation patterns

District	Reported visits	Percentage of sample reporting	Actual visits	Percentage of sample visiting	Difference
Greater Victoria	4106	80.2	4379	85.5	5.3
Cowichan Valley	1269	24.8	2574	50.3	25.5
Nanaimo	2292	44.8	3016	58.9	14.1
Alberni-Clayoquot	1804	35.2	N/A	—	—
Comox-Strathcona	1020	19.9	1129	22.1	2.2
Mt. Waddington	418	8.2	575	11.2	1.4
Gulf Islands	506	9.9	N/A	—	—

N/A: Not applicable.
Source: P.E. Murphy and C.P. Keller (1990), p. 56.

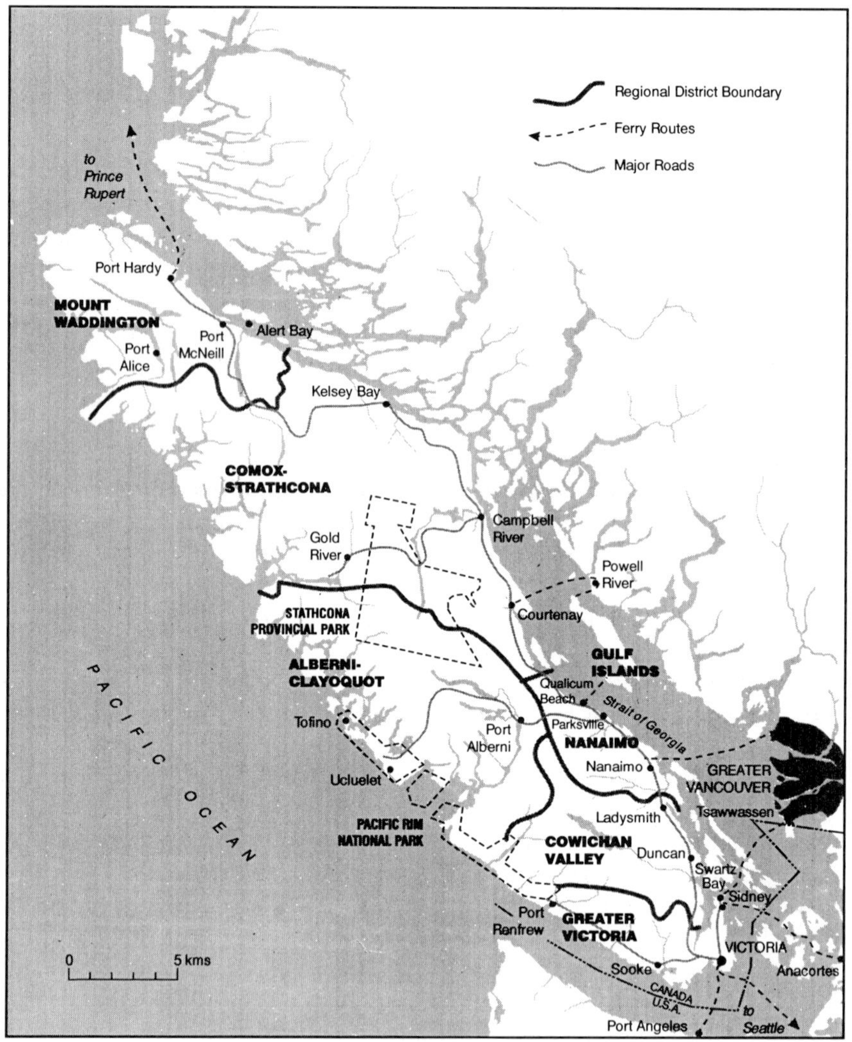

Figure 14.4. Tourist districts of Vancouver Island and environs

Cowichan and Chemainus Valleys district, containing the towns of Duncan and Chemainus, received 25% of the tourist visits, and 20% reported visiting the Comox-Strathcona district. The relatively high value of 35% for the Alberni-Clayoquot district can be explained by the presence of the Pacific Rim National Park in that area which brings a lot of business to the small communities of Tofino and Ucluelet. The anticipated decline in reported visits continued as distance increased from the two major gateway districts, with the northernmost district of Mount Waddington recording the lowest visitation rate of 8%. The Gulf Islands had nearly as low a rating, with a 10% visitation score. This reflected not so much their distance from the major gateways but the relative difficulty and expense in reaching them via small local ferries.

The reported visits represent the tourists' awareness of the routes and attractions on Vancouver Island, but when they are travelling in new areas it is quite natural for them to miss some attractions and urban destinations in a perceptual sense as well as in a reporting sense. To offset such inaccuracies, the tourists' reported travel patterns were checked against their reported arrival and departure points for spatial inconsistencies. This allowed for the creation of a data bank representing their actual travel patterns. This was done for five of the seven districts. It was not possible to check the reported visits to the Alberni-Clayoquot and Gulf Island districts because they are isolated regions possessing neither a single gateway nor a direct connection between gateways to act as a checking source. Table 14.2 shows the actual travel patterns, which were compared to the reported visitations.

It is apparent that all five districts and their associated urban cores were underreported, some by a much larger proportion than others. For example, the lowest level of inaccurate reporting was recorded in the two most northerly and least visited districts of Mount Waddington and Comox-Strathcona, while the highest was in the Cowichan and Chemainus Valleys to the south. This may be explained by the relative size of the districts and the opportunities they provide to develop awareness. The two northern districts are very large with slow driving along two-lane highways, which give the visitors plenty of time to develop place awareness. In contrast, the Cowichan and Chemainus Valleys traverse is relatively quick via a four-lane highway, and its intermediate location between the two distinctive urban centres and gateways of Victoria and Nanaimo could make it easy to miss, in a perceptual sense. The same explanation of size and opportunity could be offered to explain the inaccuracy differences between Victoria and Nanaimo. Victoria is much larger with a much bigger selection of tourist attractions and activities in its own right, whereas Nanaimo is used more as a stop-over for people travelling to the Pacific Rim national park or up-island.

When the differences between reported and actual travel were broken down into a comparison between island residents and island visitors, it was expected that the island visitors would have more inaccuracies because of their unfamiliarity with Vancouver Island. This proved to be the case in all but one district (Table 14.3). The island visitors proved to be the most unaware of the Cowichan Valley and apparently were the major cause for that district's overall poor accuracy rating (Table 14.2). Likewise, island visitors were responsible to a large extent for the perceived visitation distortions in the other districts which supports the lack of familiarity hypothesis.

The one exception to this hypothetical relationship was the Greater Victoria experience, where the island residents had a 10% differential between their reported and actual visits, compared to only 7% for the island visitors. One possible explanation for this could be that some island residents were using Victoria as their exit point on a more extensive vacation trip, and since the ferry

Table 14.3. Visitation differential for islanders and island visitors

	Islanders (n = 243)			Island visitors (n = 4843)		
	Reported	Actual	Difference (%)*	Reported	Actual	Difference (%)*
Greater Victoria	79	87	10.1	4016	4281	6.6
Cowichan Valley	80	89	11.3	1184	2479	109.4
Nanaimo	113	156	17.3	2154	2852	32.4
Alberni-Clayoquot	133	N/A	—	1665	N/A	—
Comox-Strathcona	95	97	2.1	920	1027	11.6
Mt. Waddington	30	34	13.3	385	538	39.7
Gulf Islands	37	N/A	—	469	N/A	—

*% Difference = (Actual × 100)/Reported.
Source: P.E. Murphy and C.P. Keller, p. 58.

terminal is on the northern outskirts of the city some may not have noted the city as part of their vacation itinerary. However, this must remain as speculation since the data-collection process was self-completing questionnaires rather than survey interviews.

ISLAND VACATION VALUE

It has been noted that islands are synonymous with isolation, so by definition more time, effort and money is needed to reach them than many alternative destinations. In the ever-increasing competitiveness of global tourism, islands will need to justify why they are worth that extra sacrifice. They will need to demonstrate value.

One of the first lessons to be learned from the literature is "though marketing managers are interested in what influences consumers' perceptions of value, researchers rarely have investigated or measured the concept of perceived value" (Dodds *et al.*, 1991: 307). A reason for the lack of investigation lies in the complex and individual interpretation of value. At the basic level it would involve a visitor's perception of the quality of tourist facilities, the quality of service and their relationship to the prices charged. The concept of a perceptual variation of value among visitors is widely appreciated by the industry and has been described by Morrison (1989: 16) as: "Value represents a mental estimate that customers make of a hospitality or travel service's ability to satisfy their needs and wants. Some customers equate value closely with price, other do not. Price is not the only indicator of value." Bearing these measurement and interpretive difficulties in mind, Tourism Victoria has examined the question of value in its recent exit surveys, which complement the satisfaction scores referred to earlier.

Tourism Victoria has asked value questions in a variety of ways throughout the

Table 14.4. Perceived value of a Victoria vacation (%)

	Victoria Very good and good value	Comparison with US trip	Much better and better
Accommodation	54.3		
Restaurants	52.6	Quality of vacation	50.4
Local transport	50.8		
Local tours	55.2		
Attractions	64.9	Value for money	38.0
Gift and souvenir shops	36.9		
Recreation activities	59.5		
Overall trip value	65.4		

Source: Tourism Victoria, Summer 1993 Exit Survey.

questionnaires left for completion by departing visitors at local ferry and airport terminals. Long-standing questions on whether Victoria "has good value for money" or "reasonable prices" placed among the general satisfaction questions have drawn disappointing results in the past. Visitors who strongly agree with such statements generally fall below Tourism Victoria's *ad hoc* target of 50% or better. In order to probe this issue more completely the most recent exit survey, conducted in the summer months of 1993, asked a greater variety of questions.

Once again the positive response rate for the two relevant satisfaction questions was disappointing, with 36% indicating strongly agree or agree to "good value for money" and 32% to "reasonable prices". However, when they were asked in the very next question to rate the various components of their Victoria visit in terms of value for money, defined for them as the quality received for the amount paid, the results were significantly different. Table 14.4 indicates that Victoria's visitors felt far more positive about the value received when the question was posed in this manner. The highest rating was for the overall trip, which was intended to capture the scenic strait trip to the island plus the island travel that 23% of them included on this visit, with a score of 65%. The visitors were asked also to compare their Victoria visit with a United States' trip, since for many this would have been their prime international alternative. Of those who responded, 50% considered this Victoria visit had been much better or better quality than a US trip, yet only 38% considered it had offered better value for money (Table 14.4).

Overall these preliminary examinations of value for a Victoria vacation on Vancouver Island confirm how difficult it can be to measure perceptions of such personal and complex products like vacations. The response to value appears to be influenced both by the components considered and by the way the questions are posed. It is apparent that the summer 1993 visitors were generally content with the value received from all the investigated components except for gift and souvenir shops. Whether this reflects the prices or the types of merchandise offered cannot be determined at this stage. Their summated value experience for Victoria differed considerably between the two responses given. When asked about Victoria specifically the positive response was 36% and when asked about the overall trip to Victoria it was 65%. This suggests that the island and ferry trips may have augmented the Victoria vacation experience and that Victoria's new promotional emphasis on being a gateway to the island will be on target. But more research will be needed to confirm such a relationship.

SUMMARY

The link between island and urban tourism is a strong one and one which should be explored more fully in the future. Many island destinations around the world are in reality urban destinations due to the historical pattern of their settlement and the resulting infrastructure development. Even large islands like Vancouver Island still find the bulk of their tourism business takes place in the major gateway cities and towns, while a substantial portion of the outdoor recreation pursuits are also linked to neighbouring settlements.

If tourism is to accommodate the visitor and benefit the residents then more attention should be paid to island–urban linkages. This comes out very clearly in this short commentary on the Vancouver Island situation. We find urban settlements of all sizes and economic backgrounds are waking up to the opportunities of tourism. The capital city is attempting to spread its already considerable tourism business over a longer season, and small resource towns are turning to tourism to diversify their local economies or to replace lost enterprises. The importance of linking these developments together via an effective highway and promotional system can be seen in the current lost opportunities for some of the subregions of Vancouver Island. It is particularly frustrating for the Cowichan and Chemainus Valleys district to have thousands of tourists pass through its area without stopping. Finally, all islands must be conscious of the increasing competition for the tourist business and being by definition insular and on the fringe of major markets, they must strive to offer value in order to attract visitors over the water. Although research into value indicates it will be a difficult concept to measure, there seems to be some evidence that it involves more than just price. Consequently there is hope for those island towns which can offer exceptional or unusual vacation experiences, for such qualities still appear to be valued and sufficient to draw visitors that extra mile.

It is hoped that this elementary discussion of the relationships which exist between island and urban tourism will encourage further investigation and development of this synergistic partnership. This in turn may help the microcosm societies of our islands prepare themselves more thoroughly for the delights and frustrations of modern tourism.

REFERENCES

Ashworth, G.J. (1989) "Urban Tourism: An Imbalance in Attention". In C. Cooper (ed.), *Progress in Tourism, Recreation and Hospitality Management*. London, Belhaven, 33–54.

British Columbia (1981–89) *Tourism Highlights*. Victoria, BC, Ministry of Tourism.

Broadway, M.J. (1993) "Montreal's Changing Tourist Landscape". *Canadian Journal of Urban Research*, **2**, 30–48.

Dodds, W.B., Monroe, K.B. and Grewal, D. (1991) "Effects of Price, Brand, and Store Information on Buyer's Product Evaluations". *Journal of Marketing Research*, **28**, 307–319.

Foster, H.D. (1979) "Relief, Drainage and Natural Hazards". In C.N. Forward (ed.), *Vancouver Island: Land of Contrasts*. Victoria, BC, Department of Geography, University of Victoria, 51–69.

Islands Protection Society (1984) *Islands at the Edge—Preserving the Queen Charlotte Islands Wilderness*. Vancouver, Douglas and McIntyre.

Jansen-Verbeke, M. (1988) *Leisure, Recreation and Tourism in the Inner Cities*. Netherlands Geographic Studies No. 58, Nijmegen, University of Nijmegen.

Marshall, Macklin, Monaghan Ltd. (1979) *Technical Report of the Province of British Columbia Tourism Development Strategy*. Victoria, Ministry of Industry and Small Business Development.

Morrison, A.M. (1989) *Hospitality and Travel Marketing*. Albany, NY, Delmar.

Murphy, P.E. and Keller, C.P. (1990) "Destination Travel Patterns: An Examination and Modelling of Tourist Patterns on Vancouver Island, British Columbia". Leisure Sciences, **12**, 49–65.

Murphy, P.E. (1992) "Urban Tourism". In M.A. Khan, M.D. Olsen and T. Var (eds), *VNR's Encyclopedia of Hospitality and Tourism*. New York, Van Nostrand Reinhold, 790–797.

Pearce, D. (1987) *Tourism Today: A Geographical Analysis*. Harlow, Essex, Longman.

Pollock, A.M., Turner, A. and Crawford, G.S. (1975) *Visitors'74: A Study of Visitors to British Columbia in the Summer of 1974*. Vancouver, B.C., Research.

Smith, B.J.N. (1987) *The Imaginative and Experiential Significance of the Island*. Unpublished Ph.D. Dissertation, Department of Geography, University of Victoria.

Wood, W. (1993) "Partnership in action—the Cowichan and Chemainus Valleys Ecomuseum Heritage Region Project". *Proceedings of the Heritage Interpretation International Third Global Congress*. Honolulu, University of Hawaii, 447–450.

15 Rejuvenation Planning for Island Tourism: the Bermuda Example

MICHAEL V. CONLIN
Bermuda College, Bermuda

For years, Bermuda has generally been considered and, indeed, considers itself as one of the premier island tourism destinations in the world. From its beginnings in the late 1800s, Bermuda tourism grew significantly through to the late 1970s and appeared to remain strong through the 1980s. The basis of the island's tourism business was a narrowly defined segmentation strategy aimed at the high end of the vacationing market. Policies to protect Bermuda's market position as an upscale destination were adopted and adhered to rigorously (Archer and Riley, 1990). There was a feeling among the major players in the industry that this strategy resulted in Bermuda being a truly unique destination without significant competition.

However, with the onset of the recession at the turn of this decade, Bermuda's tourism industry began to falter in the early 1990s. As a result, a national debate ensued regarding the future of the industry on the island. The debate, in its simplest form, consisted of two positions. The economic cyclists believed that the erosion of arrivals and profitability which began to receive attention in 1991 was caused solely by the downturn in the economy of the United States and exacerbated by the international nature of the recession. This position held that the future success of the industry in Bermuda would be based on a continuation of the existing policies which would, it was predicted, maintain the island's dominance in the narrow, high-end market.

The other side of the debate believed that while the economic-cyclical argument went a significant way to explaining the downturn, the island's tourism industry had not responded to changes in the international tourism industry and might have a range of structural disadvantages which would hinder a full recovery. This position mirrored the changes to the tourism industry in the 1970s which Murphy had identified: "There has been evidence of a slowdown in growth rates during the 1970's, part of which may be attributed to the recession, but part of which can be linked to changing demographic profiles and consumer preferences . . . Tourists now expect and demand more because they are experienced travelers" (1985: 166).

Notwithstanding the fact that some researchers have pointed to Bermuda as a model for sustainable growth (de Albuquerque and McElroy, 1992), the situation which the island found itself in by 1992 called for immediate action. Bermuda's

Island Tourism: Management Principles and Practice
Edited by Michael V. Conlin and Tom Baum

response to that situation is the subject of this chapter. The result of the downturn in Bermuda's economic activity was a call in the spring of 1992 by the island's premier for an examination of the two major economic divisions within Bermuda's economy, namely tourism and international business, as well as a search for new areas of appropriate economic activity. The Commission on Competitiveness, comprised of five senior business leaders, was assigned the responsibility of co-ordinating the sector analyses. The Commission operated from the summer of 1992 through the summer of 1994 and reported its findings to the Premier in March 1994.

The tourism sector analysis was managed by the Tourism Planning Committee, one of the three units of the Commission, and the process which the Committee adopted in conducting its research was comprehensive and nationally inclusive in its scope. It was clearly founded on the principles of community involvement as originally espoused by Murphy (1985) which found further support (Haywood, 1988) and which now form the basis for many tourism policy analyses, development and implementation strategies.

This chapter will discuss the response of Bermuda in 1992 to the downturn in its tourism industry within the context of the destination's traditional tourism policy. The chapter will review the history of tourism in Bermuda up to the end of the 1980s and consider the policies which contributed to its success. It will then discuss the process of analysis adopted by the Tourism Planning Committee to respond to the downturn, the findings of the Committee and its recommendations for change in Bermuda's tourism policy. Many of the recommendations engender current themes in tourism planning, and it hoped that Bermuda's experience can serve as a model for any island destination which has reached a mature stage of development.

THE DEVELOPMENT OF BERMUDA TOURISM POLICY[1]

Prior to the 1890s tourists to Bermuda had been limited to a few adventurous types, the most famous of them being Mark Twain. It is to Mark Twain that is attributed the famous quotation that "Bermuda is Paradise, but you have to go through Hell to get to it" (Zuill, 1973). Twain was referring, of course, to the fact that Bermuda was then essentially a winter resort for travellers from Canada and the northeastern United States. A visit entailed a generally uncomfortable sea voyage across the Gulf Stream in winter, ironically a time when today's cruiseship operators will not sail to Bermuda. Another visitor prior to the 1880s was Walter Aitken who, somewhat ironically, came to Bermuda in 1874 to investigate the possibility of developing Bermuda as a winter resort to complement his plans for developing the White Mountains in New Hampshire as a summer resort. Aitken took over the management of the Hamilton Hotel, at the time the only hotel developed for the tourist trade to Bermuda. Originally conceived in 1851, the hotel did not open until 1863 and the American Civil War ensured that it was not profitable until it came under Aitken's management (Zuill, 1946).

For all intents and purposes, tourism really began in Bermuda in the 1880s with the opening of the Princess Hotel on the outskirts of the city of Hamilton in Pembroke Parish. The *Princess Hotel*, which even today is considered to be the grand dame of Bermuda hotels, marked the first significant investment in facilities to house and cater to the needs of visitors (*see Figure 15.1*). The hotel was opened on 1 January 1885, and from the beginning its capacity was strained. Indeed, accommodation for early tourists to Bermuda was in such short supply that an old passenger vessel, the SS *Trinidad*, was moored in Hamilton harbour in 1905 for six weeks as a temporary "floating" hotel, much to the chagrin of its "guests" (Zuill, 1946).

As tourism increased prior to World War I, the industry expanded to meet the demand. The Princess Hotel expanded from its original hundred rooms and became a centre for Bermudian society. The monopoly on steamer service to the island, held by the Quebec Steamship Line, was successfully challenged and, by the outbreak of hostilities, Bermuda was additionally served by the Royal Mail Packet Company and the Bermuda Atlantic Steamship Company, both offering regular service out of New York. In 1910, the Bermuda Atlantic Steamship Company offered round trips to Bermuda for as little as $10.00 (Zuill, 1946). This may have been the first time that an attempt was made to cater to a less affluent segment of the tourism market, and it failed. Bermuda simply did not have the type of accommodation or amenities for other than well-off visitors.

Figure 15.1. The Southampton Princess Hotel, sister property to the Hamilton Princess Hotel. This 700-room hotel, opened in 1972, was the last major facility built in Bermuda

BETWEEN THE WARS

Following World War I, tourism grew dramatically. In 1920, 13 327 people visited the island. By 1930, visitors coming to stay in Bermuda's hotels had more than tripled to 46 463. In 1930, an additional 7668 visitors came as part of a sea-voyage holiday, some of the earliest cruiseship tourists. By 1937, regular visitors totalled 58 646 and a further 24 169 visitors came on cruises (Zuill, 1973).

One of the principal forces driving tourism in Bermuda was the English shipping company, Furness, Withy & Co. In 1920, the company opened the Bermudiana Hotel in Hamilton and several years later, the Castle Harbour Hotel and Mid-Ocean Club, both in the prestigious Tucker's town area of St. George's Parish. These hotels formed part of the company's integrated tourism plan in which it owned and operated both the means of transportation to Bermuda and the accommodation and amenities for visitors when they arrived. Supporting this expansion was the financial boom of the 1920s. Catering as it did to "well to do Americans", it was during this period that Bermuda cemented its reputation as an up-scale destination (Zuill, 1973).

The rise in tourism was matched by a corresponding decline in the importance of the island's agricultural economy. Long famous for its onions, exports fell from 153 000 crates in 1914 to just 21 570 crates in 1925. In 1919, the island exported 91 777 barrels of potatoes but by 1925, the total had dropped to just 23 448 barrels. Clearly, the economy of the island was changing, and the major change was tourism.

Before the onset of World War II, one other event of great significance for Bermuda's tourism industry took place. In 1938, Pan American Airways teamed up with Imperial Airways (a predecessor of BOAC) to offer flying-boat air service to the island. Coupled with the creation of Kindley Airfield during the war by the United States Air Force, and the subsequent opening of the facility for commercial traffic after 1945, this event effectively marked Bermuda's entry into the age of air travel. It was to have a dramatic effect on the island and, in particular, the tourism industry.

TOURISM DEVELOPMENT SINCE 1945

Following World War II, Bermuda began seriously to develop its tourism industry as a matter of national policy. Tourism promotion was then the responsibility of the Bermuda Trade Development Board, an executive body of the government. In 1945, it expanded its New York office, which had been opened in the late 1920s, and opened an office in Toronto in 1947 to respond to the potential market in Canada. An office was officially opened in London in 1945, and other offices in Chicago, Boston and Atlanta were opened, the last in 1981.

In 1968, the Bermuda Trade Development Board ceased to exist and the Department of Tourism was created. During the mid-1980s, the marketing of Bermuda overseas was reorganized with the New York office taking responsibility for all North American marketing activities through the other offices. Marketing activities in other markets such as Continental Europe and Britain are now done through agreements with marketing agencies (*Bermuda Report*, 1988).

A number of trends have characterized Bermuda's tourism industry since 1945. It has grown dramatically to the point where it is now the country's major industry in terms of employment and continues to equal the island's international business sector in terms of Gross National Product. It has completely reversed its traditional role as a winter resort and now has its highest visitor arrivals during the summer season. Air travel has long since become the predominant means of travelling to the island. Most significantly, the market segment which Bermuda caters to has not changed since the industry's beginnings over one hundred years ago and since 1945 has become the basis for the country's tourism policy.

GROWTH OF THE INDUSTRY

In the period from 1949 to 1979, tourist arrivals in Bermuda grew tenfold from 54 899 to 599 145. During this period, three trends were evident: the percentage of air arrivals increased, the percentage of cruiseship arrivals increased dramatically and traditional arrivals by ship virtually disappeared. In 1949, air arrivals accounted for 51% of total arrivals, whereas conventional ship arrivals were 42% of the total. In 1956, air accounted for 69%, conventional ship arrivals accounted for 18%, with cruise visitors accounting for 13% of the 109 131 visitors that year.

Following 1956, the trend toward air and cruise arrivals continued accompanied by a continuing decrease in conventional ship arrivals. By 1979, air accounted for 76%, cruise 24%, with only 686 hotel-based visitors arriving by ship out of the total of 599 145 visitors. Table 15.1 illustrates these trends.

During the 1980s, tourism continued to dominate the island's economy. This period saw several swings, but arrivals continued to be strong. In 1980, arrivals reached a new high of 609 556, but this was followed by five years in which arrivals decreased, with 1984 representing the lowest level in this period at 528 871. This was a period of recession in North America and was also marked by labour unrest in Bermuda which directly affected the tourism industry. In 1987, another record was reached with 631 314 arrivals, but since then total annual arrivals have suffered from the effects of a declining economy in North America, the Gulf War and other factors which relate to the changing international tourism market. Table 15.2 lists all arrival data for this period.

BERMUDA TOURISM POLICY

During the 1960s and 1970s, Bermuda examined the type of tourist market it wished to continue attracting and concluded that it would be in the country's best interest to preserve its image as an upscale resort destination (Riley, 1991). As a result of

Table 15.1. Historical picture of Bermuda arrivals, 1949–1979

Year	Air	Ship	Cruise	Total
1949	28 258	23 231	3 410	54 899
1950	37 609	26 558	3 649	67 816
1951	57 185	23 745	11 136	92 066
1952	57 394	25 089	10 583	93 066
1953	65 591	24 096	13 814	103 501
1954	68 408	23 360	15 036	106 804
1955	74 802	21 128	14 721	110 651
1956	75 211	19 809	14 111	109 131
1957	86 313	16 256	18 415	120 984
1958	92 479	15 960	22 382	130 821
1959	96 682	12 833	32 815	142 330
1960	99 295	11 992	40 119	151 406
1961	113 280	10 371	46 971	170 622
1962	124 098	9 173	59 531	192 802
1963	132 689	8 954	62 538	204 181
1964	137 985	7 122	43 885	188 992
1965	180 752	6 513	50 517	237 782
1966	205 534	5 064	46 174	256 772
1967	235 392	1 771	44 004	281 167
1968	265 378	2 064	63 937	331 379
1969	279 262	1 725	89 933	370 920
1970	301 604	1 172	86 138	388 914
1971	318 371	939	93 637	412 947
1972	338 574	1 208	81 168	420 950
1973	384 474	767	82 015	467 256
1974	420 089	1 132	110 347	531 568
1975	411 783	739	99 602	512 124
1976	449 359	678	108 837	558 874
1977	439 454	1 571	131 830	572 855
1978	419 028	756	131 682	551 466
1979	458 095	686	140 364	599 145

Source: *A Statistical Review of the Years 1980–1989*, The Bermuda Department of Tourism, 1991, Table 20.

numerous studies, a number of policies which would preserve this image were adopted and continue to be the foundation of the country's tourism policy.

MORATORIUM ON DEVELOPMENT

The most important policy was one which directly limited growth in carrying capacity by imposing a moratorium on the construction of new hotels and the maintenance of a 10 000-bed ceiling. This policy still forms the basis of development for Bermuda's tourism industry and is enforced through a phasing

Table 15.2. Total arrivals by month

	1980	1981	1982	1983	1984	1985	1986	1987	1988	1989
Jan.	11 948	11 885	8 345	10 597	9 536	9 021	8 237	9 994	11 297	9 184
Feb.	25 026	20 886	15 112	19 279	15 362	14 696	16 034	18 156	15 351	15 862
Mar.	47 524	41 556	31 921	38 358	33 955	34 046	34 539	38 447	34 659	31 454
Apr.	52 511	58 676	57 705	50 112	51 021	48 048	44 276	50 175	42 416	41 970
May	74 171	52 217	78 045	73 798	68 064	68 735	69 037	81 808	76 424	68 649
Jun.	67 224	63 430	66 173	69 931	61 370	72 248	75 472	82 348	75 672	71 079
Jul.	61 757	58 983	66 258	67 470	62 484	70 722	81 721	83 064	78 961	70 120
Aug.	70 530	64 387	64 920	75 250	66 966	76 419	82 991	83 666	82 610	74 407
Sep.	68 402	55 754	54 148	58 645	60 048	61 492	65 342	71 096	64 186	57 333
Oct.	67 097	56 262	55 627	54 316	53 976	50 881	61 315	61 505	56 053	58 271
Nov.	43 744	35 987	31 525	34 887	30 322	27 873	34 299	33 452	30 268	30 972
Dec.	19 622	15 243	14 687	15 067	15 767	15 409	18 650	17 603	17 321	20 294
Total	609 556	535 246	544 466	567 710	528 871	549 590	591 913	631 314	585 218	549 595

Source: *A Statistical Review of the Years 1980–1989*, The Bermuda Department of Tourism, 1991, Table 1.

scheme which maintains the 10 000-bed ceiling and allocates available space within the ceiling to the stronger properties which maintain high standards.

The policy has been overruled on two occasions. In the late 1970s, the government gave permission for Bermuda College to construct a 64-room resort hotel on the island's south shore. Named the Stonington Beach Hotel, the property is adjacent to the College's Hotel School and serves as the training facility for students in hospitality programmes. The government also agreed in 1989 to allow the Ritz-Carlton group to construct a 400-room resort property, also on the south shore. However, the deteriorating financial condition of the industry world-wide and the continuing objections of local residents have caused the project to be postponed indefinitely. Notwithstanding the above exceptions, the moratorium continues to be in effect, and its emphasis continues to be the strengthening of existing properties and the improvement of their occupancies.

GRADING POLICY

The emphasis on controlled, upscale development was further strengthened by the Department of Tourism's grading plan introduced in 1988 designed specifically to link the renewal of hotel licences with the maintenance of high-quality standards. Under this plan, properties are required to meet high standards of cleanliness, attractiveness and offer defined levels of amenities in order to ensure the renewal of their operating licence. Clearly, conventional mass tourism plays no part in Bermuda's tourism policy as to property development.

TIMESHARE POLICY

The conservative approach which the policies on development and standards attest to are mirrored by the country's policy with respect to timesharing properties. During the 1980s, two hotel properties received permission to convert to timesharing, and permission was granted in 1981 to York-Hannover, the Canadian developer, to construct a timesharing resort in the town of St. George. Since then, a moratorium has been placed on any further timesharing development until the government can assess its role as a tourism product. This policy is contrary to that of many other island resort destinations which have embraced the timesharing concept, not always with positive results. In this sense, the policy is an indicator of the control which Bermuda exercises over innovative development in addition to traditional development.

CRUISESHIP POLICY

As indicated earlier, cruiseship arrivals have played a major part in Bermuda's tourism since its inception. This segment reached its high point in 1988 when arrivals totalled 158 368. However, concern about overcrowding on the part of hoteliers, and related impact to the island's image resulted in Bermuda adopting a restrictive policy in 1988. This policy limited cruiseship arrivals to 120 000 during the high season of May to October, and allowed only four scheduled cruiseships weekly between Monday and Friday. The policy also allowed for up to 12 additional occasional callers. Figure 15.2 shows the impact of cruiseships on Front Street, the main thoroughfare of the capital city of Hamilton.

The rationale for such a restrictive policy was to reduce the pressure on Bermuda's tourism infrastructure and to maintain the image of the island as an upscale destination (Riley, 1991). To further bolster these objectives, visits were only awarded to high-standard cruise operators such as the Royal Viking Line, Chandris Celebrity Cruises and Royal Caribbean. Figure 15.3 shows the Royal Caribbean Line's *Song of America* and the Norwegian Cruise Line's *Dreamward* alongside Front Street in the capital of Hamilton.

In 1989, the year the restrictive policy began to take effect, cruiseship arrivals fell to 131 322 and in 1990 actually fell below the 120 000 ceiling with a total of 113 000. As a result of this decrease and the deterioration in the tourism industry generally, the government raised the ceiling in the early 1990s to 150 000. This relaxing of the policy was designed to offset the drop in air arrivals which had been occurring since the 1987 high. This policy and its recent amendments again underscore the extent to

Figure 15.2. During the summer weeks, two cruiseships can be accommodated alongside Front Street, the main thoroughfare of the capital city of Hamilton. It results in significant crowding which hoteliers feel detracts from the peaceful ambience of the island

Figure 15.3. Bermuda has long been a favourite destination for cruisers. This picture shows the Royal Caribbean's *Song of America* and Norwegian Cruise Lines *Dreamward* tied up alongside Front Street, the main thoroughfare of the capital of Bermuda, the city of Hamilton

which the maintenance of a narrow market approach form the basis of Bermuda tourism. Policies are flexible, striving always for a balance between arrivals and profitability. The focus is always on extracting the maximum return from the least number of visitors.

BERMUDA'S TYPICAL TOURIST

Bermuda's tourism policy achieved what it set out to do in terms of the type of tourism which it sought to attract. Its emphasis on controlled development, a flexible approach aimed at maximizing profitability as opposed to sheer numbers of arrivals, and a market concern for the maintenance of the product and the country's infrastructure has resulted in a very narrowly defined market.

By origin

By far, the majority of visitors to Bermuda come from the United States, both by air and by cruiseship. As Table 15.3 illustrates, the mix of visitors by country of origin has not changed significantly since 1980. In 1980, US arrivals accounted for 86.4% of air and 93.6% of cruiseship visitors. In 1989, the corresponding numbers

Table 15.3. Total arrivals by country of origin

	1980	1981	1982	1983	1984	1985	1986	1987	1988	1989
USA	535 499	475 247	480 593	500 156	463 315	489 940	525 159	561 960	514 098	473 919
Canada	36 240	29 920	31 998	37 811	39 533	35 277	34 495	34 149	34 058	35 480
UK	21 820	18 201	19 314	16 598	15 002	13 907	15 952	17 308	20 103	24 118
Europe	8 558	5 963	6 413	7 444	6 016	4 910	4 128	5 422	7 844	6 169
Other	7 979	5 915	6 148	5 701	5 005	5 556	12 179	12 475	9 115	9 909
Year										
Regular	491 640	429 801	420 288	446 864	417 461	406 687	459 711	477 877	426 850	418 273
Cruise	117 916	105 445	124 178	120 846	111 410	142 903	132 202	153 437	158 368	131 322
Total	609 556	535 246	544 466	567 710	528 871	549 590	591 913	631 314	535 218	549 595

Source: *A Statistical Review of the Years 1980–1989*, The Bermuda Department of Tourism, 1991, Table 2.

represented 84.0% and 93.2% respectively. In total, US arrivals accounted for 87.9% of visitors in 1980 and in 1989 they accounted for 86.2% of the total.

This situation is even more exclusive when US visitors are considered in terms of where in the United States they come from. In 1980, 81.0% came from the mid-Atlantic and north-east regions. By 1989, visitors from these two regions still accounted for 74.5% of the US total. The south-east region increased during this period from 6.1% to 10.9% of the total. Table 15.4 illustrates these trends.

By age

Table 15.5 indicates that visitors to Bermuda are getting older. Much of the change is due to the decline in younger visitors during the annual Spring Break. During the early 1980s, Bermuda could expect over 10 000 students to visit, but in recent years students coming in the spring amount to fewer than 4000 annually. While these numbers are not significant in absolute terms, there may be long-term consequences of not establishing an early linkage with the affluent, young college market.

By season

The shift to Bermuda as a summer destination is also borne out by Table 15.2. The majority of visitors come in the period of May through August, and in spite of continuing attempts to promote the shoulder and off seasons, little success had been achieved through to the early 1990s.

By education

The Bermuda visitor is increasingly more educated. In 1980, 50% of air arrivals had graduated from college and by 1989 this had risen to 70%. Also, by 1989, 34% of visitors had completed some post-graduate education (*Statistical Review*, 1991, Table 21).

By income and occupation

Consistent with its upscale image and corresponding levels of accommodation and amenities, Bermuda visitors enjoy substantial incomes. In 1989, 72% of visitors reported family income in excess of $40 000 annually, with one-third of visitors (32%) reporting annual family incomes in excess of $75 000. In the same year, 74% of visitors considered themselves to have white-collar occupations while only 9% considered their occupations to be blue collar. Of these, most described themselves as working in service or craft areas (*Statistical Review*, 1991, Table 23).

THE SITUATION IN THE EARLY 1990s

By the end of the 1980s, an attitude pervaded Bermuda's tourism industry that it was unique, not really subject to competition or to the changes in the international

Table 15.4. Air arrivals by region (%)

US	1980	1981	1982	1983	1984	1985	1986	1987	1988	1989
Mid-Atlantic	53.8	52.6	53.1	53.5	52.5	52.3	49.6	50.0	51.8	50.7
North-East	27.2	27.4	25.9	24.3	25.6	25.8	25.3	24.9	23.9	23.8
South-East	6.1	7.7	8.1	8.6	8.5	9.1	10.4	10.2	10.1	10.9
Mid-West	6.8	6.7	7.0	7.2	7.4	7.2	8.4	7.8	8.2	8.4
West	6.1	5.6	5.9	6.4	6.0	5.6	6.3	7.1	6.9	6.2
Total	100.0	100.0	100.0	100.0	100.0	100.0	100.0	100.0	100.0	100.0

Source: *A Statistical Review of the Years 1980–1989*, The Bermuda Department of Tourism, 1991, Table 7.

Table 15.5. Air arrivals by age group (%)

	1980	1981	1982	1983	1984	1985	1986	1987	1988	1989
Under 19	10.9	12.2	13.0	12.8	8.5	8.5	7.6	8.6	8.3	7.3
20–29	21.6	22.2	22.9	20.8	18.5	18.4	15.7	16.0	15.8	14.2
30–39	19.8	19.9	20.5	21.5	22.0	22.6	22.7	22.9	22.9	22.8
40–49	17.5	17.4	17.1	17.1	19.6	19.7	22.1	22.2	22.9	23.4
50–59	17.5	16.5	15.5	15.2	16.2	15.5	15.5	15.3	15.2	15.8
Over 59	12.7	11.8	10.9	11.9	15.3	15.2	16.4	15.1	14.9	16.5
	100.0	100.0	100.0	100.0	100.0	100.0	100.0	100.0	100.0	100.0

Source: *A Statistical Review of the Years 1980–1989*, The Bermuda Department of Tourism, 1991, Table 10.

Table 15.6. Bermuda tourism arrivals and expenditures, 1990–1993

Year	Arrivals ('000s)			Expenditures ($ millions)		
	Air	Cruise	Total	Air	Cruise	Total
1990	434.9	112.6	547.5	467.9	22.2	490.1
1991	386.7	128.2	514.8	423.9	31.7	455.6
1992	375.2	131.0	506.2	410.5	32.5	443.0
1993	412.4	153.9	566.3	NA	NA	NA

Sources: *Commission on Competitiveness Final Report*, 1994, p. 48 and *Bermuda in Perspective*, 27 January 1994.

tourism market. This attitude led to complacency, an antipathy to innovation and a decreasing of service quality. This was accompanied by a significant downturn in business which Table 15.6 illustrates. In 1991, the total number of visitors to the island dropped by 32 700 from the 1990 total of 547 500. While this represented only a 5.9% decrease, the most significant drop was in the number of hotel-based visitors. Whereas in 1990, 434 900 visitors stayed in hotels, by 1991 the number dropped to 386 700, a decrease of 11.0%. Given that hotel-based visitors in 1991 represented an average daily expenditure of $225 compared with cruise visitors whose average daily expenditure was $70, the impact of the downturn in hotel-based visitors was catastrophic (*Commission on Competitiveness*, 1994: 54).

In 1992, the situation stabilized to some extent, but a small decrease of 11 500 in hotel-based visitors, representing a 2.9% decline, was still experienced. Although the relaxed cruiseship policy saw a small increase in 1992 of 2800 visitors, the overall total in 1992 was still less than 1991, amounting to 506 200, the lowest annual visitor arrival since 1973. Perhaps most significantly, the total tourism expenditures decreased from US$490.1 million in 1990 to US$443.0 million in 1992.

The creation of the Commission on Competitiveness and the Tourism Planning Committee can be understood in the light of these data. For the first time in recent memory, Bermuda actually experienced a small level of unemployment in the hospitality sector and allied economic areas such as retailing. This resulted in a decrease in the granting of work permits, and the expatriate population of the island dropped by approximately one-half during this period. While this alleviated some of the employment concerns for Bermudians, it created other social consequences including a diminishing of rental revenues, a significant source of income for a substantial number of Bermudians.

THE COMMISSION ON COMPETITIVENESS

The mandate of the Commission on Competitiveness reflected these fundamental concerns about national competitiveness and social consequences in a rapidly changing international economy:

> The Commission's mandate originated from concern over the economic performance of Bermuda during the 1980s and early 1990s amid signs that Bermuda's competitiveness was trailing other countries and jeopardizing . . . standard of living. The mandate also recognized the tremendous changes which were taking place outside of Bermuda and the impact these changes were having on Bermuda's traditional sources of foreign exchange revenues (*Commission on Competitiveness*, 1994: 4).

As stated earlier, the Commission was charged with examining the tourism and international business sectors as well as exploring new areas for economic activity on the island. Figure 15.4 shows the organizational chart of the Commission and its components. Examination of the tourism sector was co-ordinated through the four-person Tourism Planning Committee. The Committee chairman was not a tourism industry person but rather a senior banker who enjoyed an island-wide reputation for sound planning ability. The other members of the Committee reflected various constituencies within the industry, the public sector and tourism

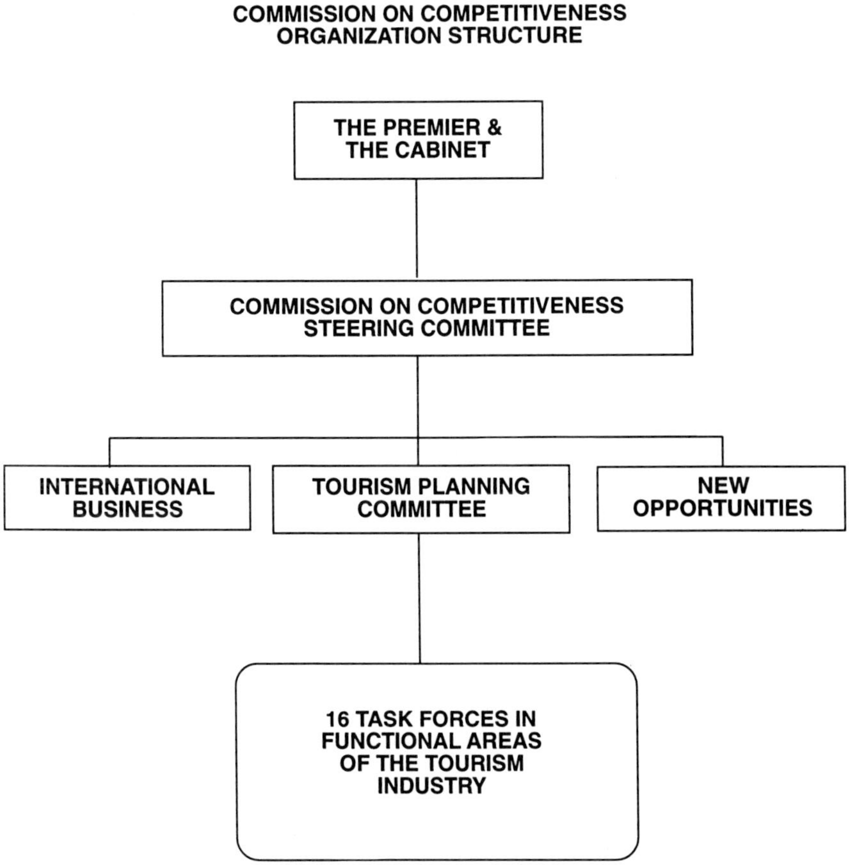

Figure 15.4. Rejuvenation planning for island tourism; the Bermuda example

education. In this way, it was felt that the Committee represented a wide range of stakeholders in Bermuda's tourism industry and its economy generally. The Committee's composition, as such, reflected the integrated approach to economic planning which the Commission itself had adopted.

The Committee decided at the onset of its investigation to employ an open, inclusive process for gathering information, formulating alternatives and establishing recommendations. This was considered essential since the Committee believed firmly that the population of the island was a fundamental component of Bermuda's tourism product. It was felt, therefore, that any successful investigation resulting in a strategic plan would need to have the support of the population, or at the very least, the broad range of stakeholders in the tourism industry. As Haywood observes:

> . . . in the way tourism is planned . . . the underlying theme is a call to include a greater degree of public participation. The rationale is as follows—the positive and negative aspects of tourism (economic, social and ecological) have their most profound impact in and on host communities. Whenever tourism activity is concentrated in time and space, builds rapidly, dominates a local economy, disrupts community life, endangers the environment, and ignores community input, the seeds of discontent are sown. Whenever the residents' thresholds of tolerance for tourism and tourists are exceeded, host–tourist encounters sour, and the industry has a tendency to peak, fade and self-destruct (1988: 105).

Accordingly, the Committee formed 16 Task Forces, chaired by prominent local stakeholders, in a range of functional areas associated with the industry. The range of Task Forces is indicative of the sophistication of the industry in Bermuda and is listed in Table 15.7. Membership of each Task Force ranged between four and 12 persons and the number of individuals who, at one time or another in the process, were involved with the active investigations of the Committee numbered in excess of 120 persons. In this sense, the work of the Committee was indeed a community activity. The planning process employed by the Committee utilized a 7-stage model: (a) project initiation; (b) participation and data input process; (c) strategy co-ordination; (d) strategy consultation; (e) the strategic plan; (f) implementation, and (g) review of benefits. The planning process is seen in more detail in Figure 15.5.

Table 15.7. The Task Forces of the Tourism Planning Committee, Bermuda Commission on Competitiveness

Air service	Cultural tourism
Cruiseships	The environment
Entertainment	Business travellers
Physical plant	Tourism research
Restaurants	Marketing
Service quality	Shopping
Sports	Tourism awareness
Tour boat operations	Transportation

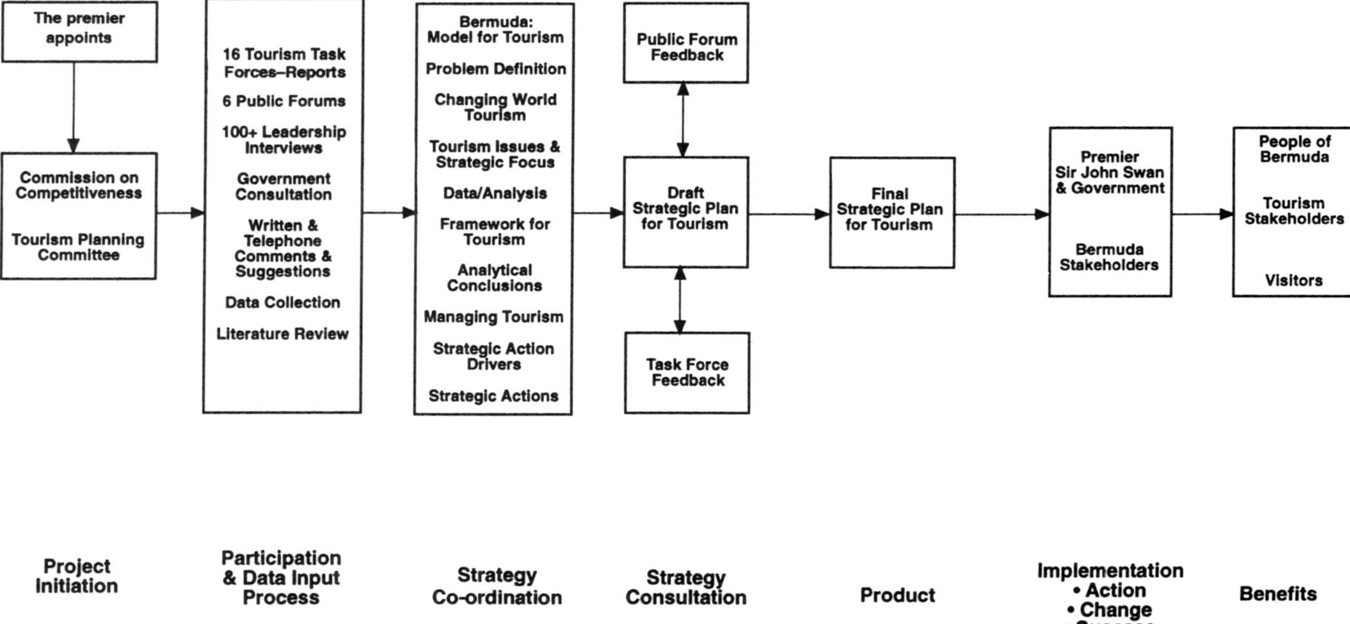

Figure 15.5. Rejuvenation planning for island tourism: the Bermuda example Source: LDR International

In addition to the formation of the 16 Task Forces, community and stakeholder input was solicited through the planning process at the participation and data input phase. Senior stakeholders in the island's tourism and related industries were consulted using a focus group format. In this way, anyone who had a role to play in the development of Bermuda's tourism policy or its industry had an opportunity to contribute to the Committee's deliberations. Likewise, the Committee was able to benefit from the counsel of respected individuals with a depth of experience in the planning of tourism stretching back to the 1960s. In addition to the focus groups, the Committee's external consultants, LDR International of Columbia, Maryland, conducted over one hundred interviews with senior leaders in the tourism industry, both in Bermuda and in its source markets. True community participation was sought through six public forums organized in various areas of the island. Advertised well in advance, these forums attracted significant numbers of the general public with an interest in or concern for Bermuda's tourism industry. The input from these meetings was recorded and incorporated by the Committee in its deliberations. Coupled with the input from the Task Forces, the Senior Stakeholder Focus Groups, and the leader interviews, the Committee was able to draw upon a broad range of historical and current community input in reaching its conclusions.

CONCLUSIONS

As a result of its examination, the Tourism Planning Committee reached the following conclusions:

1. Bermuda has been a model for developing tourism as a basis for a prosperous economy. Its success in the past should provide confidence that Bermuda tourism can improve in the future.
2. The economy and quality of life in Bermuda are dependent upon tourism. The current declines in tourism are serious and will not correct themselves without concerted effort. Nothing can adequately replace tourism in the island's economy, not even a greatly expanded international business sector.
3. Changes in world tourism, including new products, choices and competition, will dictate many of the circumstances to which Bermuda will have to adapt.
4. Bermuda is dependent upon the United States for its tourism market. It is losing its share of this market, and not primarily because of the US economy or international conflicts. The US market cannot be satisfactorily replaced with some other source market such as Europe or the Far East.
5. Bermuda's essential tourism product, the large hotels, are losing business and this is the primary reason for the decline in tourism revenues. These declines have resulted in losses in jobs, income, and domestic business throughout Bermuda. The large hotels have not been profitable as a group since 1987 and have seen their occupancies drop on average from 68.0% in 1987 to 55.9% in 1992 (*Commission on Competitiveness*, 1994: 62).

6. The cruiseship visitor cannot replace the staying visitor for economic impact on the island. The data presented above attest to this.
7. Seasonality is a problem in Bermuda, but its pattern has not changed significantly in recent years. It appears worse because all tourism has declined including the shoulder and off-season.
8. There are concerns for the lack of tourism awareness and appreciation for tourism in Bermuda. Some Bermudians do not respect the need to accommodate tourists on the island.
9. Management/labour problems on Bermuda, of serious concern in the tourism industry, exacerbate issues of hotel profitability, labour recruitment, costs and respect for the tourism industry.
10. Bermuda has major deficiencies in providing shopping, dining, entertainment and recreational experiences to the tourist. These include inadequate product, information and access. Bermuda has not capitalized on its many assets like natural resources, marine environment, culture and heritage.
11. Bermuda is overpriced in many respects and does not meet price/value expectations of visitors.
12. Bermuda's problems are not the result of inadequate marketing or promotion but rather, inadequate product policies and price/value issues.
13. Bermuda's source market is small, exclusive and affluent. It is a market sought after by much of Bermuda's competition, including destinations in the US. It is no longer valid to assume that Bermuda does not have any serious competition for this market niche.
14. Bermuda must accept the need for fundamental change. It cannot dictate the terms of world tourism. This will require significant investment of resources and effort. There are no simple, single or quick fixes for improving the tourism industry in Bermuda (*Commission on Competitiveness*, 1994: 81–82).

Having reached these conclusions, the Tourism Planning Committee made the following major recommendations:

1. The management of the tourism industry needed to be changed in a way which would result in more emphasis on product policy and development through a comprehensive planning process which would incorporate the input of various sectors of the industry. This recommendation included a consideration of the role which the Department of Tourism currently plays in the management of the tourism industry and suggestions for an expanded role to include some level of responsibility for strategic planning and product policy determination and implementation through a Policy Coordination Council appointed by the premier, Tourism Action Councils representing various sectors of the industry and a Tourism Education Council to co-ordinate education, training and tourism awareness activities. The Committee also presented various options for restructuring the Department including the QUANGO (Quasi-Autonomous Non-Governmental Organization) concept which would provide it with greater responsibility and more autonomy.

2. The tourism product requires enhancement in terms of accommodation and eating facilities, events, transportation, amenities, retailing, development of public places and recreational activities. The Committee recommended the creation of the Bermuda Development Fund to attract domestic investment in the tourism industry and to provide capital for small business operators to enhance their services. The Committee also recommended that much of the enhancement co-ordination should utilize the services of national bodies such as the Bermuda Chamber of Commerce, whose membership has a direct stake in the improvement of the tourism industry.
3. Recognizing that management/labour relations have bedevilled the industry for two decades, the Committee recommended that a Task Force on Employment be created to try and depolarize the two sides to this ongoing conflict through the greater dissemination of information, education and development of innovative human resource strategies including worker empowerment, involvement and recognition schemes.
4. Given the importance of the large hotels to the continued viability of the industry, the Committee recommended that the profitability of the hotels be improved through efforts to expand the season including the use of innovative packaging based on emerging trends in the travel market such as cultural and ecotourism niches. It also recommended that the cost structures for hotels be reviewed within the context of Bermuda's highly oligopolistic economy and that relief be sought to allow the hotels to become more competitive.
5. Price/value considerations are critical for repeat visitation and the Committee recommended that value-added strategies including the offering of a greater range of no-cost or sponsored activities should be incorporated into the island's tourism product. It further emphasized the need for a review of the island's cost structures as mentioned above in order to bring costs in line with competing destinations, at least to the extent that this is possible.
6. In its adoption of an inclusive planning process, the Committee recognized the fundamental role which the population of the island plays in the determination of the quality of the product and the level of service provided for tourists. Accordingly, the Committee made a major recommendation relating to the issue of tourism appreciation including the creation of the Tourism Education Council and programmes of education, human resource development within the industry and the creation of national programmes of certification and recognition, all of which were considered to be part of enhancing the view which the population has of the industry and its value as a career choice.
7. Although the Committee, along with the travel industry, recognized the superior reputation of the island for marketing, nonetheless the Committee recommended that greater use be made of database marketing techniques and co-operative advertising. The Committee also recommended that on-going research be conducted into the emerging niches in order to provide a basis for determining whether there are market opportunities which would fit with Bermuda's resources.

These recommendations were presented in detail with timelines and identified the organizations in the community which the Committee felt should have the responsibility for ensuring their implementation.

POSTSCRIPT

Given the underlying debate mentioned earlier between the economic cyclists and the structuralists, it is not surprising that implementation of the Committee's recommendations has been slow. Notwithstanding the broad community input which the Committee's recommendations reflect, their implementation in such a small community has implicit political consequences. Given that the government must consider the recommendations along with a plethora of other recommendations relating to international business and new ventures, all within the political arena, it is inevitable that trade-offs will need to take place and compromises sought. This will take time.

In the meantime, the industry has enjoyed somewhat of a resurgence. Total arrivals in December 1993 amounted to 18 368, an increase of 17.2% over the 1992 level of 15 674. Similarly, in January 1994, arrivals amounted to 9268, an 11.2% increase over the 1993 level of 8331. For February, the comparable figures are 16 360 in 1994 compared with 14 841 in 1993 or an increase of 10.2%. While these latest arrival levels are not quite back to those of the halcyon days of 1987, they are respectable and have given support to the economic cyclist position. Nonetheless, arrival data does not always translate into profits, and there is a suspicion within the industry that a number of properties have been discounting significantly in order to achieve occupancy. Data in support of this contention, however, is not available and it remains to be seen if the resurgence will restore the profitability of the large hotels. What is clear is that the length of advance booking is becoming much shorter than in the past, indicating that the visitor's purchasing decision is more impulsive. It is also the case that the average length of stay is continuing to erode. In 1993, the average length of stay in registered commercial properties was 5.2 days which compared with 5.6 days for 1992. The member properties of the Bermuda Hotel Association reported a similar drop from 4.7 days in 1992 to 4.5 days in 1993 (*Bermuda In Perspective*, 1994: 5).

This chapter has presented a model of inclusive, community-based planning for tourism in a small-island destination. The findings of the Tourism Planning Committee are probably indicative of those which any analysis of a mature destination would uncover. The recommendations for improving the tourism product are reasonable yet innovative. They do not seek to reposition the destination but rather to build upon its existing strengths within a context of a changing tourism market. The recommendation calling for more industry participation in policy setting is consistent with a trend occurring in many jurisdictions. In that sense, the model is very contemporary and responds to the problems which mature destinations face in a manner which is not likely to lead to further erosion of the product for short-term gain. Rather, the aim is to rejuvenate the industry in a manner consistent with the community's wishes and the market's demands. The key will be the extent to which there is a will on the part of stakeholders and policy setters to make the necessary changes recommended by the Commission on Competitiveness.

NOTE

1 Pages 182–192 relating to Bermuda's tourism development are drawn substantially from Conlin (1993).

REFERENCES

Archer, B.H. and Riley, C.W. (1990) "Bermuda: The Role of Tourism Research". In C.P. Cooper (ed.), *Progress in Tourism, Recreation and Hospitality Management. Volume Two*. London, Belhaven, 96–103.

Bermuda in Perspective: An Analysis of Monthly Visitor Statistics (1994) The Bermuda Department of Tourism, 27 January.

Bermuda Report (1988) Department of Information Services, Government of Bermuda, Second Edition.

Commission on Competitiveness. Final Report (1994) Available at the Centre for Tourism Research and Innovation, Bermuda College, P.O. Box DV356, Devonshire DV BX, Bermuda.

Conlin, Michael V. (1993) "Bermuda Tourism: A Case Study in Single Segmentation". *Journal of Travel & Tourism Marketing*, **1**(4), 99–112.

de Albuquerque, K. and McElroy, J.L. (1992) "Caribbean Small-Island Tourism Styles and Sustainable Strategies". *Environmental Management*, **16**(5), 619–632.

Haywood, K. Michael (1988) "Responsible and Responsive Tourism Planning in the Community". *Tourism Management*, June, 105–118.

Murphy, Peter E. (1985) *Tourism: A Community Approach*. London, Routledge.

Riley, Cordell W. (1991) "Controlling Growth While Maintaining Your Customer Base". *Proceedings of the 22nd. Travel and Tourism Research Association Conference*, Long Beach, California, 65–73.

A Statistical Review of the Years 1980–1989 (1991) The Bermuda Department of Tourism.

Zuill, William (1946) *Bermuda Journey*. Glasgow, The University Press.

Zuill, W.S. (1973) *The Story of Bermuda and Her People*. London, Macmillan Education Limited.

16 Island Specialty Retailing: the Clocktower Centre at Bermuda's Royal Naval Dockyard

BERT WINTERBOTTOM
LDR International Inc., USA

INTRODUCTION

Specialty retailing has traditionally been an important part of the island resort tourism experience. As tourism has grown, many island town centres have become specialty shopping places. Good examples include Old San Juan, Puerto Rico; Charlotte Amalie, St. Thomas, USVI; Marigot, St. Martin; and Front Street in Hamilton, Bermuda. At the same time, many large resort hotels have established small specialty "malls" featuring branch or "twig" stores from the town centre. Only in the past decade or so has there been an interest in developing new free-standing specialty retail centres. In part, this results from the generally small domestic market and the seasonality of the visitor market.

Specialty retail in town centres is an important part of the "island experience", but only if the town centre is a great place—safe, clean, authentic and with a good mix of attractions, public spaces, pubs, restaurants and retail shops. The importance of tourism and town centres can be summarized as follows:

- The environment is what attracts the visitors
- Successful downtowns are successful destinations
  - People oriented, busy
  - Quality, attractive places
  - Safe and inviting spaces
  - Concentrated, accessible
  - Critical mass of activities
  - Special shopping places
- Visitor Domain
  - Information and interpretation
  - Ease of access, transit
  - Hotels, overnight facilities

Island Tourism: Management Principles and Practice
Edited by Michael V. Conlin and Tom Baum

Uniqueness and image, authentic
Value and opportunity
Rich experience, day and night

Recently, as a part of broader tourism development efforts, island town-centre retailing is being given more attention. New small specialty centres are being developed and some international airports are now providing distinctive specialty retailing as part of the "duty free" experience. The Clocktower Centre at Bermuda's Royal Naval Dockyard provides an excellent example of how a small independent specialty retail opportunity, properly developed and managed, has become financially successful and has contributed to a major new interest in the Island's West End by visitors and Bermudians alike.

The Clocktower Centre at Dockyard is being developed and managed by one of Bermuda's most successful QUANGO's (Quasi-Autonomous Non-Governmental Organization), The West End Development Corporation (WEDCO). By creating a great place for people, WEDCO has established a new tourism destination and a great place for Bermudians. Based on professional market research and sound specialty retail planning, WEDCO has created a real specialty centre in a remote location on the island. A realistic leasing strategy, a strong entrepreneurial spirit and sound management have created a success story that resulted in a "Royal Opening" in 1990 and continues today as the third phase of development is being successfully implemented.

This project provides many lessons in creating a specialty retail centre about which the local retailers said "it won't work!" These lessons include the importance of planning; a strong management team with a clearly defined mission; control of the property; attention to serving local needs; creating a quality image; focus on creating concentration and critical mass; and bringing the product on-line at just the right time.

THE SETTING

The Island of Bermuda is strategically located only about 600 miles from the East Coast of the United States, with its hugh potential market population of almost 90 million people. Bermuda is really a collection of large and small islands tied together by bridges, so that the total land area is only about 22 square miles with a total population of almost 60 000 people. The Royal Naval Dockyard and the Clocktower Centre are located at the extreme west end of Bermuda. Hamilton, the capital and principal city of the island, is located approximately in the middle; and the international airport and the historic town of St. George are located on the east end of the island. The distance between the Dockyard and St. George is approximately 21 miles.

The Royal Naval Dockyard, as its name implies, is part of a larger British military complex that existed at Bermuda's West End for more than 150 years. The Dockyard is located on Ireland Island North, which has been designated as a tourism destination and a mixed-use commercial, cultural and recreational area for the benefit of Bermudians and visitors.

The Crown purchased the land at the end of 1809 and Dockyard was built as protection against the threat of American intervention, which was a particular concern to the British Admiralty during the War of 1812, when work at Dockyard had just started. The construction project included stone fortifications, the original Great Wharf, the North Breakwater, the Commissioner's House, Casemate Barracks, and a large number of supporting residential and storehouse buildings.

The Victualling Yard buildings were completed in 1848, including the Dockyard Terrace, providing housing for the key operation officers of the Dockyard. Today the Victualling Yard is an important part of Dockyard and plays a strong supporting role to the East Storehouse building, now known as the Clocktower Centre. The Clocktower building was built in 1856 and represents a dramatic example of 19th-century military architecture. No construction of historical significance took place in the Dockyard area after 1907.

By the year 1900 Dockyard was the most important employment centre on the Island. After World War II, the practical and strategic importance of the Naval Dockyard was greatly diminished. In 1956 the Royal Navy was able to accommodate its entire operation on 26 acres, constituting the HMS *Malabar*, located adjacent to Dockyard. Little or no development activity occurred at Dockyard for several decades, other than its designation as a Free Port under the Free Port Act of 1956. With that designation it was hoped that the area would become a major industrial and manufacturing trading centre.

In 1979 an initial development plan for the West End was prepared by the Bermuda government. In 1982 the West End Development Corporation (WEDCO) was established by the government to "manage and develop this area with the view to the progressive improvement of the social and economic conditions obtaining there" (Section 4 of The Act of Incorporation). The WEDCO mandate was to have responsibility for approximately 214 acres on the four islands that represent the West End: Watford Island, Boaz Island, Ireland Island South and Ireland Island North.

One of the first official acts of WEDCO in 1982 was the commissioning of a new development plan and the employment of local and international consultants to provide assistance. The West End Development Plan 1984 has served for a decade as the primary policy and development guidance mechanism for the Dockyard area. A part of the Development Plan included analysis of the Dockyard as a potential retail shopping centre prepared by The Rouse Company's American City Corporation. A relatively small specialty retail centre was determined to be feasible at the Clocktower Building at that time.

THE SPECIALTY RETAIL SHOPPING CONCEPT

In 1987 the WEDCO management group was ready to proceed with development of specialty shopping-centre space in the Clocktower building. In view of considerable local scepticism about the potential for shopping facilities at Dockyard, the decision was made to employ an American firm, LDR International, Inc., to review the 1984 American City Corporation market research and market forecasts and to prepare a predevelopment feasibility study, retail analysis and strategy for the Royal Naval Dockyard, along with a new and more specific landscape development strategy. The LDR strategy provided the market research support and themed leasing strategy required for development of what was to become the Clocktower Centre.

WEDCO management emphasized the importance of carefully assessing the local Bermudian market, as well as the visitor market. A major WEDCO objective was to create a place for Bermudians, as well as visitors. In addition to looking at market support for retail development, the LDR research carefully looked at the competitive retail market framework, establishment of a retail mix and a suggested retail and marketing strategy. The final element of the LDR work included an implementation strategy and conditions of development.

Conventional wisdom: "it won't work!"

The predevelopment feasibility analysis involved leadership interviews throughout the island with particular emphasis on the major retailers. This was done in conjunction with an analysis of the competitive framework on the island. Retailing in Bermuda is primarily concentrated in the city of Hamilton, with smaller groupings in St. George and Somerset. Retailing has traditionally been a major attraction in Bermuda, with Hamilton's Front Street being viewed by most visitors as a specialty centre.

At the time of the survey, Hamilton had about 156 retail stores, with a broad mix designed to serve visitors and Bermudians. St. George had 47 shops and Somerset 15. In addition, the major hotels had 36 shops. Hamilton retailers suggested that the Front Street shops cater about 70% to visitors and 30% to Bermudians (see Figure 16.1). Hamilton's Reed Street, which is one block behind Front Street, had a ratio of about 50/50. Over the years Hamilton has become much more tourist-oriented, particularly as the number of cruise visitors has increased. The cruise visitor does not have the same impact as the regular "air" visitor. As a result, the shops on Front Street have become more oriented to T-shirts and lower-end retail items. The traditional major retailers struggle to maintain their high-end image but they too are changing.

While only a small amount of retailing is located on board the cruiseships, they have an impact on retail sales in Bermuda. They typically carry three or four retail gift shops of approximately 200–400 square feet each. Although these retail shops are forced to close while in port, their prices are often lower than Bermuda's and therefore, purchases are made on the return trip from Bermuda. Cruiseship visitors are encouraged to comparison shop. Hotel shops, which cater exclusively to the visitor market, are comprised of about 25% apparel and accessories, 39% other retail shops, and 36% restaurants. Sales are reported to be higher in a quality hotel environment due to the higher income levels of visitors to those locations. Most of

Figure 16.1. Hamilton's Front Street

the larger retailers (department stores) on Front Street have "twig" stores or branches located at each of the smaller centres and in some of the hotels. Most "twig" stores appear to be primarily oriented to visitors and thereby carry a large proportion of smaller gift items.

As a result of the competitive assessment and leadership interviews, several interesting retail issues were identified. It was generally thought by Hamilton retailers that retail sales growth would be static in the future and smaller, less experienced merchants would have some degree of difficulty while major anchor retailers would likely remain profitable. The lack of quality sales and mid-management personnel was then providing a difficulty for employers. It was also reported to be more difficult to hire employees for the outlying locations. An additional issue was the number and type of cruiseships docked in Bermuda. There was some sentiment expressed that the income level of clientele from certain cruiseships was well below the average of residents and regular (air) visitors. The major retailers were uniformly negative about locating branch or "twig" shops at Dockyard. More than one Front Street merchant said "it won't work!"

The market: locals and tourists

The WEDCO management and Board have had a consistent policy that the retail development and outdoor environment at Dockyard should be new, different and of interest to Bermudians as well as visitors. There has been no attempt to compete directly with Hamilton's Front Street retailers. As a result, the planning for the new shopping centre focused on creating something new, different and special that would be financially viable.

The visitor market in the 1987 study analysed 1986 and prior visitor data. In 1986, the total number of visitors to Bermuda was 591 868. While this was more than the preceding two years, it did not approach the banner year of 1980 when visitation exceeded 609 000. Of the 1986 figure of 591 913, there were 459 666 regular "air" visitors and 132 247 cruiseship visitors. The objective of the Bermuda Department of Tourism at that time, and of most Bermudians was to see approximately 500 000 regular visitors annually and approximately 130 000 cruise visitors. The cruiseship visitation level is carefully regulated by the government in response to the rise and fall of air visitors and the politics of the day. As shown in Figure 16.2, seasonality is a problem for a year-round retail operation.

The resident market was comprised of the number of households in primary and secondary market areas identified for the study. The area Somerset and the West End was considered as the primary market and the area from Somerset to and including Hamilton was considered as the secondary market. The total number of households within the two areas was 20 300. The market size and expenditure rate for a proposed retail facility at the Royal Naval Dockyard is shown on Table 16.1.

As shown in Table 16.2, this produced projected retail sales to which were applied assumed productivity rates (US dollars per square foot of retail sales), which in turn produced estimated supportable gross leasable area (GLA) in square feet. The projected retail sales for Dockyard amounted to $4.8 million, with an average productivity level of $250 per square foot that results in a potential demand for retail space amounting to 19 282 square feet. A similar exercise was conducted for food and entertainment which produced a demand for an additional 10 849 square feet, for a total 30 131 square feet for the initial phase of the centre. The

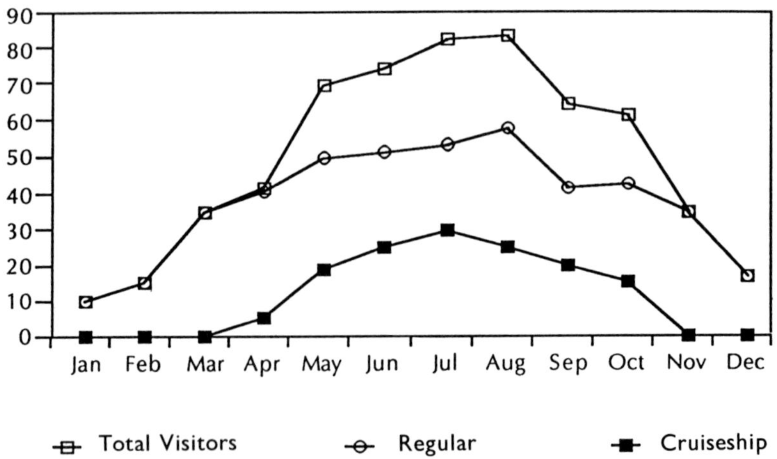

Figure 16.2. Bermuda Visitor Arrivals by Month in 1986

Table 16.1. Market size and expenditure rate, Royal Naval Dockyard, Bermuda

	Market size	Retail ($)	Food and entertainment ($)
Regular visitors	475 000	102.5	99.39
Cruiseship visitors	115 000	95.67	22.93
Cruiseship berth	25 000	95.67	22.93
Total cruiseship	140 000	95.67	22.93
Total visitors	615 000	———	———
Resident households	20 300	2069.70	2017.82

*All dollar figures are expressed in constant 1986 US dollars.
Source: LDR International, Inc.

Table 16.2. Retail sales, Royal Naval Dockyard, Bermuda (1986 US dollars)

	Total expenditures ($)	Dockyard capture rates (%)	Projected sales ($)	Productivity ($)	Supportable GLA (sq. ft.)
Regular visitors					
Primary	12 804 813	15.0	1 920 722	250	7 683
Secondary	35 882 688	3.0	1 076 481	250	4 306
Total	48 687 500		2 997 203		11 989
Cruiseship visitors					
Visitors	11 002 050	5.0	550 103	250	2 200
Berth	2 391 750	20.0	478 350	250	1 913
Total	13 393 800		1 028 453		4 114
Resident households					
Primary	8 822 961	6.0	529 378	250	2 118
Secondary	33 191 137	0.8	265 529	250	1 002
Total	42 014 098		794 907		3 180
Total retail	104 095 398		4 820 562		19 282

Source: LDR International, Inc.

study reported that when fully developed, there was the potential to capture approximately $7.7 million in retail sales, as measured in 1986 dollars.

Retail mix and leasing strategy

The next step in the process was the preparation of a retail mix for the centre and a leasing strategy. The idea was to focus on developing and leasing ground-floor space in the Clocktower Building and subsequently expanding to another building behind and immediately adjacent to the Clocktower Building. The retail mix suggested for the Dockyard project appears, in retrospect, to be a model for island specialty retail development. The focus was on creating small shops and using push carts and kiosks during peak seasons so that the available retail space could shrink during the off-season (November through March). Only a limited number of large retail shops (those averaging 2000 square feet in size) were suggested as anchors. This proved unwise since all of the major Hamilton retailers declined to participate in the first phase of development at Dockyard. Consequently, the focus was much more on small shops and a smaller first phase of development.

The retail mix proposed for dockyard is summarized on Table 16.3. As shown, retail types were identified with suggested average size, number of shops and total square footage for each category. This was backed up by projected sales in dollars per square foot, sales per store and total anticipated sales. As shown, the retail space was projected to produce approximately \$4.9 million in retail sales, with an additional \$2.9 million in food and beverage sales, for a total of \$7.8 million.

The marketing and leasing strategy that evolved was to create a small, intimate retail place with a good mix of small retailers. A second concept suggested a fresh food market which currently did not exist in Bermuda. This would be very different from a typical supermarket with a baker making fresh breads on premises, as well as stalls for meat, poultry, fish and produce. A part of this idea actually worked and became an anchor with an excellent bake shop and patisserie. This particular shop became "the place" for coffee and cakes at the West End.

The leasing strategy was simple and straightforward. Based on a retail architectural layout for a portion of the ground floor of the Clocktower Building, WEDCO staff would begin recruiting potential Bermudian entrepreneurs. The focus was on helping Bermudians get into the retail business. The response was overwhelming but not from the traditional retailers.

Clocktower Centre at Dockyard

The theme for the marketing strategy was equally simple and straightforward. The term "Royal Naval Dockyard" conjures up all kinds of images for both residents and visitors alike. "Royal Naval Dockyard" and "Dockyard" was to be used in a positive fashion in all marketing and promotion efforts. It was also recommended that the retail space have its own distinctive theme within the Royal Naval Dockyard (see Figure 16.3). A number of different themes were discussed and the "Clocktower Centre at Dockyard" was finally selected (see Figure 16.4).

Condition of development

While the Clocktower Centre appeared to have good potential for success, the consultant advised WEDCO that there were some prerequisites or conditions of development that would have to be met, over time, to assure success. These conditions are summarized as follows:

- Enhanced ferry service to and from Hamilton, particularly in the evenings and weekends. This is still a problem.

Table 16.3. Retail mix, Royal Naval Dockyard, Bermuda

Retail type	Avg. size	Number	Sq. ft.	Sales/sq. ft. ($)	Sales ($)	Total sales ($)
Retail space						
Large retail space	2000	5	10 000	225	450 000	2 250 000
Small retail space	500	12	6 000	275	137 500	1 650 000
Kiosks	250	10	2 500	300	75 000	750 000
Push carts	100	8	800	300	30 000	240 000
Total retail			19 300			4 890 000
Food space						
Restaurants	4000	2	8 000	260	1 040 000	2 080 000
Fast food	500	5	2 500	320	160 000	800 000
Total food and entertainment			10 500			2 880 000
Total			29 800			7 770 000

Figure 16.3. Retail shop and shoppers in the centre's new Victorian Mall

Figure 16.4. Clocktower Centre

- Early investment in quality site and building improvements (complete).
- Improved bus service (complete).
- Support for expansion and enhancement of Dockyard, Craft Centre, Island Pottery, Maritime Museums and Shopping Centre as a visitor attraction (complete).
- Encourage additional new public attractions (well underway with submarine ride, entertainment venue, pub and restaurants).
- Establish aggressive marketing and promotion campaign (underway).

Action Agenda

The plan for Dockyard and the shopping centre included a three-year, 21-point "Action Agenda" designed to facilitate plan and programme implementation beginning in 1988. While some slippage in the schedule occurred, WEDCO was able to implement a large part of the action plan in order to achieve a "Royal Opening" in 1990. Planning for expansion and upgrading continues as does implementation.

CREATING A GREAT PLACE FOR PEOPLE

Bermuda's West End and Dockyard, in particular, represent a special and important environmental resource for this small island and its people. The general nature of the 1984 Development Plan was detailed and brought to life in a new landscape plan prepared in 1988 and implemented on a phased basis by WEDCO using planting from its own nursery. The first priority was to reduce the amount of cement, stone and gravel surface and replace it with grass. This "greening" of Dockyard had an immediate positive impact on its image. It almost immediately became cooler, softer and more user friendly (see Figure 16.5).

Creating a quality environment

The landscape was further reinforced with a themed signage programme, period lighting and ornamental stone and ironwork. Roadways and pedestrian paths and sidewalks were installed along with designated parking. A tent pavilion was added for summertime use and push cart and kiosk vendors to service the new cruiseships that began landing at Dockyard in 1989.

Dockyard became a new Bermuda attraction destination for cruise visitors as well as other visitors who come by ferryboat from Hamilton and by bus or taxi from the resort hotels. The concentrated mix of Maritime Museum, traditional pub, restaurant, working waterfront, specialty shopping and a great themed maritime environment has become another Bermuda success story as judged by visitors and Bermudians alike.

Creating a unique shopping experience

WEDCO began the initial phase of shopping centre development with about 4000

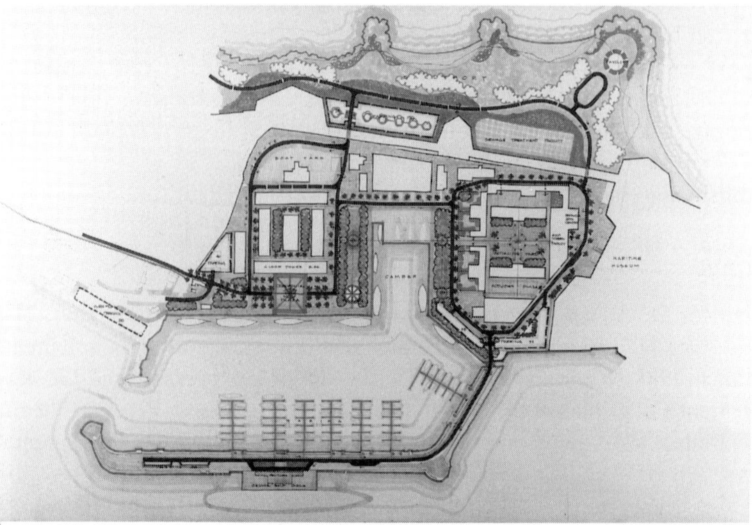

Figure 16.5. Dockyard Landscape Plan

square feet of retail space on the ground floor of the Clocktower Building. The authenticity of the historic building was maintained by keeping the design simple and utilizing the heavy, exposed beams, stone walls and stone floors. Small shop spaces facing a central corridor were created with a system of wood/metal partitions. Ceiling fans and drop lighting were provided from a darkened ceiling.

WEDCO assisted the new entrepreneurs with shop design and marketing advice. The emphasis was on authenticity, colour and simplicity. In July 1990, the Clocktower Centre opened its Phase I development with a "Royal Opening" at which HRH Princess Margaret participated. After an initial year of operating experience, WEDCO began plans for the next phase of development. This was to include about 3600 square feet of new retail space. The Clocktower Centre was on its way to becoming a special place for Bermudians and visitors.

Performance to date

Phases I and II of the Clocktower Centre encompass a total of 7663 square feet that houses 19 shops and employs just over 40 staff, exclusive of management. The shops range in size from 68 square feet (artist gallery) to 1386 square feet (bakery/coffee shop). Retail sales in 1993 were estimated at $1.9 million, up to just over $1 million from the first year of operation in 1991. Overall productivity is at a good healthy rate of $247 per square foot for retail sales. Both management and tenants are pleased with these initial results.

The third phase of development scheduled for opening in early summer 1994 included 12 additional shops in 4915 square feet. This brought the total space up to just over 12 500 square feet. In addition to the new retail space, additional plans are being developed for a bed and breakfast operation, a kiddie world attraction, a mini-brewery and expansion and development of the multi-purpose hall on the second floor of the Clocktower Building into the adjacent Sail Loft building. All of these activities combined, when implemented, will firmly established Dockyard as a major tourism destination on the island.

LESSONS LEARNED

The Clocktower Centre at Bermuda's Royal Naval Dockyard provides an excellent case study for successful island specialty retailing. The experience at Dockyard provides many lessons for Bermudians and other island destinations. These can be briefly summarized as follows:

- *A special development entity may be required.* Very often in the limited market provided on most island locations, the private sector either cannot or will not develop specialty retailing of the quality and quantity to have a real impact. Use of a quasi-public development corporation or QUANGO provides the perfect vehicle for a public/private partnership that can effectively wed private-sector expertise with public-sector funding capability.
- *Strong, centralized management of the process is essential.* In the case of WEDCO, there was consistently strong leadership from the chairman and board, as well as the executive staff. The organization mission was clearly defined and adhered to.
- *Careful predevelopment feasibility planning is essential.* There must be the prospect of success measured in real market research that the public- and private-sector investors can believe in. Predevelopment feasibility planning should include market research, concept and theme, leasing strategy, marketing plan and development/management strategy. Having the same organization in place to manage predevelopment feasibility planning, development and operations management seems to be critical.
- *Control of the property and the buildings is a must* so that planning and development, as well as ongoing maintenance, can be of a uniformly high quality.
- *The retail facility and the retail mix should be carefully designed to accommodate local needs as well as those of tourists.* A tourist-only facility will not attract locals and the tourists can make the difference in creating a successful local retail operation that might not exist otherwise.
- *Combining the retail space with other visitor attractions and amenities is very important.* Creating a special place with a concentration and critical mass of facilities, activities and people is very important.
- *Creating a consistent readily identifiable theme and image is important.* A heritage motif can work well as can the creation of a new special kind of place. A special quality image is what counts.

- *Timing of development is very important.* Meeting the market with the first phase of development calls for a sensitivity not to over-build or under-build the initial space. The initial plans should also include the opportunity for phased future development. Subsequent expansions should also be carefully timed to meet the market and be co-ordinated with other development activities in the area, i.e. opening of other visitor attractions.

The success of the Clocktower Centre at Dockyard is best measured in the tremendous response accorded the announcement of the third phase of retail development with decisions by seven Hamilton stores to open outlets there. Recent research by WEDCO indicates that almost 80% of Bermuda's more than 400 000 visitors now come to Dockyard during their stay on the island.

In addition to creating a great retail opportunity, WEDCO has created a great place on the island for people to come and enjoy an outstanding outdoor environment. It is one of the few places on the island that is distinctly oriented to the pedestrian who can stroll at leisure in a nicely landscaped space surrounded by sky and sea with distant landscapes across the water. Importantly, it is "a fun place" to visit which does not require a ticket to get in. As with most specialty shopping, the idea is to create an environment and experience that will compel the visitor to shop even though that is not the purpose of the visit. In this sense, Dockyard is probably the most successful place on the island.

17 Destination on the Edge? the Case of the Cook Islands

PETER BURNS
AND
ROBERT CLEVERDON
University of North London, UK

This chapter describes tourism planning and development in a particular island microstate (such political entities being, as Wilkinson (1989) notes, worthwhile studying as they "do seem to constitute a relatively distinct subset") and analyses the key role that airlines play in framing its tourism system. Links are drawn between strategic route planning of airlines and the power of such exogenous decision taking to cause tourism arrival targets (planned by government to take account of socio-cultural and environmental concerns) to be overtaken by enthusiasm for tourism growth "as it comes—while it comes".

INTRODUCTION

In terms of industrial growth and diversification, the Cook Islands shares certain characteristics common to many island microstates, including:

- limited land area, wide geographic spread of the islands and distance from markets;
- high shipping costs which raises the price of imports and places exports at a competitive disadvantage;
- scarcity of industrial raw materials coupled with reliance on a limited range of primary commodity exports;
- small, fragmented domestic markets that lack "critical mass"; and
- a labour market characterized by a limited skills base and reliance on expatriates.

Such economies are characterized by the acronym MIRAB (Milne, 1992) and comprise: *outward migration* (MI); a dependence on high levels of *remittances* resulting from the migration (R); overseas *aid* (A) receipts (often from a former colonial/administrative power) to cover trade deficits and a reliance on government

Island Tourism: Management Principles and Practice
Edited by Michael V. Conlin and Tom Baum

bureaucracy (B) for job creation. Milne argues that for many Pacific island microstates, this dependency situation will almost certainly continue as almost the only viable economic option in the short to medium term.

REGIONAL TOURISM TRENDS

Given that regional airline routings have created something of a paradox in that there is a necessary mutuality between the island nations and yet increasing competition, it is important to place Cook Islands tourism in the context of regional tourism trends. Total international tourist arrivals reached 500 million in 1993, having grown at an annual rate of 7.2% over the period 1950–1993. The East Asia and Pacific Region (the World Tourism Organization (WTO) geographic grouping which includes the Cook Islands) achieved a rate of growth more than double the global average, i.e. 14.5% a year between 1950–1993. Even in 1993, however, only 13.7% of total international arrivals were in the East Asia and Pacific Region; albeit, this share was up from below 1% in 1950 (WTO, 1994a, b).

The 1980s and early 1990s saw a global slowing down of tourism growth rates. However, the East Asia and Pacific region maintained its momentum more successfully than other regions, i.e. 1980–1993 average annual growth rates were 4.3% (global) but 9.5% for the East Asia and Pacific Region (WTO, 1994a, b).

The Pacific Islands have been less successful in tourist arrival growth rate terms than the overall East Asia and Pacific Region. The 1980s' growth rate in tourist arrivals in Pacific Islands was 7.5% a year, while in the five years from 1987 to 1992, the region's rate of expansion (4.5% per annum) was even below the increase in global international arrivals (6.1%). The Cook Islands account for less than 2% of total arrivals in the South and Central Pacific (excluding Hawaii) (TCSP, 1993).

GEO-POLITICAL AND DEVELOPMENT CONTEXT

Given Wilkinson's (1989) suggestion that "the smaller the microstate, the greater the probability that tourism will come to dominate the social and economic environments", it is important to illustrate just how small the Cook Islands is. Geographically, it comprises 15 islands divided into two broad groups spread over 2 million square kilometres of the Pacific Ocean. The total land area of these islands is 244 square kilometres. The largest island, and centre of government, is Rarotonga with a land area of 67 square kilometres. The total population is approximately 17 500, of which 9700 live on Rarotonga. This relatively low level of population is bound up with the propensity for migration, principally to New Zealand, to take place. Cook Islanders are full New Zealand passport holders and as such have complete right of entry and abode in New Zealand. In this sense, it is very different from other Pacific island microstates such as Tonga, Western Samoa and Kiribati.

Government socio-economic development planning (Cook Islands, 1982) requires policies and programmes to be guided by two principles:

- to achieve fiscal independence by ensuring that an increasing proportion of the national budget comes from local sources;
- to channel a greater measure of development assistance to the rural, outer islands of the country.

In fulfilment of these aims, the government has identified three "frontline" industries for the nation's future development: tourism, agriculture and marine resources. It believes that the purposeful pursuit of these can yield very tangible results to benefit all parts of the country. Other government policy in relation to development includes the commitment to localization of posts currently held by expatriates and the encouragement of Cook Islanders living overseas to return to the country.

In relation to tourism, the government developed 10 key points. These emphasized: incorporating private-sector inputs to policy formulation; developing healthy working relationships between private- and public-sector tourism enterprises; encouragement for the industry to upgrade standards; increased focus on Cook Islands' Maori participation in the tourism sector (as employees and entrepreneurs); and increased marketing budgets for the Cook Islands Tourist Authority (CITA).

ORIGINS AND CHARACTERISTICS OF TOURISM IN THE COOK ISLANDS

Two related events mark the beginning of significant tourism in the Cook Islands: the completion of the Rarotongan International Airport in 1975 and the opening, some two years later, of the 151-bedroomed Rarotongan Resort Hotel. Tourist arrivals in the Cook Islands rose three and a half times, from under 10 000 in 1976 to over 34 000 in 1990 (with strong growths between 1976 and 1980 and again between 1983 and 1988). Over the same period, the supply of hotel rooms increased from 198 to 691. Tourist statistics to February 1994 indicate a strong visitor arrivals' trend since 1990 (CITA, 1994b), despite three years of global recession and the Gulf War. The growth rate in international tourist arrivals in 1991, 1992, and 1993 was 16.9%, 25.1% and 5.7% respectively—though it should be noted that the strong growth in 1992 can be partly attributed to the Cook Islands being the venue for the 1992 South Pacific Festival of Arts. This event alone added an estimated 2000–3000 of the total arrivals. In 1993, a total of 52 868 tourist arrivals were recorded (CITA, 1994a).

Tourism development during the 1970s and 1980s proved generally unsystematic. This led to fluctuations in the pattern of tourism facility growth, particularly accommodation. As a consequence, accommodation occupancy levels went as low as 50% in 1988—with profit levels proving unreliable. This in turn caused two major problems for the sector. First, standards of operation for all types of touristic activity became inconsistent; and second, the poor profits meant a generally low level of re-investment in business operations including investment in human resources (RPT-ESG, 1991).

Among the key performance indicators and characteristics of Cook Island's tourism are the following:

- New Zealand has, historically, been the dominant source of visitors, though its share dropped from 58% in 1980 to 42% in 1991. New Zealand residents (including Cook Islanders) made up only 27% of total arrivals in 1993 (i.e. 14 277), when it was overtaken by the Europe/UK source region.
- Australia recorded the fastest overall growth during the 1980s. By 1991 it accounted for over 15% of total arrivals (6073) but declined during the following two years, i.e. 5806 arrivals or 11% in 1993.
- New Zealand and Australia see the Cook Islands as a short-haul destination, with most visitors from these two markets on a single destination package holiday of between one and two weeks, though there is also a significant VFR tourist flow of Cook Islanders resident in New Zealand or Australia.
- During 1990/91/92/93 the US market showed growth rates of 32.5%, 0.8%, 35.3% and 30.5%, the poor performance of 1991 being attributed to the "stay at home" response of Americans to the Gulf War. In 1993, US arrivals in the Cook Islands reached 7790.
- Canada and Europe/UK arrivals both grew rapidly in the early 1990s. Canadian arrivals grew at an average annual rate of 24.3% between 1989 and 1993, while the corresponding increase over this period for Europe/UK was 32.7% per year.

Tourism expenditure (excluding air fares) in 1988 was calculated to be US$46.00 per night (total of about US$447 per trip). Estimated total gross receipts (total visitor expenditure) to the Cook Islands in 1990 was determined by 34 218 visitors with an average spend of NZ$859 equivalent to NZ$29.4 million. The leakage factor in 1984 was calculated at 58%, i.e. some 42% of tourism expenditure was retained in the Cook Islands (Milne, 1987), while in 1990 it was calculated to be in the region of 46–54% (RPT-ESG, 1991). The improved 1990 leakage rate was probably due to the rapid expansion of small-scale entrepreneurs selling a range of home-produced goods (such as printed garments, carvings and fruits, etc.) to the tourists.

STRATEGY FOR FUTURE TOURISM DEVELOPMENT

The 1991 Cook Islands Tourism Master Plan (RPT-ESG, 1991) documented the official government position on tourism and made a number of key statements about the future direction and profile of tourism for the Cook Islands. It also made the general point that quite apart from any cultural considerations, the Cook Islands cannot sustain any form of mass tourism by reason of its small land mass and low population. While the Plan predicted supply side growth from the current 620 rooms to 1100 rooms by the year 2000, it also made the caveat that this increase was liable to be in fits and starts rather than in the form of steady, year on year growth. The new Sheraton will add 189 rooms in one go, the three Polynesian-style hotels recommended for Aitutaki will add about 120 rooms in three distinct periods, while a small 15-room property was suggested for the outer island of Manihiki. The main thrust of the Plan, particularly in relation to Rarotonga, was to consolidate and upgrade rather than suggest significant growth. In the case of the fragile outer islands, the Plan strongly recommended strict control of tourism: the inhabitants lead remote lives and as a consequence have very little awareness of tourism. Development should be on the basis of "for the islands, by the islands, as they want it".

During the early part of the 1990s, the Cook Islands was on the verge of another period of tourism growth: direct-flight air service capacity from the US West Coast which was only re-introduced in 1990 (after a break of eight years) was, in 1994, providing 860 seats a week while at the same time, the much delayed Sheraton rescheduled the opening of its resort hotel on Rarotonga for late 1994, setting the scene for a dramatic increase in the country's room stock which will go up by over one quarter from 735 to 925 rooms.

MARKETS: MAIN ORIGINS AND TRENDS

The Cook Islands' source markets for tourists showed widely varying performance during the 1980s and early 1990s. While overall growth was strong (10.3% a year average increase in arrivals between 1983 and 1993), long-haul origins considerably out-performed the primary short-haul market of New Zealand. The combined Europe/UK market increased by over a quarter each year during the 1980s. By contrast, New Zealand (excluding Cook Island Maoris resident there) arrivals grew by just 2% a year over the same period. Arrivals from the USA also grew at a rate well above the average, though Canada's rate of expansion was not so high (though strong in 1989–93). The other principal short-haul market—Australia—showed fluctuating growth: strong in the mid-1980s, weak in the early 1990s (apart from 1991) as illustrated in Table 17.1.

There were two key contributory factors to these general trends:

- the strength of the economic recession in Australia and New Zealand which was most pronounced in the way that it hit tourist flows in the 1990–1993 period;
- changes in the direct air services offered between the major source markets and the Cook Islands.

CHANGING INTERNATIONAL AIR TRANSPORT ACCESS

The successful development of many tourism destinations is enmeshed in reliable air access. "A destination can fail or succeed depending on decisions taken by a

Table 17.1. Tourist arrivals, by country of residence, 1983 and 1993[b]

Origin	1983		1993		Average annual growth 1983–1993 (%)
	'000 arrivals	%	'000 arrivals	%	
New Zealand	10.5	53.2	14.3	27.0	3.1
Cook Islanders	1.6	8.0	3.4	6.4	7.9
non-Cook Islanders	9.0	45.2	10.9	20.7	2.0
Australia	2.1	10.7	5.8	11.0	9.5
Cook Islanders	(a)	(a)	0.6	1.0	(a)
non-Cook Islanders	2.1	10.7	5.3	10.0	9.5
USA	1.9	9.6	7.8	14.7	15.2
Canada	2.5	12.5	4.0	7.6	5.0
Europe/UK	1.8	9.1	17.5	33.2	25.5
Other Pacific Islands	0.6	3.1	2.6	4.9	15.7
Asia	0.2	1.0	0.7	1.3	12.3
Other countries	0.1	0.7	0.2	0.2	2.4
Total	19.8	100.0	52.9	100.0	10.3

Notes: (a) Not separately available; included in total for "Other countries"; (b) columns may not aggregate to given totals owing to rounding.
Source: CITA.

single airline" (Poon 1993: 326). Poon goes on to cite examples where financial difficulties of major US carriers (Eastern Airlines, Pan Am) caused several "major loss[es] in seat capacity" to several Caribbean island nations (Barbados, Bahamas, Turks and Caicos Islands). Butler and Waldbrook (1991: 9) describe access as the "result of a combination of physical transportation linkages as well as the accessibility provided by ease of purchase". In the case of the Cook Islands, linkages to (or isolation from) metropolitan tourism markets have been, and continue to be, dominated by foreign carriers: for reasons implicit in this chapter, there is no realistic chance of this situation changing.

Ikeda, *et al.* (1989: 2–21) noted that the limited international air service schedule to the Cook Islands restricted access and was not convenient for shorter stays, but in a sense this "restriction" may be seen as positive in that longer-staying visitors tend to generate a higher level of spend. This paradox serves to illustrate air transport's critical role in the development of microstates located long distances from their existing and potential markets. The nearest source market for the Cook Islands, Auckland, is 3012 kilometres away. Table 17.2 shows flying times from other major generating locations illustrating the much reiterated point that remoteness is one of the characteristics of many island microstates.

In 1988, there were just seven international air service connections a week: i.e. from Auckland (three direct, one via Nadi, Fiji) and one each from Sydney,

Table 17.2. Flying times to Rarotonga based on Feb. 1994 schedules

Flight routing	Journey time
Auckland	3 h 50
Sydney via Apia	13 h 10 (incl. three stops)
Los Angeles via Honolulu	13 h 05
Los Angeles via Papeete	11 h 20
Los Angeles (non-stop)	9 h 40

Source: *ABC World Airways guide.*

Honolulu and Apia (Western Samoa). In order to set the context of how airline scheduling and traffic flows have shaped Cook Islands tourism in relation to its various source markets, it is worth briefly looking at each major market:

New Zealand

The New Zealand market has been consistently well served with direct flights operated by Air New Zealand and, for short periods in the mid- and late-1980s by Cook Islands-based ventures: 1986/87, Cook Islands International; 1989/90, Air Rarotonga.

Australia

Air services between major Australian centres and Rarotonga saw many changes during the 1980s and early 1990s. Polynesian Airlines (the airline of neighbouring Western Samoa) has operated services through Apia for several years, though schedules often necessitated overnighting *en route*. For a short period in the mid-1980s, the Cook Islands operated a national carrier (Cook Islands International) which flew direct between Australia and Rarotonga. Early 1994 Polynesian Airlines' schedules featured flights from Sydney and Melbourne with a connection in Apia, creating the most traveller-convenient service for some years.

Significantly, the Australian market has performed best for the Cook Islands when there has been a direct air service. There were substantial increases in arrivals in the mid-1980s, but then a fall-off in demand with loss of Cook Islands International's service. In the eight months (June 1993–January 1994 inclusive) following the commencement of Polynesian Airlines' new schedule, the Australian arrivals in the Cook Islands rose 23% over the corresponding period a year earlier.

USA and Europe/UK

The initial direct Los Angeles–Rarotonga air service (via Honolulu) was launched by Air New Zealand in September 1978. This once-a-week service was operated for four years up to October 1982, when it was withdrawn. No other direct US–Cook

Islands air service was operated until late 1980s when Hawaiian Airlines launched a Honolulu–Rarotonga service, connecting in Honolulu with its service from the northwest US cities of Portland and Seattle. This service was withdrawn in 1991.

The major impetus to US–Cook Islands tourist traffic came with the introduction of a service to tap the growing market out of California. In November 1990, Air New Zealand commenced a 200-seat (*B767*) weekly service Auckland–Rarotonga–Honolulu–Los Angeles and return, with guaranteed connection in Los Angeles with its London service thereby linking up two major markets with a highly reputable and reliable carrier. This was supplemented in October 1991 with a 430-seat (*B747*) weekly service Auckland–Rarotonga–Papeete–Los Angeles and return. In August 1993, Polynesian Airlines commenced a Los Angeles–Rarotonga service (on to Apia) with 235 seats (*B767*), with a key marketing strategic aim being to link up with Lufthansa's Frankfurt–Los Angeles service, again targeting the US and European markets.

Table 17.3 shows that in less than three years, weekly air seat supply between Los Angeles and Rarotonga rose to 865. Though none of these seats are dedicated to Rarotonga–all are on free sale–a significant proportion of travellers on these services are bound for the Cook Islands, as several non-stop Auckland–Los Angeles (and return) services are available for travellers between these two "end points".

Canada

Historically, there has been no direct air service between Vancouver and Rarotonga, most Canadians transiting via Honolulu or Los Angeles, creating a less convenient air schedule than available for the US market (and even the Europe/UK

Table 17.3. Growth in weekly seat capacity, Los Angeles–Rarotonga

		USA		Europe/UK	
Year	Weekly seat capacity ex Los Angeles[a]	'000 arrivals	% change on previous year	'000 arrivals	% change on previous year
1990	200 (from November)	4.4	32.5	6.0	6.5
1991	630 (from October)	4.4	0.8	8.4	39.9
1992	630	6.0	35.3	13.7	62.8
1993	865 (from August)	7.8	30.5	17.5	27.9

Note a: with seasonal variations.
Source: CITA and authors' own research/calculations.

market). This is illustrated by the relatively inconsistent rate of increase for tourist arrivals from Canada during the two years prior to 1994 (i.e. a fall of 4.3% in 1992, a rise of 7.5% in 1993).

AIRLINE ROUTING, TOURISM PLANNING AND *REALPOLITIK*

Over a decade ago, de Kadt (1979) warned against discussing tourism without reference to the global network of political processes that determine development. Britton (1982) in discussing the articulation of international tourism and Third World destinations took up the theme: "Dependency . . . [is] a process of historical conditioning which alters the internal functioning of economic and social sub-systems within an underdeveloped country. This conditioning causes the simultaneous disintegration of an indigenous economy and its reorientation to serve the needs of exigenous markets" [internal disarticulation].

The case for applying this to the dependency situation in which many island microstates are placed in respect of their tourism development and international airlines is quite compelling. Many such countries, including the Cook Islands with its ill-fated venture with Cook Islands International, have made the painful discovery that the prestige of having their own national carrier is outweighed by the financial liability arising from the absence of the economies of scale to compete with metropolitan country airlines. There are two main alternatives available to small-island destinations, which have identified tourism as an important tool for economic development.

The first is to operate a national carrier and be prepared to subsidize it as part of the national tourism marketing effort. There are some outstanding successes of this type. Air Mauritius has grown successfully as a "niche carrier" totally committed to the development of the island's tourist traffic. It operates non-stop Europe services and carries 53% of total passenger traffic to the island. The support of the government of Mauritius for its national airline is consistent with its pursuit of high-spending, upmarket tourists and a ban on charter services. Air Lanka is another success, though under quite different circumstances. During the period when Sri Lanka's tourism sector was severely depressed as a consequence of the ethnic troubles on the island (the mid- and late 1980s), and major carriers like British Airways and Swissair ceased operations, Air Lanka kept Sri Lanka on the tourist map.

The second alternative for governments is to place a reliance on foreign airlines, with the key task for the destination's aviation and tourism authorities being to "manage" these operators so that they are in line with the country's requirements for the tourism sector. This entails: licensing the amount of capacity which the destination's facilities require and which can be sustained; and working in co-operation with the carriers in marketing efforts to ensure that the country's and the airlines' marketing strategies and programmes are fully consistent with each other.

The first of these two alternative international air transport strategies is not a realistic option for the Cook Islands. There are "small-country" islands and island microstates: Sri Lanka and Mauritius fit into the former category; the Cook Islands into the latter. The future of the tourism sector of the Cook Islands is inextricably interwoven with Air New Zealand and other foreign carriers.

CONCLUSION

The 1991 Tourism Master Plan provided a series of strategic guidelines for the development of tourism in the country. These were framed by the notion of "controlled and orderly development" (RPT-ESG, 1991) and included the idea of a moratorium on all new tourist development on the main island of Rarotonga but allowed for "natural" increases in existing small-scale properties and the development of perhaps three small mid-scale (30–60 rooms) Polynesian-style resorts on the second island of Aitutaki. The Plan recognized the need to increase hotel occupancy rates before allowing further tourism developments ameliorating the perennial chain of events whereby low profits lead to low reinvestment which in turn leads to poor maintenance which then creates an unfavourable, or downmarket image for the destination. The Plan was clearly set up to counter negative aspects of tourism development and in that respect went some way to addressing general criticisms of tourism planning (Murphy, 1985; Getz, 1986). Such criticisms are well encapsulated by Wilkinson's (1989) observations on tourism and planning in island microstates which introduces the term "folly", which he describes as being:

> the pursuit of governments . . . of policies contrary to their own interests, despite the availability of feasible alternatives . . . (e.g., neglecting to clean polluted beaches, building unattractive hotels, mining beach sand, permitting enclave resorts which provide little local benefit). The spirit of the concept of folly seems to be eminently appropriate in much tourism development, *frequently because of the absence of reasoned government policies and practices related to tourism* (Wilkinson, 1989) (our italics).

It might be argued that for the Cook Islands, the added "follies" (which cannot be explained on the grounds of "absence of reasoned policies") are:

- the Government's uncritical embracing Air New Zealand's substantial contribution to tourist flows;
- the active pursual of the controversial Sheraton project.

This has resulted in increased visitor arrivals in 1992/93 at targets well above those set by the officially endorsed Plan.

The pressure for development is being compounded by inflows of Cook Islands Maoris, previously resident in New Zealand, returning home partly as a result of New Zealand domestic policy changes (introduced in April 1991) which reduced social security and unemployment benefits (these changes were, themselves, partly the result of New Zealand's recession).

While the Cook Islands has traditionally maintained a good and close working relationship with Air New Zealand, the goals of a commercial airline and an elected government are not the same: the government sets tourist arrival targets which are appropriate to economic goals and social/physical carrying capacity, while Air New Zealand's goal remains directed towards satisfying its shareholders. In a sense, we can conclude that while governments can set socio-environmentally sensitive visitor arrivals targets, these can be over-ridden by exogenous corporate forces; for this particular microstate, a boardroom decision taken in Auckland (while no doubt discussed with the Cook Islands government) created a major change in supply.

The Cook Islands now finds itself a "destination on the edge", not only in terms of geographic location but, more importantly, on the edge of its physical and social capacity to carry more tourists. The reality for many microstates is that whatever the level or quality of planning, the tourism profile, growth patterns and systems are all fundamentally determined by the *realpolitik* of international carriers; the volume of passengers carried and their ability to reach the destination rests ultimately on the quality of the relationships between the microstate governments and the metropolitan carriers.

REFERENCES

Britton, S. (1982) "The Political Economy of Tourism in the Third World". *Annals of Tourism Research*, **9**, 331–358.

Butler, R.W. and Waldbrook, L.A. (1991) "A New Planning Tool: the Tourism Opportunity Spectrum". *The Journal of Tourism Studies*, **2**(1), 2–14.

CITA (1994a) *Tourism Marketing Update: January*. Rarotonga, Cook Islands Tourist Authority.

CITA (1994b) *Tourism Marketing Update: February*. Rarotonga, Cook Islands Tourist Authority.

Cook Islands (1982) *Development Plan 1: 1982–1985*. Rarotonga, Planning and Economic Development.

de Kadt, E. (1979) "Social Planning for Tourism in the Development Countries". *Annals of Tourism Research*, **6**(1), 36–48.

Getz, D. (1986) "Models in Tourism Planning: Towards Integration of Theory and Practice". *Tourism Management*, March 1986.

Ikeda, G., Collison, F. and Choy, D. (1989) *Tourism Development in the Cook Islands*. Manoa, East–West Center (draft).

Milne, S. (1987) *The Economic Impact of Tourism for the Cook Islands*. Occasional Publications 21, Auckland, University of Auckland.

Milne, S. (1992) "Tourism and Development in South Pacific Microstates". *Annals of Tourism Research*, **19**, 191–212.

Murphy, P. (1985) *Tourism: a Community Approach*. London, Routledge.

Poon, A. (1993) *Tourism, Technology and Competitive Strategies*. Wallingford, CAB.

RPT-ESG (1991) *Cook Islands Tourism Master Plan*. London, Economic Studies Group.

TCSP (1993) *Annual Report*. Suva, Tourism Council of the South Pacific.
Wilkinson, P. (1989) "Strategies for Tourism in Island Microstates". *Annals of Tourism Research*, **16**(2), 153–177.
WTO (1994a) *Tourism in 1993: Highlights*. Madrid, World Tourism Organization.
WTO (1994b) *Global Tourism Forecasts to the Year 2000 and Beyond: Vol. 4—East Asia and the Pacific*. Madrid, World Tourism Organization.

18 Tourism Development in the South Indian Ocean: the Case of Mauritius

PHILIPPE WING
University of Ulster, UK

INTRODUCTION

Among the small-island economies, Mauritius is not only already a well-established tourist-receiving country in the Indian Ocean but also on the highly competitive world market. The development of tourism facilities, more particularly the accommodation sector, has been stimulated by the private local sector and overseas interests with a low level of government intervention. The powerful indigenous private sector dominated by the plantocracy, which has been diversifying into the other economic sectors because of the volatility and instability prevailing in the international market for primary resources, had targeted tourism as a potential growth industry even before Mauritius achieved its political independence in 1967. The pioneering role was undertaken not by the government, as is common in most developing small-island states, but by the local private sector.

Although the tourism industry is dominated by the private sector, the Mauritian government has been involved in the provision of financial incentives to attract both local and foreign investment, in establishing a high level of political stability which has become the envy of African and other developing countries. But after years of a *laissez-faire* approach, the government must be prepared to take a more active role since the industry cannot be allowed to be self-regulated and the capacity of the island is limited. The appointment of a minister exclusively responsible for tourism in the new cabinet in 1991 indicates a new approach to tourism development. The government must define the future of tourism development by formulating policies towards the type and scale of tourism.

PROBLEMS OF TOURISM DEVELOPMENT

The size of the island means that tourism cannot be allowed to expand indefinitely as tourism is bound to give rise to a large number of conflicts. The local population

Island Tourism: Management Principles and Practice
Edited by Michael V. Conlin and Tom Baum © 1995 John Wiley & Sons Ltd

is incapable of competing against the hotel establishments which can pay a higher price for land, local produce and other materials. This unfair competition has led to higher prices on the local market and to a high level of inflation. However, the development of tourism has been assisted by the enterprising local private sector and the latter's willingness to exploit new commercial opportunities. But some of the traditional values are being threatened by both tourism and the media. This is inevitable since contact between hosts and guests is bound to create advantages and disadvantages to the local society.

The narrow economic base has been diversified and broadened, and reliance on the export of primary resources has been abandoned. The government has successfully diversified into other economic sectors, more particularly the export of manufactures and the development of tourism. Unlike other small-island state economies, Mauritius does not rely entirely on tourism for its economic development; tourism ranks only third after the industrial sector and agriculture in terms of gross foreign exchange earner. This broadly based economy is less vulnerable than those small-island states solely dependent on tourism. But the level of intersectoral linkage is still low, implying that the tourist industry is still importing a high level of supplies to service the tourist industry.

One of the main reasons why tourism has been successfully developed can be attributed to the high level of political stability and to the success of parliamentary democracy. Since independence, with the exception of the odd ethnic incident, the different racial groups which form the Mauritian society have been able to co-exist in relative harmony. In other countries, racial discord has been common because of the inability of the poor people to earn a decent living. Fiji is a prime example of a small-island state which has been severely affected by racial problems, resulting in the decline of the tourist industry. Mauritius's neighbours, more particularly Madagascar, the Seychelles and Comoros, have failed to develop their economy or their tourism industry because of sporadic conflicts. Overall, Mauritius has benefited substantially from the troubles of its neighbours and its East African competitors.

GEOGRAPHICAL SITUATION

Mauritius lies in the Indian Ocean. The principal island, from which the country derives its name, is located about 800 kilometres east of Madagascar, 250 kilometres from Reunion, its nearest neighbour, and 2400 kilometres from the East African coast. The other main islands are Rodrigues, Agalega and Cargados Carojus. Both Mauritius and Rodrigues, which together with Reunion form the Mascarene Archipelago, are of volcanic formation. Mauritius has no known mineral deposits and several attempts to discover oil in the Mauritian Exclusive Economic Zone (EEZ) have so far proved unproductive. Mauritius claims sovereign right to the 17th largest EEZ in the world or some 345 000 miles of the Indian Ocean, based on the international 200-mile EEZ. Being an island can be advantageous if such abundance of maritime resources can be commercially exploited.

The land rises from the coast to a central plateau, varying in altitude from 900 feet to 2400 feet, and bounded on the north, west and south by mountains. Numerous small rivers are found throughout the island, most of them are short, fast-flowing torrents descending from the central plateau to the sea. Some of the large waterfalls are not only major attractions for the visitors but have been harnessed to supply hydroelectric power. Measuring 38 miles by 29 miles approximately and with a land area of about 720 square miles, the island is surrounded almost entirely by coral reefs. Within these reefs are lagoons, ringed by beaches of white coral sand all around the island, without interruption in the south where the coral sands give way to steep rocky coast.

Mauritius has a tropical maritime climate which is conditioned by south-east trade winds. The lowlands are tropical; the hot and wet season lasts from December to April, and during those months there may be cyclones (see Table 18.1). The latter are important factors in the development of the economy and of tourism because cyclonic weather can destroy the agricultural sector and cause damage to tourism facilities. Cyclones are an exogenous factor which has been responsible for the poor performance of the tourist industry generally in the past. No measures can be taken against this element, but tourist facilities must be constructed in such a way to withstand the cyclonic pressures. Generally the probability of tourists experiencing one is so low that their occurrence has little impact on tourism with the possible temporary disruption of services.

HISTORICAL DEVELOPMENT OF THE TOURISM INDUSTRY

The history of Mauritius is fraught with confusion and no one exactly knows who first visited the island. Portuguese sailors visited Mauritius in the early 16th century although it had been known to Phoenicians, Malays and Arabs. Dutch sailors, who named the island in honour of Prince Maurice of Nassau, established a small colony in 1598 but abandoned it in 1710. Five years later, the French claimed Mauritius, renaming it Ile de France and it became a prosperous colony. In 1767, the French government assumed direct control and the island became a naval base during the Napoleonic wars. In December 1810, Mauritius was captured by the British naval

Table 18.1. Mauritius—Meteorological data

Daily maximum temperature (°C)	25.3–31.4
Daily minimum temperature (°C)	18.5–24.2
Rainfall (millimetres)	18.0–222
Rainy days	4.0–14
Bright sunshine (daily hours)	7.1–8.5

Source: Mauritius Meteorological Office, 1991.

force because of its strategic position in the Indian Ocean. Four years later, British rule was confirmed by the Treaty of Paris although the British chose to retain the French institutions including French law. This is the main reason why although English is the official language, French is more widely spoken.

Historically, it can be argued that the development of tourism can be traced to the times when ships from the maritime powers from the 14th to 18th centuries were in transit. The Dutch did not attempt to colonize the island, but France turned it into a prosperous colony. During the French colonial period, a small number of French visitors were attracted to Mauritius which they found very congenial for rest and relaxation. Prior to 1952, all visitors wishing to visit the island had to use sea transport, but this changed when in that year the Australian national airline, Qantas, started to operate the first commercial flights on a fortnightly basis between Australia, Mauritius and South Africa. In 1957, the tourism industry received a boost when South African Airways joined the same route on a weekly basis.

The development of air transport transformed the remoteness of the island as it became more accessible. Air transport is the most important element in the development of tourism since prior to air connections, Mauritius had to depend on sea transport. It made it faster to travel to the island. However, international tourism itself did not take off until 1970, when new hotels were built to accommodate the increasing number of visitors and when the metropolitan airline companies started to operate.

TOURIST TRENDS

Mauritius has emerged as the most important tourist destination in the Indian Ocean. From a base of 68 000 foreign visitors in 1973, this had risen to nearly 350 000 in 1993. The tourist industry has become the third most important after manufacturing and agriculture. The main objective of the government and of the Mauritius Government Tourist Office (MGTO) is to continue to attract high-income visitors whose economic impacts are acknowledged to be more beneficial to the local economy than low-spending visitors. Unlike other small-island economies, Mauritius's private sector has always been a key player in the economic development of the island. For over a hundred years, the private sector has been present in all the economic sectors. In the other Indian Ocean islands, it is the government which has been responsible for the development of tourism; without the intervention of the state, tourism would not have been developed because of the absence or weakness of the private sector.

The strength of the private sector is such that the government has been compelled to intervene to curb its power. Although the private sector is generally regarded as having played the pioneering role in initiating tourism development, the colonial government had come to the realization that the economy should be diversified and consequently that tourism should be used for this end. Prior to political independence, it had been recognized that tourism could be developed on the same scale as in successful Caribbean islands. But the colonial government did not have to initiate the development of tourism in Mauritius as it did in the Seychelles; the latter did not have the basic infrastructure and superstructure to attract the international tourists.

In 1960 there were practically no suitable hotels of reasonable international standard. Thirty-two years later, there are at least 80 hotels of international standard. The policy makers of the colonial government were sceptical about the tourism potential of the island because of the distance that exists between Mauritius and the main European tourist market and of the remoteness and isolation of the island. Even at that time tourists from Europe had a wide choice of sea, sun and sand holidays, especially in the Mediterranean countries. Competition existed and Mauritius, with an infant tourist industry, had to find the means to attract the long-haul tourists. The major problems can be identified in terms of communication and superstructure.

The plan by the private sector to build a hotel with the financial assistance of the colonial government gave rise to a debate among the decision makers. Hypothetical questions arose such as whether it would be of any use or it would be a waste of public money. Would a first-class hotel attract many people so far off the beaten track (Mead, 1968, 147). These pessimistic views, germane to the development of tourism, were well founded at the time because tourism was a relatively new industry in Third World countries. There were also economic alternatives which could have been developed in lieu of tourism. With the rapid technological development of air transport, the distance between Mauritius and the main tourist-generating countries has shrunk. Currently, it is well connected with Europe, South Africa and Reunion but connection is poor with the mainland African countries.

The level of tourist traffic has increased substantially since 1993, which has been regarded as the most successful year. But for how long will Mauritius be able to sustain this growth? Mauritius has not been severely hit by the current world recession as such because of its ability to take advantage of the political situation of many of its competitors. Many African destinations which are generally regarded as competitors to Mauritius do not enjoy the same high level of political stability. For instance, Kenya's tourist industry is being affected by political instability as there is growing dissatisfaction with the current government. Furthermore, the image of Kenya as a safe tourist destination has been severely tarnished after a spate of attacks on European tourists. Such attacks have resulted in bad publicity in the European media. Many tour operators are replacing Kenya with safer destinations, more particularly Mauritius. There is a high level of substitution but Mauritius must be cautious because there is a tendency for the government to be paying too much heed to maximizing the tourist traffic as opposed to optimizing it.

Although the future of tourism looks bright at the moment, Mauritius is still vulnerable to changes in taste, fashion and pricing. It is a situation which the government needs to watch because after years of tourism growth in the Caribbean, those small islands are facing increasing competition from other destinations (*The*

Courier, 1992: 65). The MGTO and the minister of tourism want to diversify their markets. There is a recognition that there must be a broad market base because reliance on a single trigger market can be more dangerous to the economic stability of the island. In spite of the world recession which has severely affected the Caribbean islands, the tourist industry is confident that its performance will not be affected and that Mauritius will be able to capture a bigger share of the tourist market in 1994.

Efforts are also being made to penetrate the Arab and Japanese markets. But these markets must be approached with care because of their own "environmental bubble" whereby they need things, food and fixtures which are familiar. Even some of the European destinations have found it difficult to cope with their special requirements. High investments have been needed to refurbish hotels to the demands of the Japanese market. In the 1970s, the promotion of Mauritius emphasized the uniqueness of its beaches, but such campaigns prove unproductive. Potential visitors were not attracted by such promotion campaigns because a beach is a homogeneous product which can be easily substituted. Currently, the emphasis of the campaign is on the aggregate quality of the product in terms of the friendliness of the people, the shopping experience, the quality and variety of the food and the relative safety of the visitors.

Mauritius is well connected with the outside world, with numerous scheduled flights daily and the development and expansion of international air services by Air Mauritius. The isolation and remoteness of Mauritius is a thing of the past. The authorities have exploited this enormous advantage which it has over its neighbours in the Indian Ocean. The rapid growth of tourism was accompanied by the expansion of the industrial sector, and tourism has been closely linked with the other economic sectors. The main rationale for tourism development is purely economic as tourism has been financing the other economic sectors for development purposes. Tourism has become a central support to economic development.

CONCLUSION

Tourism has become an important economic plank for development in a large number of small island states. In some, tourism has become the dominant tool for economic survival as it has emerged as *the* economic activity. In Mauritius, the government has realized since independence that tourism cannot be seen as the only panacea for all its economic malaises by successfully diversifying into the industrial sector. Tourism as an important earner of foreign exchange and creator of employment has alleviated these problems. Although at the embryonic stage of tourist development there was a conspicuous absence of planning despite the inclusion of tourism in all the development plans, the situation has changed because the government is attempting to minimize the detrimental impacts of tourism on society, economy and the environment.

It must be pointed out that the participation of the sugar estates in the development of tourism in Mauritius has resulted in tourism linking up with the agricultural sector, the latter supplying fresh food produce to the former. This unique partnership is beneficial to the local economy because of the low level of leakage. After all, if benefits are to be maximized, there must be a reduction in the import content of the tourist sector.

REFERENCES

Mead, G.E. (1968) *Economic and Social Structure of Mauritius*. London, Frank Cass.
The Courier (1992) "Country Reports: Mauritius", No. 135, Sept–Oct, p. 65.

19 Small-scale Tourism Development in Bali

VERONICA H. LONG
AND
GEOFFREY WALL
University of Waterloo, Canada

> "I know they're doing it in Ubud, but I don't think they are doing it here—yet," a Balinese restaurant owner informed us, ". . . but, I have seen people from Ubud buying black magic to use on their competitors."

Visitors to Bali are struck by the tranquil people, the ceremonial attention to religious practices and the splendour of the landscape. Known as "The Last Paradise", "The Morning of the World" or the "Island of the Gods" (Turnbull, 1982; Oey, 1990; Picard, 1990a), many visitors to Bali come to experience the mystical beauty and "other worldliness" that Bali appears to offer. Visitors leave the island laden with souvenirs representing Balinese cultural manifestations as well as photographs of ceremonies, religious processions and dances—developed instantly at the one-hour processing services dotting the island.

Most tourists to "utopian" Bali are unaware that the pursuit of this nirvana is bringing a rush of development to communities hoping to better themselves through acquisition of the tourist dollar. Tourism in Bali is referred to by resident intelligentsia as "*Arus deras yang melanda Bali*", i.e. "a violent current that is flooding Bali and undermining its foundations" (Picard, 1990a). While the small-scale nature of much of this development allows it to go unnoticed by most visitors, associated community tensions and other tourism impacts could grow to extinguish the serenity that is sought and expected in Bali.

In order to avoid past mistakes, current tourism development advocates promote "appropriate" or "alternative" tourism. The industry calls for ecotourism (D'Amore, 1993), while planners and developers talk about sustainable development (Nelson *el al.*, 1993). Even tourists, in disdain of the image of a "tourist," insist on being called "travellers." Although the *will* is clearly present, the terms are many and confusing and the *way* to appropriate tourism remains unclear.

For a number of reasons, small-scale, community-based tourism development is heralded as a means of avoiding the industry's excesses (Rodenburg, 1980; Woodley, 1993). Resident participation and the resulting economic gains is one

Island Tourism: Management Principles and Practice

Figure 19.1. Tourists photographing a tooth-filing ceremony

highly touted benefit (Rodenburg, 1980; Jenkins, 1982). Small-scale development is also considered to be more benign than "mass" tourism as it places less stress on social and physical systems (Jenkins, 1982; Wilkinson, 1989). Although this may be so, others such as Cohen (1982), Deardon (1993), Smith (1993), and Woodley (1993) are cautious in their endorsement of small-scale tourism.

This chapter seeks to further the understanding of small-scale tourism development issues. This will be done by presenting a case study of small-scale development in a Balinese *banjar* (neighbourhood). Tourism in Bali and, in particular, the Ubud region will be introduced in order to describe the development forces which are present. In addition, as a *banjar* is the focus, the formal governmental structure of which it is a part will be described. This will be followed by the presentation of the research project and results. The chapter concludes with discussions of the implications for tourism in Bali and of the issues associated with small-scale tourism development.

GENERAL BACKGROUND OF TOURISM IN BALI

Since the 1920s, Bali has received visitors interested in its culture and environment. Tourism to Bali began with visitors who disembarked from a weekly Dutch Royal Packet Navigation Company (KPM) steamship. These visitors numbered several thousand annually by the end of the 1930s (Picard, 1990b; Sutton, 1991). At the same time, a colony of foreign artists and anthropologists became established in the interior of the island in the vicinity of the village of Ubud (Universitas Udayana and Francillon, 1975; Picard, 1990b; Sutton, 1991) (see Figure 19.2). These resident

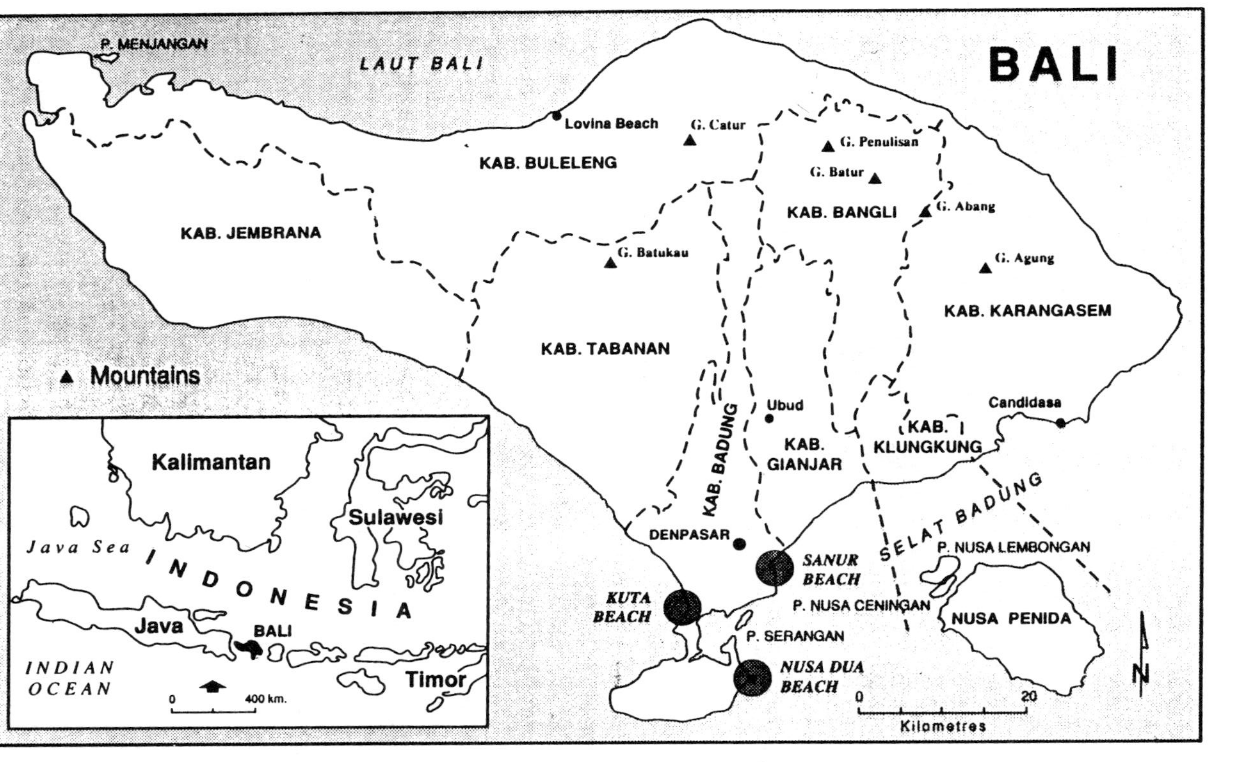

Figure 19.2. Map of Bali indicating main tourism areas

expatriates were experts in a number of cultural fields including painting, music and dance, and they encouraged the arts in the area and helped spread the word regarding the attractiveness of the region.

In 1969, with the construction of the Ngurah Rai International Airport, mass tourism began in earnest and tourism arrivals increased dramatically. While official plans concentrated development in Nusa Dua, Kuta and Sanur, nodes of spontaneous development occurred in villages such as Candi Dasa, Lovina and Ubud. Although tourism to all parts of the island has increased, 80% of all tourist accommodations, and 90% of all star hotels are found in Badung Regency in the south, especially in Kuta, Sanur and Nusa Dua (Dibnah, 1992) (Figure 19.2).

Currently, Bali attracts visitors for two major types of tourism. The first is comprised of activities based on sun, sea and sand where tourists come to swim at beaches, surf the world-class waves and dive in the coral reefs and shipwrecks. The second is referred to as "cultural" tourism in which visitors experience Balinese culture through such activities as dance and gamelan performances, shadow puppet shows and visits to temples and religious ceremonies.

While tourists to Bali come from all parts of the world, the two types of activity tend to draw particular nationalities (Universitas, Udayana and Francillon, 1975). Australians, who come on charter vacation packages and can be found mainly in the vicinity of Kuta Beach and Sanur (Mabbett, 1987) make up a large proportion of the recreational market segment. Visitors from Europe and North America, and possibly Japan, on the other hand, constitute the majority of the cultural tourists. While these tourists can be found in all parts of the island, they are especially concentrated in and around Ubud.

Tourism in the Ubud area

The Ubud region is noted as the centre of cultural arts in Bali (Santosa, 1980; Manuaba *et al.*, 1988). Although the research discussed in the chapter was done in the nearby village of Peliatan, tourism in the village of Ubud has such a great impact on the surrounding area that it must be discussed as it provides the context for the development in Peliatan.

The village of Ubud, famous for its painters, is surrounded by the villages of Mas, Tegallalang and Peliatan which are known for woodcarving, contemporary art and dance respectively (Mantra, 1991). The region is comprised of several scenic river valleys with beautiful panoramas of terraced rice fields. The cultural and physical factors combined endow the Ubud region with an extraordinary number of aesthetic attractions.

Although official government plans concentrated tourism development in the southern part of Bali, a substantial amount of small-scale tourism business development has occurred within Ubud and in the surrounding region. The Table 19.1 shows the growth of tourism in the Ubud district between 1987 and 1990 (the Ubud district includes Peliatan).

Tourism in Peliatan is heavily integrated with that of Ubud due to its geographic

Figure 19.3. University students dressed to perform traditional dances for tourists

Figure 19.4. Cremation ceremony with tourists and tourist bus

Table 19.1. Number of tourists in the Ubud District by year

Year	Number of tourists
1987	16 676
1988	16 651
1989	20 323
1990	40 706

Source: Ubud District Police Department.

location and complementary tourism attractions. The two villages are literally side-by-side with no visible separation which often causes tourists confusion. Peliatan and Ubud complement each other with Peliatan offering "a smaller and quieter version of Ubud" (Dalton, 1990). Tourist guidebooks often list Peliatan as an alternative place to stay when visiting Ubud (Dalton, 1990; Wheeler *et al.*, 1989; Oey, 1990; Black and Hanna, 1991; Charle, 1991). In addition to providing a tranquil atmosphere, tourists to Peliatan can also visit art shops and dance performances.

PLANNING AND DEVELOPMENT OF TOURISM IN BALI

Government institutions in Bali

Tourism planning, policy making and development strategies occur at most levels of government. To comprehend tourism development fully in Bali, one must understand the complex governmental structure and accompanying tension in which it occurs. The following scheme represents the hierarchy of government agencies in Bali:

CENTRAL GOVERNMENT OF INDONESIA

PROVINCIAL GOVERNMENT OF BALI

KABUPATEN (Regency)

KECAMATAN (District)

DESA (Village)

Desa Adat (Customary) and *Desa Dinas* (Administrative)

BANJAR (Neighbourhood)

The 13 677 islands which make up the country of Indonesia are divided into 27 provinces. Indonesia is mainly Moslem, but the province of Bali is Hindu which makes it culturally unique. The Indonesian central government, located in Jakarta on the island of Java, appears to stress the tourism potential of Bali because of the foreign exchange which this brings (Francillon, 1990; Picard, 1990a).

Ironically, although tourism in Bali is based substantially on its culture, control of major tourism developments is largely in the hands of the non-Balinese central government of Indonesia. While the province of Bali does have a tourism ministry and struggles to maintain some control over planning and development, financial restrictions and limiting regulations imposed by the powerful central government inhibit large-scale planning initiatives and policy development by provincial agencies (Noronha, 1976; Picard, 1990a). Furthermore, officials in Jakarta are responsible for much of the research, planning and marketing associated with tourism. The central government is also responsible for public participation regulation and infrastructure planning and development (Picard, 1990a).

The province of Bali is divided into eight regencies. Below the regency level, individual districts pursue policies which aim to attract as much tourism as possible to their respective areas (Dibnah, 1992). Within districts are villages which have two types of administration. The first, *Desa Adat*, refers to the traditional form of community organization employed by Balinese people for centuries. It relates to an area which contains three distinct temples and has rules of membership related to land tenancy and birth. Religious beliefs and customary values and procedures are incorporated into activities and organization. The second type of administration, *Desa Dinas*, was established during the period of Dutch colonization and serves as a part of the national governmental structure (UNDP, 1991).

Banjar institutions

Villages are usually divided into *banjars*, each *banjar* having a *bale banjar* (banjar meeting room) and associated rules of membership. The ethic of *Gotong Royong* (mutual co-operation) forms the basis of the *banjar* institution. Membership in a *banjar* involves participation in various activities and organizations including youth groups, ceremony preparations and temple maintenance. These organizations and their social obligations have created a unique and strong form of social cohesion in Balinese society (Noronha, 1976; Mantra, 1991).

The role of *banjars* in tourism development has not been addressed in formal tourism planning (Dibnah, 1992). Nevertheless, some *banjars* have been involved in tourism. In Sanur, Ubud and Legian, the *banjars* use tourism to make money (Udayana, 1975; Noronha, 1976; Mantra, 1991). In Sanur, a beach-front art market was established by the *banjar* to try to capture some of the economic benefits of the tourism that had invaded their neighbourhood (Noronha, 1976). Dance troops and gamelan orchestras have also been formed to perform for groups of tourists while providing individual *banjars* with a source of revenue.

Tourism planning

A tourism master plan for Bali, called the SCETO report, was written by a consortium of French consultants in 1971. The work was sponsored by the United Nations Development Program (UNDP) and the International Bank for Reconstruction and Development (IBRD). This plan emphasized tourism development in the south while allowing for day-trip excursion routes to be developed into the interior of the island. The concentration of development was designed to protect the Balinese culture which was understood to be one of the main attractions of the island (SCETO 1971; Rodenburg, 1980).

The SCETO report has been frequently criticized for the lack of Balinese input. While a plan for tourism development is outlined in the report, there is a lack of attention to the overall development needs of Bali (Picard, 1990a). It was regarded by some Balinese as a plan which was imposed upon them by the central government. In response, the Balinese government held a seminar in which the concept of "cultural tourism" evolved and was embraced as the official type of tourism to be supported and promoted. It represented a way in which the Balinese could participate in the tourism industry which was being driven by the central government and foreign consultants (Picard, 1990b).

In 1988, the Balinese government changed its approach to tourism development planning and produced the Spatial Arrangement Plan for Tourism Areas (SAPTA). This new plan adopted a policy of spreading economic benefits to all parts of the island and designated 16 areas as tourism development sites. This new approach allows for a more equitable distribution of the opportunities provided by tourism and, at the same time, represents a more realistic reflection of the actual development taking place on the island.

In spite of the plans, spontaneous development by island residents can be seen throughout Bali. The intent of the planners was to develop luxury tourism, catering to upper-income tourists, but an unanticipated market segment of young, low-budget tourists also developed and other foreign visitors were interested in experiencing the culture more closely than was possible from five-star hotels. As tourism increased, Balinese residents found ways to become involved. As much of the initial "official" development was concentrated on large-scale hotels built by outside investors, the "homestay" was developed to cater to other market segments (Noronha, 1976) and can be seen as being made possible by weak development control mechanisms (Dibnah, 1992). Many residents opened small-scale businesses, typically restaurants, "homestays", souvenir shops and art and craft manufacture. Many of these businesses could be termed "informal sector" activities (Cukier-Snow and Wall, 1993).

Homestay development

Termed by Rodenburg (1980) as "craft tourism", "homestays" are characterized by their small size, and tend to be family-owned and operated. "Homestays", sometimes called "*losman*", are the typical type of accommodation provided by resident Balinese. They are usually cheap and include a room with two single beds, a bathroom, and breakfast.

Homestays are the predominant form of accommodation in the Ubud area. While this is due, in part, to official plans which concentrated the majority of large-scale accommodations in the Denpasar, Kuta and Sanur region, tourists to the Ubud region tend to be seeking a more intimate experience with Balinese culture. Homestay accommodations afford the desired views of traditional housing compounds and family life. The widespread development of homestays not only represents a supply of inexpensive accommodation to serve a low-budget market, but it also demonstrates the demand of tourists for interaction with the Balinese. As Stringer (1981) points out, bed and breakfast accommodation is seen as being not only a commercial transaction but as a form of socio-cultural relating as well.

RESEARCH PROJECT

As small-scale development is prevalent in most areas of Bali, it needs to be better understood in order to increase the effectiveness of planning efforts. This research project was undertaken with this aim in mind. The study took place in one of the *banjars* in the village of Peliatan, near Ubud, where a great deal of small-scale tourism development was occurring.

Fieldwork took place in 1991. One of the researchers chose to live in a homestay in Peliatan because of its reputation as a traditional community in the hope of learning about typical Balinese lifestyles. Upon moving to the *banjar*, however, the researcher noticed a rapid and widespread development of homestays and decided to investigate the phenomenon of their development.

The research was both exploratory and descriptive. It was exploratory in that it sought to investigate the little understood phenomena of development forces in *banjars* and to identify important issues. It was descriptive in that it documented tourism development in a *banjar*.

The *banjar* was composed of 200 families living in housing compounds located along two parallel roads running between two rivers. In this *banjar* there were 26 homestays, three restaurants, six stores selling souvenirs and six *warungs* or foodstalls. The *banjar* will not be mentioned by name to maintain the confidentiality of informants.

Research methods

The data-collection techniques of participant-as-observer, in-depth/key-informant interviewing and survey questionnaire were used for various types of data collection, using verbal communication in English and Indonesian.

The participant-as-observer role was employed to gain an in-depth understanding of homestay development and operation. In order to understand life and community dynamics, one of the researchers lived in a homestay, in the study *banjar*, for three months. From this situation, the daily operation and co-ordination of the family in the management of the homestay could be observed at close range.

In-depth, key-informant interviews were used to explore ideas, questions and specific issues. By living in the *banjar*, the researcher was able to have repeated contact with particular individuals for a series of informal interviews. A survey questionnaire was used in order to provide a comprehensive documentation of the *banjar* tourism development. This survey was conducted at the end of the field stay when the field researcher was familiar to many of the *banjar* residents and was able to speak enough Indonesian to conduct interviews.

The following is a list of the survey questions asked in each accommodation establishment:

1. When did this homestay/*losman*/bungalow open?
2. How many rooms for rent are here?
3. What are the prices per room?
4. Is there hot and cold water?
5. Who owns the homestay/*losman*/bungalow?
6. Who works in the homestay/*losman*/bungalow?
7. Do you have plans for the future?
8. How did you learn how to manage the homestay/*losman*/bungalow?

Twenty-five of the 26 lodging establishments in the *banjar* were surveyed. The remaining establishment was physically separated from the rest and had been in operation much longer than the majority, offering a slightly different type of service. Of the 25 establishments surveyed, one was excluded from the analyses. This facility was owned by a Dutch national and was a four-star hotel/bungalow complex with a swimming pool; as a tourism facility it was quite distinct from a homestay.

Study results

The results of this research will be presented in the order of the survey questions. A discussion of their implications, supplemented with information from key-informant interviews and participant-as-observer observations follows in the ensuing section.

The following is a presentation of the survey data.

LENGTH OF TIME IN OPERATION:
- range of one month to 18 years;
- two were under construction, near completion;
- not counting the one which had been in operation 18 years, the average length of time in operation was 14 months;
- 11 had been in operation one year or less.

NUMBER OF ROOMS FOR RENT:
- available rooms ranged from one to nine;
- the average number of rooms was four;
- 17 had four or fewer rooms.

PRICES PER ROOM:

- prices ranged as follows (in rupiah):
  - single 5000–20 000 cold water and 10 000–30 000 hot and cold water;
  - double 10 000–20 000 cold water and 12 000–30 000 hot and cold water;
- average price per room:
  - single, 9000 cold water and 19 000 hot and cold water;
  - double, 13 000 cold water and 22 000 hot and cold water;
- four homestays had both hot and cold water.

OWNERS OF THE HOMESTAYS:

- every homestay except one was owned by the resident family.

WORK IN THE HOMESTAY:

- in 12, or half, of the homestays the family members did the work;
- 7 had hired help;
- in three, family members worked as well as hired help.

PLANS FOR THE FUTURE:

- 16 wanted to add one or more rooms;
- two wanted to add hot water.

WHERE HOMESTAY MANAGEMENT LEARNED:

- 12 had previous experience in some sort of tourism business or in tourist areas;
- two admitted to not really knowing what they were doing but learning as they went.

Thus, it is apparent that the majority of accommodation establishments were small, cheap, family-operated businesses of recent vintage.

IMPLICATIONS OF THE RESEARCH

Balinese involvement in the small-scale tourism industry is applauded by many academics. It is seen as a way in which residents can participate in an industry which is dominated by the central government and outside investors (Jenkins, 1982; Sutton, 1989; Francillon, 1990). Although this participation is laudable, this research project uncovered some interesting dynamics which indicate that there may be reason to use caution in small-scale tourism development.

This survey examined only one type of small-scale business, the homestay, but several issues arose which may be applicable to small-scale tourism development in general. The issues are as follows: (1) cultural integrity; (2) demands on family life; (3) *banjar* cohesion; (4) economic benefits; (5) carrying capacity; (6) rapid rate of development; (7) process of diffusion; and (8) planning. The following discussion addresses the issues raised by the research in the study and relates them to views expressed in current literature on tourism development.

Cultural integrity

The impact of tourism on Balinese culture has long been a source of concern and debate among many authors (Udayana, 1975; Noronha, 1976; and Picard, 1990b). While Lansing (1974), McTaggart (1980), Mabbett (1987) and McKean (1989) suggest that tourism does not have a negative impact on Balinese society, Francillon (1990) describes it as a "tragedy". The researcher observed small-scale tourism to be a threat to cultural integrity in various ways.

Impact on participation in ceremonies and rituals

As in many religions, some rituals are undertaken by specific members of the household. Traditionally, the woman of the household makes an offering at the family temple three times each day. The researcher observed the husband and children making this offering when the woman was too busy with homestay duties.

Ceremony participation seems to have been affected by the tourism industry as well. Other researchers have found that those who work in the tourism industry do not have enough time to participate in ceremonies or that ceremonies have to be held when tourism workers can fit them into their schedules (Suthna *et al.*, 1989). As a result, the ceremonies are shortened to accommodate the workers' needs (Udayana, 1975). Participation in traditional religious ceremonies in Batubulan is often interrupted by the need of *banjar* members to perform dances elsewhere for tourists (Udayana, 1975).

Change in "form and function" of traditional Balinese housing compounds

The conversion of rooms to rented rooms and the tendency to add rooms whenever and wherever possible has altered the traditional form and function of Balinese housing compounds. Traditional compounds and *bales* (rooms) are arranged in a pattern reflective of Balinese culture respecting their Hindu cosmology (Budihardjo, 1986; Eiseman, 1990). Each *bale* is used by family members during certain stages of their life cycles. The researcher observed several families using spare *bales* as homestay rooms, shops and restaurants. The use of these for homestay purposes reflects a change in culture values associated with traditional architecture.

Intimate contact with foreign cultures

Much attention has been given to the interaction of tourists and the on-site population (Noronha, 1976; McKean, 1989; Turnbull, 1982). Homestays open families to intimate exposure to outsiders. The researcher noted homestay families regularly including tourists in *banjar* ceremonies. In addition, it was observed that women who operated homestays often allowed guests to accompany them while shopping at the local market. Cultural tourism is seen to be more intrusive than the much eschewed, superficial, mass tourism (Universitas Udayana and Francillon,

Figure 19.5. Resident building additional rooms in his family compound

1975). Independent tourists, who comprise the majority of the homestay market, tend to stay longer than group tourists and have more intensive interaction with the local Balinese (Rodenburg, 1980).

Culture as a tourism resource

There is great debate about the consequences of Balinese culture being used as a tourism attraction. Some claim it is causing a revitalization of arts and crafts and strengthening the culture (McTaggart, 1980; McKean, 1989). Others believe that tourism is causing the commoditization of culture (Universitas Udayana and Francillon, 1975; McTaggart, 1980). Evidence was observed which supports both sides of the debate. McKean (1989) claims that there is "revitalization" of culture as the number of people that practise arts and crafts, the number of dance troupes and the number of music ensembles have all increased and more people are able to support themselves as artists. Both daughters of the field researcher's homestay family came home from their university accommodation on weekends to participate in dance performances. Residents often learn increased details about their culture in order to explain them to tourists (Manuaba *et al.*, 1988). The field researcher often saw the father of her homestay family explaining various aspects of Balinese life and culture to guests.

Picard (1990b) argues that the doctrine of cultural tourism espoused by the central government is turning Balinese culture into a "touristic culture". He suggests that the strategy of "cultural tourism" is infusing the values of culture with those of tourism because culture is something which characterizes the society and also serves as a tourism product. Culture has become accessible to tourists, turning its "heritage" function into a "capital" function to promote economic development

(Picard, 1990a). The researcher noted objects from religious ceremonies and cultural artifacts for sale to tourists in local craft shops. Ceremonies were also "for sale" to tourists. A tour guide from outside the study *banjar* capitalized on *a banjar* cremation ceremony by importing a busload of paying tourists. Dances intentionally designed for foreign audiences are now considered traditional by the Balinese themselves. Thus the question of the impact of tourism on the culture could be considered irrelevant since tourism is now an integral part of Balinese culture.

Demands on family life

The impact of homestay operation on family life and traditional occupations was also seen to be an issue. All but one of the homestays was owned by a resident family. Of the resident families surveyed 15 (62%) indicated that they did the work involved with managing and operating the homestays while seven (29%) said that hired help did the work. It is suspected, however, that some managerial duties are still undertaken by resident owners.

In addition to attending to homestay operation duties, owners maintained traditional employment and upheld *banjar* responsibilities. Homestay ownership increased household workloads. As has been reported in other tourism areas (Smith, 1993), this has implications mainly for women who do the cooking, cleaning, laundry and shopping. Children who helped their mothers were also affected by the increased workload. With the increased responsibilities of homestay management, the participation of complete homestay family units in village events was often prohibited since at least one member of the household had to remain in the compound to operate the business.

Banjar cohesion

The introduction of tourism to the *banjar* has been accompanied by new forms of interaction among *banjar* members. The system of *gotong royong* (mutual aid) is disappearing and being replaced by a wage system. Turnbull (1982) discusses the threat of a cash economy and loss of reciprocity in human relationships on the essence of Balinese culture. The researcher observed that tourism did indeed bring in social forces that threatened *banjar* cohesion. At the same time the traditional processes of *banjar* social interaction and co-operation were used to mitigate the threats.

Increased banjar *conflict*

Banjar members found themselves in a new type of interaction with their neighbours' competition. Some researchers have detected a certain amount of negative competition among art shops in Ubud (Udayana, 1975). In the course of the field research interviews, several respondents talked about the ill-will caused by competition among homestays. Periodically, guests changed homestays, causing owners to believe customers had been enticed away by other homestay owners when they had found a style of accommodation that they preferred or when they had joined friends staying in another homestay.

Increased banjar *co-operation*

Increased intra-*banjar* conflict was accompanied by increased intra-*banjar* co-operation. As Walle (1993) states: "Traditions help people cope with 'future shock.'" This was the case in the study *banjar*. With the realization that tourism issues needed attention, a *banjar* tourism organization (P3T) was formed. The organization had the goals of co-ordinating promotional efforts to strengthen the flow of tourism to the *banjar*, co-ordinating efforts to protect the environment and addressing issues causing conflict.

In-migration of outsiders

Not only is there the fear that the presence of large numbers of foreign tourists will cause major socio-cultural impacts but that the numerous workers attracted by the tourism industry will weaken social cohesion (Sutton, 1989). Other studies indicate that in-migration occurs with tourism development in Bali (Rimbawan and Utama, 1989). Within the *banjar*, the researcher noted several new *banjar* occupants engaged in tourism activities. Since the *banjar* is traditionally a blood-related community, these "outsiders" represent a shift in community demographics.

Economic benefits

It is often thought that small-scale tourism development provides the maximum amount of benefits to the on-site population (Rodenburg, 1980; Jenkins, 1982; Sutton, 1989). Such participation, with much of the economic benefit going directly to Balinese communities, is seen as a force which strengthens the culture of Bali (Udayana, 1975; McKean, 1989; Sutton, 1989; Mantra, 1991). Small-scale enterprises can succeed economically with small numbers of tourists and can provide direct economic benefit to operators (Rodenburg, 1980). The researcher observed some of the claims of economic benefits to be true but saw reason to question them as well.

Ease of entry in small-scale enterprise

True to the claims of the literature on small-scale development, homestays tend to involve a relatively low initial capital outlay (Rodenburg, 1980; Jenkins, 1982). In the study *banjar*, the business was accessible to anyone with an extra room or to anyone with space to build one. Some families used the rooms of children away attending school as homestay rooms. As was found by Jenkins (1982), the facilities demanded by the low-budget tourist market are not extensive and homestays with few rooms and no hot water were accepted as standard tourist accommodation.

Unclear economic benefit to individual operators

Homestay operators also often lack skills necessary to manage tourism businesses properly, such as a knowledge of accounting (Manuaba, *et al*., 1988). Also, the actual prices paid for rooms often varied due to the fact that bargaining is prevalent in most business transactions in Bali. The data on room prices reflects a survey response and not necessarily what was actually paid by guests. Given the variability of prices, it is questionable if operators were able to budget effectively. These factors make it difficult to determine the profitability of homestay operations.

Carrying capacity

Although all benefited from the quiet, neighbourhood atmosphere which also attracted tourists to the *banjar*, there was no mechanism to protect it from the associated development. One of the first projects of P3T was to erect a large sign where the *banjar* street intersected a major tourist thoroughfare with the goal of increasing visitation to the *banjar*. Butler (1980) states: "tourist attractions are not infinite and timeless, but should be viewed and treated as finite and possibly non-renewable resources." Healy (1991) discusses the similarity of "tourism resources" to "common property". As the scenic rice fields are being transformed into homestays, restaurants and art shops at a rapid pace (Sutton, 1991), it is possible to imagine a "tragedy of the commons" scenario as the carrying capacity of tourism resources is surpassed.

Seventeen of the 24 respondents (71%) indicated a desire to build more rooms. As this survey only pertained to existing homestays, it is unknown how many other families were planning to build homestays in the *banjar*. The expansion of the existing homestays, however, would affect the already changing "tranquil" atmosphere of the *banjar* (see Figure 19.5).

Another aspect of carrying capacity involves the spatial arrangement of tourism facilities in the *banjar*. Some new land uses may be incompatible with traditional land uses and zoning may become an issue. The researcher was informed of conflicts between those in traditional family homes and those in tourism operations. It was explained that there were complaints about household animals making noise, and that there was a rumour that 60 animals (chickens and dogs) had been poisoned in order to eliminate noise that was bothering guests. The problems seemed to come from both directions as the noise from homestays and restaurants was also a source of complaint by non-homestay households. The separation of these activities would not only remove the benefits associated with integration but would require some form of zoning regulation. Currently there is a lack of sufficient zoning regulations and staff to enforce them in local government (Noronha, 1976; Dibnah, 1992).

Increased development by homestay operators in the study *banjar* would threaten the market niche it occupied. The "authentic" nature of the area may be lost, and as a result the neighbourhood may become indistinguishable from other *banjars* in the Ubud–Peliatan area. The central street of the *banjar* was already being compared by residents and visitors alike to a busy commercial street, Monkey Forest Road, in Ubud. The changes in market niche would mean that instead of complementing the tourist attractions in the Ubud area, the *banjar*'s services would be in direct competition with them.

Rapid rate of development

Some see a rapid rate of change imposed by tourism development as a destructive force on culture (Universitas Udayana and Francillon, 1975). Slow, incremental development is often recommended as it allows impacts to be absorbed by the resident community (de Kadt, 1979; Shafi, 1986; Cater, 1987). With 26 out of 200 families already operating homestays and 11 of those having been developed in the last year, the survey data indicate homestay development is occurring at a rapid pace.

While there is no indication that this rate of development will continue, there is the possibility that the lack of zoning and development regulations will permit an increase in development. The amount of tourism to Bali was expected to increase by 15% per annum from 1989 to 1994 (Repelita V, as cited by Dibnah, 1992). Many Balinese residents may try to profit from the opportunities afforded by such a high growth rate. *Banjar* residents who perceive an economic gain from homestay development will want to participate in the benefits enjoyed by their neighbours. How well the *banjar* will absorb the impacts associated with rapid development is unknown.

Informal diffusion process

Small-scale tourism is usually seen as community-based tourism (Woodley, 1993). One problem with many communities where tourism development occurs is that residents are unaware of how they can be involved (Manuaba *et al.*, 1988; Long, 1989). This study clearly shows that widespread involvement by Balinese villagers in tourism enterprises is occurring. Few of the homestay operators had formal training but had learned how to manage the operations in diverse ways. Some learned as they went along, some watched their neighbours, while others worked in tourism-related businesses such as art shops, restaurants or *losmans*.

The results suggest an informal process of diffusion. This diffusion could be seen on two levels: (1) at the island-wide level people move among tourism areas learning new skills and developing new ideas for tourism enterprises; and (2) at the level of the *banjar* skills and ideas are shared among members.

Knowledge of networks of innovation diffusion could prove useful to tourism planners to disseminate information necessary to enhance the goals of tourism development and management. On the other hand, it may be precarious to depend on informal networks to provide adequate tourism training since inappropriate or incorrect information and practices could be dispersed unwittingly among operators.

Planning

In order to minimize negative impacts, *banjars* should be incorporated into the process of decision making in tourism development (Noronha, 1976). In Bali, it has been legislated that community organizations be involved in tourism planning and development (UU No. 9/1990 and Perda Bali No. 3/1990, as cited by Dibnah, 1992). Although there appears to be rhetoric on the importance of local community involvement in planning, it is unclear if this has actually happened in Bali. The researcher did not see any official planning which incorporated the *banjar* level of administration. *Banjar* members were left to establish their own plans and co-ordinate their own activities.

CONCLUSIONS

Small-scale tourism development can be a remedy for some of the tourism industry's ills. As this study indicates, there are many benefits that can be achieved such as widespread involvement with opportunities of economic benefit for residents and a revitalization of culture as residents become "guides" to their home society and community. At the same time, there is reason to be sceptical of the benefits of small-scale tourism development. In the study *banjar* there was evidence that it was a threat to cultural integrity, it impinged on family life, it challenged *banjar* cohesion and it had unclear economic benefits. Small-scale tourism development was occurring through a process of informal diffusion but without regard for long-term implications and possibly at a rate which was too fast.

The issues raised by this study have important implications for tourism development in Bali and for small-scale tourism development in general. One of the main issues is whether or not tourism in Bali is sustainable when it is based substantially on a culture which is being changed by the tourism it attracts. As this study showed, there are many changes occurring in Balinese life which might have implication for the culture. It is widely believed that the unique political and religious aspects of Balinese culture are its hope of maintaining cultural integrity (Universitas Udayana and Francillon, 1975; Picard, 1990b). In this study the forming of P3T in order to foster mutual co-operation (in the tradition of *gotong royong*) served to rescue the study *banjar* from being dislocated by conflicts associated with tourism.

This study also furthers knowledge about small-scale tourism development in general. Although community-based, small-scale tourism is widely lauded in the tourism literature, there is little discussion of how on-site residents actually learn how to enter the tourism industry. This study demonstrates that there is a possibility of diffusion of knowledge and skills in the informal sector of the tourism industry. This study also illuminates the conundrum of "tragedy of the commons" as community-based tourism is dependent upon a resource which is not managed and protected.

The research presented has additional implications for the importance of planning at the community level. In this case, the *banjar* is the institution which has the primary contact with the small-scale development, and formal participation of *banjars* may serve as a keystone in the debate on appropriate tourism development in Bali.

Tourism development almost always is accompanied by social and physical changes to an area. Any adoption of small-scale tourism should be in recognition of the dynamic processes specific to its nature. Failure to do so could result in the loss of resources invested and the destruction of the areas where it is developed.

As the world's largest industry, tourism has the potential to propagate extensive global benefits (D'Amore, 1988). On the other hand, if not approached properly, it could contribute to widespread global problems. This study suggests that small-scale tourism may be the solution to some of the challenges faced by tourism developers, but it is not necessarily benign. Thus, unconditional adoption and promotion of small-scale tourism development is unacceptable, and the dynamic processes which accompany it must be understood and anticipated.

REFERENCES

Black, S. and Hanna, W. (1991) *Bali*. Singapore, Apa Publications.

Budihardjo, E. (1986) *Architectural Conservation in Bali*. Yogyakarta, Gadjah Mada University Press.

Butler, R. (1980) "The Concept of a Tourism Area Cycle of Evolution: Implication for Management of Resources. *Canadian Geographer*, **24**, 5–12.

Cater, E. (1987) "Tourism in the Least Developed Countries". *Annals of Tourism Research*, **14**, 202–226.

Charle, S. (1991) *Bali: Island of Grace*. Chicago, Passport Books.

Cohen, E. (1982) "Marginal Paradises: Bungalow Tourism on the Islands of Southern Thailand". *Annals of Tourism Research*, **9**, 189–228.

Cukier-Snow, J. and Wall, G. (1993) "Tourism Employment: Perspectives from Bali". *Tourism Management*, **14**, 195–201.

Dalton, B. (1990) *Bali Handbook*. Chico, California, Moon Publications.

D'Amore, L. (1988) "Tourism—the World's Peace Industry". *Business Quarterly*. Fall.

D'Amore, L. (1993) "A Code of Ethic and Guidelines for Socially and Environmentally Responsible Tourism". *Journal of Travel Research*, **31**, 64–66.

de Kadt, E. (1979) *Tourism—Passport to Development*? Washington, DC, Oxford University Press.

Deardon, P. (1993) "Cultural Aspects of Tourism and Sustainable Development: Tourism and the Hilltribes of Northern Thailand". In J.G. Nelson, R. Butler, and G. Wall (eds), *Tourism and Sustainable Development: Monitoring, Planning, Managing*. Department of Geography Publication Series Number 37, University of Waterloo, 165–178.

Dibnah, S. (1992) "An Assessment of Spatial Arrangement Plans for Tourist Areas in Bali". Research paper Number 39, University Consortium on the Environment Publication Series, Waterloo, University of Waterloo.

Eiseman, F. (1990) *Bali: Sekala and Niskala. Volume II Essays on Society, Tradition, and Craft*. Singapore, Periplus Editions.

Francillon, G. (1990) 'The Dilemma of Tourism in Bali". In W. Beller, P. d'Ayala and P. Hein (eds), *Sustainable Development and Environmental Management of Small Islands*. Paris, UNESCO and Parthenon Publishing Group.

Healy, R. (1991) "Property Rights and Tourism Resources: Tourism Resources a Common Pools and Common Property". Paper prepared for the Annual Meeting of the International Society for the Study of Common Property, Winnipeg, 26–29 September.

Jenkins, C. (1982) "The Effects of Scale in Tourism Projects in Developing Countries". *Annals of Tourism Research*, 9, 229–249.

Lansing, J. (1974) *Evil in the Morning of the World. Phenomenological Approaches to a Balinese Community*. Ann Arbor, The University of Michigan Center for South and Southeast Asian Studies.

Long, V. (1989) "Social Mitigation of Tourism Development Impacts: Bahias De Huatulco, Oaxaca, Mexico". *Tourism Recreation Research*, **14**, 5–13.

Mabbett, H. (1987) *In Praise of Kuta*. Wellington, January Books.

Mantra, I.B. (1991) "Tourism Industrial Impact on Socio-Cultural Life in Ubud, Bali". Paper presented at the Pacific Area Travel Association Conference, Bali, Indonesia, April 1991.

Manuaba, I.B.A., Oka, T.I. and Suwena, I.K. (1988) *Meningkatkan Mutu Kepariwisataan Di Ubud Dan Peliatan Melalui Perbaikan Kemampuan Pelayanan Dan Fasilitas Industri Serta Dukungan Penduduk*. Denpasar, Bali, Udayana State University.

McKean, P. (1989) "Towards a Theoretical Analysis of Tourism: Economic Dualism and Cultural Involution in Bali". In V. Smith (ed.), *Hosts and Guests: the Anthropology of Tourism*. Philadelphia, University of Pennsylvania Press (second edition), 119–138.

McTaggart, W. (1980) "Tourism and Tradition in Bali". *World Development*, **8**, 457–466.

Nelson, J.G., Butler, R. and Wall, G. (eds.) (1993) *Tourism and Sustainable Development: Monitoring, Planning, Managing*. Waterloo, Department of Geography Publication Series Number 37. University of Waterloo.

Noronha, R. (1976) "Paradise Reviewed: Tourism in Bali". In E. de Kadt (ed.), *Tourism—Passport to Development*? Washington DC, Oxford University Press, 177–204.

Oey, E. (1990) *Bali: Island of the Gods*. Singapore, Periplus Editions.

Picard, M. (1990a) "Kebalian Orang Bali: Tourism and the Uses of 'Balinese Culture' in New Order Indonesia". *Review of Indonesian and Malaysian Affairs*, **24**, 1–38.

Picard, M. (1990b) "Cultural Tourism" in Bali: Cultural Performances as Tourist Attraction". *Indonesia*, **49**, 37–74.

Rimbawan, N.D. and Utama, M.S. (1989) *Dampak Sosial Ekonomi Pengembangan Kawasan Wisata Candi Dasa*. Denpasar, Bali, Udayana State University.

Rodenburg, E. (1980) "The Effects of Scale in Economic Development: Tourism in Bali". *Annals of Tourism Research*, 7, 177–196.

Santosa, S. (1980) *Bali, What and Where*. Bali, Guna Agung.

SCETO (1971) *Bali Tourism Study*. Report to the Government of Indonesia. Paris, UNDP/IBRD, 6 volumes.

Shafi, M. (1986) "Tourism Planning in Developing Economies". *Tourism Recreation Research*, **11**, 99–101.

Smith, V. (1993) "Privatization in Third World: Small-Scale Tourism Enterprises". In W. Theobald (ed.), *Tourism in the 21st Century: Global Issues, Trends, Opportunities*. Oxford, Butterworth-Heinemann.

Stringer, P. (1981) "Hosts and Guests: the Bed and Breakfast Phenomenon". *Annals of Tourism Research*, **8**, 357–376.

Sutha, I.G.K., Parwatha, G.O., Mudana, I.N., Sukranatha, K. and Palguna, A.A.N. (1989) *Pengaruh Pariwisata Terhadap Aktivitas Organisasi Banjar Di Desa Ubud*. Denpasar, Bali, Udayana State University.

Sutton, M. (1989) "Bali—from Five Star Hotels to Intimate 'Homestays'" *World Development*, **2**(6), 13–16.

Sutton, M. (1991). "Knowledge, Governance and Tourism: Colonial Construction of

Balinese Culture". Paper presented at 8th Annual Berkeley Conference for Southeast Asia Studies, February 1991, Berkeley, California.

Turnbull, C. (1982) "Bali's New Gods". *Natural History*, January, 191–194.

Udayana University Research Team (1975) *The Impact of Tourism on Village Development*. Denpasar, Bali, Udayana State University.

UNDP (United Nations Development Programme) (1991) *Village Level Organization in Bali: Subak, Desa Adat, Desa Dinas, and Seka*. Working Paper Number 3. Denpasar, Bali, Bali Tourism Management Project.

Universitas Udayana and Francillon, G. (1975) "Tourism in Bali—Its Economic and Socio-cultural Impact: Three Points of View". *International Social Sciences Journal*, **27**, 721–752.

Walle, A. (1993) "Tourism and Traditional People: Forgoing Equitable Strategies". *Journal of Travel Research*, **31**, 14–19.

Wheeler, T., Covernton, M. and Samagalski, A. (1989) *Bali and Lombok: a Travel Survival Kit*. Hawthorn, Australia, Lonely Planet Publications.

Wilkinson, P. (1989) "Strategies for Tourism in Island Microstates". *Annals of Tourism Research*, **16**, 153–177.

Woodley, A. (1993) "Tourism and Sustainable Development: the Community Perspective". In J.G. Nelson, R. Butler, and G. Wall (eds), *Tourism and Sustainable Development: Monitoring, Planning, Managing*. Department of Geography Publication Series Number 37, University of Waterloo, 135–147.

20 Sustaining Tourism Under Political Adversity: the Case of Fiji

PETER BURNS
University of North London, UK

This chapter sets out to do three things: first, to illustrate the often unacknowledged complexity that characterizes the political economy of island micro-states; second, to demonstrate that attitudes within resort hotels and their employment practices mirror deeper cultural tensions; and third, that the losses to national opportunities caused by tourism's downturn immediately after military coups are far more complex than a drop in visitor arrivals. Within the context of Fiji's tourism industry, the chapter will show that foreign investment in ground plant "at bargain basement prices" can reinforce structural inequities: the people of Fiji are now further than ever from playing anything other than a minor role in their national tourism industry.

INTRODUCTION: AN ISLAND PARADISE?

The general perception of community relationships in Fiji prior to the 1987 military coups was epitomized during the Pope's visit of 1986. He described Fiji as "a symbol of hope in a troubled world" (*Islands Business*, June 1987, 3). Clearly His Holiness was no more aware of the Byzantine webs of intrigue than he was of the tin-roofed sheds of poverty, both of which mark and define ethnicity, caste and social stratification in that particular tropical paradise. It is not claimed that these tensions cause more anguish than in other countries; what sets them apart is the extent to which "sweeping under the carpet" had, prior to the coups, become institutionalized.

Relationships among people working within the tourism sector, especially the hotel industry, mirror this institutionalized social sanitation, much as the relationship between Fiji and the international tourism network is a mirror of colonial times. No doubt, when the tourists' glance rests momentarily upon the smiling resort worker, the backbone of these "environmental bubbles", these "islands of affluence" (literal and metaphoric) that constitute a luxury resort, all must seem well with the world. The tourist is able to act out the variety of roles expected of him as playchild in the tropics: part Robinson Crusoe; part colonial

Island Tourism: Management Principles and Practice
Edited by Michael V. Conlin and Tom Baum

officer; part millionaire; part philanthropist; part sex-machine in the heightened atmosphere brought about by close contact with splendour, nature and noble savage.

The resort management will have connived in enhancing the fantasy. Guest contact staff such as receptionists, waiters, room staff, etc. will almost exclusively be Fijians. Back-of-house staff such as cooks, reservation clerks, accountants will, just as certainly, be Indian. The island of affluence will, to use the colonial metaphor, be governed by whites.

As in the broader context of Fijian society, the various "tribes" that make up the workforce of a luxury resort complex tolerate each other with varying degrees of jealousy and amiability. The restaurant brigade are dismissive of the coffee shop "boys"; the "girls" who make up beds in the luxury suites are sure of their superiority over the "girls" who make up beds in the standard rooms. The gardeners laugh gently at the poolside waiters and waitresses who, though dressed in smart attire, and working under a blue sky, seem to derive no benefit from it. The kitchen staff, of course, just know that they are superior to everybody else! Superficially then, all is well with the world . . . just provided that the coffee and the sun are hot, the beer and the pool are cold, and the snacks don't take too long to arrive.

The situation was first researched by John Samy, a graduate of the University of the South Pacific and an ethnic Fiji–Indian. He reported:

> Local participation in hotel employment . . . is . . . based on racial and ethnic criteria. Expatriates and Europeans occupy top-paid managerial and executive positions involving far greater economic and social benefits. This racial pattern of job distribution in the hotel is institutionalised and is based largely on prejudice and stereotypes (Samy, 1981: 67).

He goes on to describe a familiar pattern of employment specialisms being defined by race and gender. Samy's study is very detailed, but to use one or two illustrations: 100% of the bar staff were ethnic Fijians, as were 94% of the restaurant staff, as were 100% of the tour desk staff, as were 100% of the porters. In contrast, 59% of the kitchen workers were Indian, as were 80% of the accounts staff, as were 76% of the maintenance/engineering staff. Europeans accounted for 73% of administration and management while accounting for only 4% of the resort's workforce. Samy rose to the rank of First Permanent Secretary in the Department of Economic Planning and Development and was largely responsible for Fiji's 9th Development Plan before being pressured to resign, along with several other high-ranking civil servants of Indian ethnicity, following the coups.

CULTURE AND HERITAGE: THE MISSING HALF

Displays of heritage within the resort are likely to be distorted: a sort of "ethnically cleansed" version: cute, non-threatening and in the form of 35-minute cultural show by the poolside. Such shows would be *vaka-Viti*, that is to say "of Fiji". They will include a woman's *meke* (sitting dance), a spear dance and, if near to the Island of Beqa, perhaps a *vilavilairevo* (walking on hot stones, the so-called "fire walking"). What one is most unlikely to see is any reference to the 48% of the population that is of Indian origin . . . a mixture of descendants from indentured labourers and Gujerati merchants, rich in religion, myth and networks. This invisibility would be further emphasized by a visit to Fiji's National Museum in Suva. The only notion of Indian ethnic heritage is a paltry display of household goods, some handtools related to toil in the sugar cane farms and a poignant collection of faded photographs showing the workers' *lines* (barracks). So, in this "model of hope" to paraphrase the Pope, or "The way the world should be" as the theme of the 1986 Tourism Convention termed it, all was not, perhaps, as it should have been.

LIVING IN PARADISE

Ieremia Tabai, President of Kiribati, re-asserts Steve Britton's description of popular imagination leading to a perception of oceanic micro-states as being symbolic of a paradisical backwater (Britton, 1987: 113). Tabai states:

> The sooner we stop using the word Paradise the better; the Pacific islands as Paradise is just the imagination of tourist people and the media . . . Islands are full of problems. I live on one of those islands, and it's only a Paradise when you don't have to live there long. It's good to come and see the natives and so on, but I'm not sure you want to spend the whole of your life staying in Paradise. There are a lot of very real problems (Tabai, 1988).

Among these problems is the sensitivity of tourism (which many Pacific Islands States recognize as having significant growth potential and which they "expect . . . to play a significant role in . . . future development" (SPEC, 1986) to political instability. Such sensitivity was noted in a business analysis of Pacific Island tourism: "New Caledonia's tourist record in the 1980's has been one of steady decline. Political unrest and poor political relations . . . have affected the tourist trade" (EIU, 1989: 85). The report went on to identify other areas of political unrest, noting that: "the troubles in [Papua New Guinea's] Bouganville area are likely to damage perceptions of the country's *political stability as a tourist destination*" (EIU, 1989: 84) (my emphasis). In recent years, Sri Lanka, Grenada, Philippines, the Seychelles and the Maldives have all experienced political upheavals, notably military coups, which have had a negative affect on their tourism.

In the case of the Pacific, where the influence of airline carriers on tourism is strong (Britton, 1983, chapter 3), political disruption in one country can have consequences for another. The Cook Islands reported a 7.8% downturn in its visitor arrivals from the 1986 peak, due mainly to airline schedule changes, purportedly as a direct result of the first Fiji coup: "the disruptions this [coup] caused to the region's air services [were notable] since Fiji acts as a hub for Tonga, Western Samoa and the Cook Islands . . . Tonga's air arrivals from Australia fell

5% in 1987 due to the . . . constitutional crisis in Fiji [and] its affect on traffic passing through Nadi" (Britton, 1993: 93). This emphasizes the sensitivity and vulnerability of immature markets to the impacts of political disturbance.

TOURISM IN FIJI IMMEDIATELY BEFORE THE COUPS

Fiji's ninth national development plan (1985–1990) placed a considerable emphasis on the tourism sector in helping generate employment opportunities and economic growth (Government of Fiji, 1984). However, certain institutional weaknesses had been identified by outside observers, notably the reliance on metropolitan airline companies, the extent of foreign ownership and marginalization of employment opportunities for locals (Samy, 1981; Britton, 1987) Britton asserted that the structure of tourism in Fiji is:

> a mirror of deeper structural characteristics, typical of a neo-colonial economy. The encouragement of tourism by local and foreign governments and business interests has been, at least in part, a response to contradictions caused by colonization . . . Tourism [continues to serve] those local and foreign interests that dominate the country's commercial activities (Britton, 1987: 126).

This view was not reflected in the rhetoric generated by the euphoric 25th (Silver Jubilee) Tourism Convention in 1986 (FVB, 1986a). Economic Planning, Development and Tourism Minister Peter Stinson declared that the deliberations of the convention would "contribute to the buoyant mood of the industry" (FVB, 1986a). In his opening address to the convention Prime Minister Ratu Sir Kamise Mara declared: "Government is firmly committed to the tourist industry, and over the years government's help has been very positive. We have provided . . . infrastructure . . . incentives. To this encouragement there was a splendid response by the industry" (Mara, 1986).

One of the few notes of caution in the proceedings was from the Governor of the Reserve Bank of Fiji (and a later "victim" of the coup for his stand against the military), Savenaca Siwatibau. Commenting that the hotel sector appeared to be "high geared" [with] low equity and high indebtedness" (Siwatibau, 1986: 10) which was likely to be a contributing factor in the rising cost of food, beverage and accommodation, a central theme in consumer criticism of Fiji's tourism especially in the traditional source markets of New Zealand and Australia (FVB, 1986b). Bill Whiting of the Fiji Visitor's Bureau's (FVB) Sydney office reported that: "Fiji's price advantage in the Australian Market [had] been badly eroded by the collapse of the Australian dollar . . . [with] . . . Australia's Barrier Reef a far more price competitive holiday for the Aussie Tourist" (*Pacific Islands Monthly*, June 1986: 46). Whiting also reported growing concern over increasing competition from Nusa Dua in Bali and from Pacific Island neighbours such as New Caledonia and Vanuatu.

While socio-economic conditions of tourism could be seen as institutionally weak, showing vulnerability to exchange rates, natural disasters (e.g. cyclones in 1983 and 1985) and more aggressive marketing from alternative destinations, the general view from industry was positive. A journal dedicated to Fiji's travel and tourism scene indicated that the FVB was aiming to spend F$2.5 million to attract 285 000 visitors in 1987, a target 25 000 up on 1986 (*Talanoa*, February 1987: 21). FVB General Manager Malakai Gucake even expressed concern over a possible shortage of rooms in 1988. The generally optimistic mood was reflected in extensive press coverage in local and regional media (*Islands Business*, 2 June 1986; *Travelweek Australia*, 9 June 1986; *Talanoa*, Feb 1987) of a whole range of development activities such as the opening plans for the A$34 million Sheraton in Nadi; of the several new tourist business ventures; expansions and improvements to the facilities of existing plant.

POLITICAL BACKGROUND: POST-COLONIAL ERA

To gain some understanding of the political economy of tourism in Fiji, it is necessary to understand something of the complex political situation that exists. To believe that the coups took place only as a result of the victory of Timoci Bavadra's fledgling Labour Party (which tore up the hidden political agenda that the 49% Indian population would stick to business leaving politics to the Melanesians) is to misinterpret the highly complex social structure of Fiji's traditional Chiefly and land/clan systems. Ethnic Fijian focus of attention, however, has always been on the latter. It is through the *mataqali* (clan), which collectively holds land, that the Chiefs hold power: thus control over land is the material base for power. Colonial administrators saw this and perpetuated the East–West divide which survived cession to the United Kingdom and which continued to dominate post-independent politics up until the time of the coups.

As the British prepared Fiji for independence, the question arose as to how power should be handed over. The divergence of thought between colonial administrators (anxious to ensure Fijian land rights within a form of democratic framework), Fijians who simply wanted power handed back to the *Taukei* (original land owners) and the Indians who wanted a straightforward, non-racial parliamentary democracy eventually led to a complex system in which each voter had two votes by virtue of belonging to one of three Communal (i.e. racial) electoral rolls (Fijian, Indian, or "general") *and* the National electoral roll.

As far back as the 1977 elections, the rise of Fijian ethnic nationalism was evident. The traditional Fijian voting pattern (which was to support Ratu Mara's ruling Alliance Party) was broken by Sakiasi Butadroka's Fijian Nationalist Party. This allowed the Indian-dominated Federation Party to gain 26 seats against the Alliance's 24. However in the days following the unexpected result, alleged in-fighting between Federation leader Siddiq Koya and deputy leader Irene Jai Narayan caused such delays in announcing the new cabinet and naming a new prime minister that on 7 April 1977 Governor-General Sir George Cakobau re-appointed Ratu Mara as prime minister in a caretaking capacity until new elections were conducted later that year. As expected, Ratu Mara was returned to power.

Elections in September 1977 and 1982 reaffirmed the dominance of the Fijian-led Alliance Party but in a new atmosphere of racial polarity and political acrimony. However, if the overt problem of Fijian politics was fear among ethnic Fijians that they were being left behind by the Indians in the growth of business and enterprise, then the undercurrent was of resentment by clans from Western Viti Levu against the hegemony of Eastern Chiefs, notably from Bau and Lau, a resentment exacerbated by the rise of a new class of university-educated, urban-dwelling Fijians who were beginning to question the Chiefly system. This questioning, together with seemingly irresolvable damage to the Federation Party led to the formation of the Fiji Labour Party in July 1985 with Timoci Bavadra, a Fijian commoner, as leader.

By late 1986, the Labour Party had formed an electoral pact with the traditional opposition party, the Federation, in preparation for Fiji's fifth post-independence general election. The election of Bavadra's Labour Party, with its educated middle-class professionals and leftists, broke the social post-colonial political pattern and demonstrated the changes of composition in Fiji's class structure in a manner which led directly to Rabuka's first coup. Bavadra's electoral victory was met, on the whole, with what appeared to be good-natured resignation by the defeated prime minister Ratu Mara, who praised the democratic system in Fiji and wished his successor well (Ratu Mara's resignation speech reported in *Fiji Times*, 13 April 1987).

This attitude of tolerance was not to last. As the Labour Party moved to implement it's liberal-democratic policies, amid rumour of the new government uncovering "corruption at the highest level" (*Fiji Times*, 27 April 1987) and the growing unrest which "culminated in the burning of government ministers' offices" (*Islands Business*, June 1987: 15) . . . "and street demonstrations by ethnic Fijians" (*Economist*, 16 May 1987: 7). The stage for Rabuka's coup was set:

> I . . . thought . . . about the multiracial society in Fiji and the slow erosion of Fijian control of the Nation . . . While studying at the India Defence Staff College . . . I wrote a thesis on the role of military forces in the socio economic development of nations. As part of the thesis I studied coups in various African and Latin American States. It reinforced my belief that the Royal Fiji Military Forces could have a very active part to play in the socio economic development of Fiji. When the 1987 elections were announced followed by the Taukei movements action, I knew that the climate was ripe for either socialism or military intervention to preserve democracy and traditional values (*Islands Business*, September 1987: 7).

Rabuka carried out his military coup on 14 May 1987. Pacific Island neighbours were quick to react. Australian Premier Bob Hawke was reported as "condemning this attack on a government of the South Pacific and the Commonwealth, elected through the proper constitutional and democratic process" (*Fiji Times*, 15 May 1987: 2). Papua New Guinea's Premier, Michael Somare, expressed disbelief at the news of the coup: "I can't believe this sort of thing has happened in the Pacific" (*Fiji Times*, 15 May 1987: 2). New Zealand's Prime Minister David Lange stated that his government recognized "only the constitutional authority of the Governor-General" (*Fiji Times*, 15 May 1987: 3).

REACTIONS FROM THE TOURISM INDUSTRY

First reactions from the tourism industry to the coup were made public on 21 May, six days after the coup and the first day of publication after the army shutdown of the press. Radike Qereqeretabua, a well-respected hotel manager and sometime chair of the Fiji Visitors Bureau (also a rare Fijian ethnic voice in the expatriate/foreign-dominated sector) asserted that Fiji could forget about the record visitor arrivals hoped for in 1987 (*Fiji Sun*, 21 May 1987: 3) stating that "arrivals were expected to drop by 50% in the next couple of months". By July 1987, it was reported that Fiji's "economy [was] shattered . . . Tourism, the second most important industry in terms of foreign exchange and employment is at a standstill" (*PIM*, July 1987: 14). The report went on to describe how Fiji's hotel industry had the potential to lose F$80–100 million in revenue and that "a number of hotels could be forced to close down . . . [and that] . . . the industry would be lucky to reach half the F$200 million revenue from the 1985 season". Hotel occupancy rates were at a record low of 10% compared to a seasonal average of 70%.

International airlines reacted to the coup by altering schedules: Continental Airlines, the only US carrier flying into Fiji suspended flights; Qantas announced that it would carry no tourists, only Fijian Nationals or journalists; and Air New Zealand suspended flights after one of its 747s was involved in a pathetic hijack attempt. Only Air Pacific (the national carrier) and Japan Air Lines maintained regular flights.

In the face of this adversity, Fiji's 1987 Tourism Convention took place as scheduled, on 8 June, only four weeks after the first coup. Significantly, reflecting the importance being placed on tourism in the process of economic recovery, the Governor-General Ratu Sir Penai Ganilau agreed to give the opening address in which he outlined a nine-point plan for reconstruction (Ganilau, 1987: 1). The plan included liberalizing tax and duty laws on imported equipment; liberalization of development loan regulations; several moves to encourage new investment in industry and capital projects; public-sector involvement in capital projects and the final point, a F$500 000 emergency grant to the FVB to assist in marketing and crisis management.

Reserve Bank Governor Siwatibau reported in his Statement on the Economy (part of his address to the convention) that the short-term outlook for tourism was not good, visitor arrivals had already dropped and that at the time (June 1987) hotel occupancy was running at 20–30% (Siwatibau, 1986: 7).

The FVB initiated a marketing drive in Australia to recover Fiji's overseas image. Other positive initiatives came from operators and Air Pacific who offered special price deals out of Australia, and from the Fiji Hotel School, which, under the guidance of its expatriate director, initiated and developed the high-profile tourism training programme Partners in Recovery. The scheme was implemented by the Fiji National Training Council's tourism training division and was assured of full support by the Fiji Hotel Association. The scheme had something of a hidden agenda in that it was initiated as much as an industry-wide anti-depressant as it was to help with skills development during the downtime.

THE SECOND COUP: PARADISE LOST

However, in spite of growing confidence, and a general perception of the non-violent nature of the first coup, on 25 September, amid continuing unrest among various ethnic Fijian groups, notably the Great Council of Chiefs, Colonel Rabuka mounted his second coup. If the target of the May Coup was one faction of modern Fiji's political class, the Bavadra government, "a multiracialist coalition of upstart South Pacific leftists and the more familiar Indian bourgeoisie in the Federation party" (*Sydney Morning Herald*, 7 October 1987), then the second coup by contrast was against the reconstituted civilian class, represented by the trio of the Governor-General, Ratu Mara (the defeated prime minister) and Dr Bavadra (the ousted prime minister). The coup appeared to hover between outright military dictatorship and the establishment of a new political structure with credible claims to civilian legitimacy.

Warren Osmond, foreign editor of the *Sydney Morning Herald*, raised some interesting issues concerning what he identifies as Rabuka's strategic diffidence in conducting the coups, linking Rabuka's reluctance to take on the role of military dictator with his status as commoner in Fiji's traditional Chiefly system. This may have led to his preferred method of military intervention: that of forcing the civilian politicians to read and take his cues rather than the more conventional method of outright dictatorship by decree. Osmond proposed that perhaps Rabuka had developed a new style in coups: "the weak, courtly and rather gentler South Pacific Coup, minimising force and bloodshed" (*Sydney Morning Herald*, ibid.).

We can conclude perhaps that the most profound sociological pattern behind both coups was the internal struggle for power in a rapidly changing Fijian elite. As Osmond asserts:

> The Rabuka coups may well be seen by historians as phases in a historic revolt of commoners (and lesser Chiefs) against the Great Chiefs, especially their long standing and most sophisticated political leader, Ratu Mara. Even if the commoners, including Rabuka, may profess to support the traditional chiefly caste, they actually comprise a new power elite based partly in Army and also among uprooted and unemployed ethnic Fijians (*Sydney Morning Herald*, ibid.).

Fiji, with no contemporary history of overt political instability, and described by the pope in a visit some few months before the coups as "a symbol of hope in a troubled world", was generally seen as a democratic role model in the South Pacific. Given this, the reaction from the major source markets Australia and New Zealand could be described as almost resentful, as though their perception of Paradise had been shattered. As Teye (1988) asserts in his model of the potential effects of military coups on tourism, coups in countries or regions with a history of strife will have less effect on the tourism industry than those with a reputation for peacefulness. Australia, New Zealand and the United States, all issued travel advisories to their nationals, and yet there were no reported cases of harassment of tourists or resident foreigners (news reporters notwithstanding). Rabuka's peculiarly singular coup did conform to Teye's model to a some extent, but perhaps it could be argued that the model is so broad as to be axiomatic. What is important is the nature or extent of impact.

COUPS D'ETAT AND THEIR EFFECT ON TOURISM

Teye's model attempts to elucidate the impact of frequent *coups d'état* and the resultant political instability on tourism. He describes military *coups d'état* as affecting tourism in three broad areas:

- the effectiveness of the National Tourism Office
- the flow of international tourists (demand for product)
- the development of tourism resources and attractions.

These three headings form a useful framework within which to examine the affect of the two military coups in Fiji.

IMPACT ON THE NATIONAL TOURIST OFFICE

Within three weeks of the coup, press reports highlighted the need for plans to be made "to protect tourism" (*Fiji Sun*, 6 June 1987: 10). Speculation that a "positive reassuring advertising programme" (*Fiji Sun*, 6 June 1987: 10) would be launched at the forthcoming Tourism Convention proved correct. The Governor-General announced an extra F$500 000 for marketing efforts by the Fiji visitors' bureau, some of which was to be used to counteract negative marketing from Anuka Resort in the Solomon Islands which ran a campaign under the heading "Why risk Fiji?" in the *Queensland Sunday Times* (*Fiji Sun*, 6 June 1987: 10). They offered a seven-night package including meals, transfers, air fares, activities (including water sports) and baby sitting for A$1295. The last line of the advert ran: "Why risk Fiji when something better is something safer" (*Queensland Sunday Times*, reported in *Fiji Sun*, 6 June 1987). As a side note, during 1988, Anuka Resort was destroyed in an arson attack following a dispute between the traditional landowners and the Australian operators.

At the 1987 Fiji Tourism Convention, John Rowe, managing director of the Australian Tourist Commission noted in his speech to the delegates, that:

> During the past few days your discussions have centred almost totally on your immediate problems of restoring world wide identity and consumer confidence. Your experience only emphasizes to all of us in tourism the fragile and perishable nature of our industry. Whenever a tourist destination suffers a set-back, the most immediate and important step is for all segments of the industry to become a unified marketing team (Rowe, 1987: 1).

David Williams, Chairman of FVB, and project director of the massive Saweni Beach resort project, commented on rumours of plant closures saying that: "as a matter of policy, [they] are not a good thing" (*Travel Trade Australia*, September 1987). He went on to state that operators may not be so tolerant of a profit level lower than they were previously accustomed to. A senior civil servant in the government's Department of Tourism, Levani Tuinabua, expressed concern over the potential for long-term strategic marketing damage caused by relying on "fire sale promotional tactics" (*Travel Trade Australia*, September 1987). Tuinabua considered that: "promoting value for money and Air Pacific A$299 and A$399 return fares were attracting budget conscious visitors who don't have much impact on the economy. People who were reportedly heating up baked beans in their electric jugs at Mana Island resort" (*Travel Trade Australia*, September 1987).

The government once again showed its commitment to tourism in an October policy paper prepared by the Adviser (Minister) for Foreign Affairs, Filipe Bole. Of the five objectives listed in the paper the third was "the development tourism" and that the "initiatives should be programmed to the governments of those countries which are likely to understand and even support . . . Republican status" (*Island Business*, November 1987).

IMPACT ON THE FLOW OF INTERNATIONAL TOURISTS

Tourist flow was impacted for two major reasons: extremely bad publicity in major source markets and the rescheduling and cancellation of flights by international carriers. A dramatic illustration of impact is the comparison of June 1986 visitor arrivals of 18 000 with the June 1987 figure of only 5000. Government sources claim that Fiji earned an average of F$4 million each week from tourism, F$200 million in the year up to the coups. Over the same period in 1988, one year later tourism had grossed only F$70 million. This in itself raises some interesting issues in that tourism statistics are notoriously questionable, and even more questionable is the way in which such statistics are used. Could these figures have been manipulated in any way for certain interested parties (perhaps the FVB or investors from the troubled Sheraton and Saweni resorts)? While there is no evidence for such manipulation, raising the issue will serve to remind us that it is essential to consider the source of statistics and the uses to which they may be put.

The immediate impact of the first coup on the tourism industry was described in no uncertain terms. The coup "caused the total collapse of Fiji's second largest industry. Japanese visitors halved during June [1987] and dropped further during July and August. Australian, American and New Zealand tourists dropped by 71%" (*PIM*, February 1988: 43).

Inbound travel flows were affected more seriously by the 25 September (second) coup, described variously as "worst than the first" (New Zealand Premier Lange reported in *Weekend Australia*, 26 September 1987) and "a savage blow" (*PIM*, November 1987: 13). The special air fare and accommodation promotional packages coupled with the 30 June devaluation of 17% succeeded in increasing tourism from major source markets only to have these increases knocked back by a 30% cancellation rate. Sources from Fiji Visitors Bureau reported that:

> Even if the current [promotional] drive succeeds, the industry knows that cut price fares and discounted tariffs are merely short term solutions. The industry will only recover when tourists pay normal prices. Tourists attracted by cheap deals, who spend F$20 a day instead of F$100 cannot make the country solvent (*PIM*, February, 1988: 43).

In total, visitor arrivals for the year up to 31 August 1988 fell by 22.8% compared to the same period in 1987 (178 081 in 1988 against 230 734 in 1987). By November 1988, just over a year after the FVB projected 313 000 visitors by 1991, a total of which FVB thought could increase to 500 000 by the year 2000. Statistics presented to the 1988 Fiji Tourist Convention indicated that Fiji's visitor arrivals for 1987, the year of the coup, were down from the 1986 figure of 258 000 to 190 000, reducing its regional share (Papua New Guinea, Solomon Islands, Vanuatu, Tonga, Western Samoa, American Samoa, Cook Islands, Niue, Kiribati, and Tuvalu) from 57% in 1986 to 48.4% in 1987. This 9% drop is relatively significant in the context of Pacific Island tourism.

IMPACT ON DEVELOPMENT OF TOURISM RESOURCES AND ATTRACTIONS

At the time of the coups there were several projects being undertaken, ranging from the 30-bedroom Athol Hotel near the capital of Suva to the Saweni Beach development on Western Viti Levu with a projected 900 rooms in three separate resort hotels. The initial reaction to the first coup could have been described as "putting a brave face on things". Administrative and construction work went on as before. Events were, after all, described as a "benign coup". We were, after all, living in an island Paradise. These illusions were shattered some five months later. The second coup was altogether a nastier affair: a proper coup. The industry reacted with stunned silence. Once again, the Murdoch press in Australia had a field day of barely concealed racial attacks on their Pacific Island neighbour, motivated perhaps by angry resentment of "Paradise lost", almost as if these natives had no right to interfere with Australia's traditional playground. The playful, carefree, smiling Fijians were growing up, and the Aussies didn't like it.

This evident resentment by Australia and New Zealand of political action by the Fijians, is in a sense, a manifestation of the attitudinal nexus that surrounds the notion of "other". Edward Said's thoughts on this are well known (Said, 1978), and Marianna Torgovnick (1990) brings further thoughts to the debate in the introduction to her book: "'Primitives' exist for us in a series of dichotomies: by turns gentle, in tune with nature, paradisal, ideal—or violent, in need of control; what we should emulate or, alternately, what we should fear; noble savages or cannibals".

THE POST-COUPS' SITUATION

If Britton's description of metropolitan, big-capital ownership styles within Fiji's tourism industry had any value before the coups, then his assertions are now doubly relevant: in the two years immediately following the coups, the Japanese were very active in the property market. The Tokyo-based giant EIE Development Company purchased Fiji's premier resort complex Denerau Island comprising two major properties, the Sheraton and the elegant but fading Regent of Fiji (*PIM*, July 1988). Far from being concerned over these events, the then Minister for Tourism David Pickering was quoted in the same edition as being willing to talk to anyone with development proposals, "EIE is too big for us not to listen". The principal investment adviser to EIE considered that:

> EIE can use its financial might to improve not only the Denerau Island resort: [but also that] closer ties between Suva and Tokyo [would] eventually stabilize the Republic's tenuous new democracy and, ultimately, bettering Fiji's way of life . . . Fiji clearly has tremendous potential as a resort destination and EIE is willing to back that offer (*PIM*, July 1988: 40–42).

By the end of 1988 there was increased investor confidence, with the Fiji Employers' Association being quoted on the possibility of an investment boom (*PIM* December 1988: 26). The article went on further to report Westpac Bank's Chairman, Sir Eric Neal as declaring: "now is the time for capitalism in Fiji to come out of the closet".

Rodney Cole, Assistant Executive Director of the Centre for Development Studies (Australian National University), postulated that there was a need to promote a greater understanding of profit: "profit is not a dirty word" (*PIM*, December 1988: 26). The Japanese certainly seemed to agree. The *Fiji Times* of 2 July 1988 reported with a front-page banner headline that: "Japanese Buy Deuba Resort". The article, which referred to an "undisclosed sum", went on to conclude that the Japanese purchasing company South Pacific Development (SPD) had plans for setting up a 1300-room development. SPD was later reported in the *South Seas Digest* (a private newsletter on Pacific Island affairs) (16 September 1988) as intending to spend more than US$281 million on redevelopment. Earlier, the *South Seas Digest* (5 August 1988) had reported the aging Naviti Beach Resort as being sold to a Hong Kong-controlled company for a paltry US $2.8 million.

CONCLUSION

The two military coups have had a profound effect on the tourism industry in Fiji, going far beyond the immediate drop in visitors (the success of tourism cannot be defined by measuring visitor arrival figures). The most far-reaching effect will be the change in the pattern of ownership, and the increasing domination of Japanese ownership, which, with its characteristically vertically integrated nature does not bode well for Fiji's ambitions to increase the amount of revenue that stays in the country. This trend in ownership will, to a large extent, be perpetuated by the Fiji government's own actions in encouraging the national carrier in its dedicated Nadi–Tokyo route. It would appear that the Fiji government's concern over the negative effect of cheap bargain-basement holidays being sold through Australia and New Zealand would have been better directed at safeguarding the predatory tactics of large metropolitan-based companies. The ownership of plant in Fiji is further than ever away from the people; the opportunity presented by the coups to re-evaluate Fiji's position in the tourism market, to consider tourism alternatives has been lost. The ever-smiling Fijian created in the minds of mindless holiday-makers by cynical advertising executives appears to be destined to fulfil the roles of cook, gardener, housemaid and beach boy set aside for them through their post-colonial inheritance. The men will continue to thrill the tourists with frenetic spear dances and the women will continue to charm the tourists with a half-whispered *bula* greeting. They will both dream of some day returning to their village, and both will thank the good Colonel for saving their country from the Indians.

The National Museum in Suva will continue to display a distorted and undervalued representation of Fiji's Indians, who are left to ponder the proposition that 19th-century indenture has turned out to lead to 20th-century serfdom (Robertson and Tamanisau, 1988). The Indians in the resorts will remain sweating over the stoves, under the watchful eye of a German or Swiss executive chef. They will remain behind the scenes finalizing the month's profit figures and silently dream of joining Hari in Canada, or Ganesh in Australia.

REFERENCES

Britton, Stephen (1983) *Tourism and Underdevelopment in Fiji*. Canberra, Australian National University.

Britton, S. (1987) "Tourism in Pacific Island States: Constraints and Opportunities". In S. Britton and W. Clarke, *Ambiguous Alternatives, Tourism in Small Developing Countries*. Suva, University of the South Pacific.

Britton, S. and Clarke, William C. (eds) (1983) *Ambiguous Alternatives, Tourism in Small*

Developing Countries. Suva, University of the South Pacific.
EIU, (1989) "The Pacific Islands". *International Reports*, (4) 85.
FVB (1986a) *The Silver Convention: Annual Tourism Convention Delegates' Handbook*. Suva, Fiji Visitors Bureau.
FVB (1986b) *Consumer Survey of Departing Tourists* (carried out at Nadi airport, 1986).
Ganilau, Ratu Sir Penai, Opening Speech to the 1987 annual Tourism Convention.
Government of Fiji (1984) *Development Plan 9*, Department of Economic Planning and Development.
Mara, Ratu Sir Kamisese, Opening address to the 1986 FVB Tourism Convention.
Robertson, R. and Tamanisau, A. (1988) *Fiji, Shattered Coups*. Canberra, Pluto Press.
Rowe, John, *Marketing Fiji in Australia*. Paper to 1987 FVB Tourism Convention.
Said, Edward (1978) *Orientalism*. London, Routledge & Kegan Paul Ltd.
Samy, John (1981) "Crumbs from the Table". In Freda Rajotte and R. Crocombe (eds), *Pacific Tourism as Islanders see it*. Suva, University of the South Pacific.
Siwatibau, Savenaca (1986) *Some Thoughts on Fiji's Economy*. Paper to 1986 FVB Tourism Convention.
SPEC (South Pacific Economic Bureau) (1986) *Tourism*. Suva.
Tabai, Ierimia (reported in) *Islands Business*, **14**(1), 12.
Teye, V. (1988) "Coups d'Etat and African Tourism: a study of Ghana". *Annals of Tourism Research*, **15**, 329–356.
Torgovnick, Marianna (1990) *Gone Primitive: Savage Intellects, Modern Lives*. Chicago, University of Chicago Press.

Island/Island Regions Index

Subject Index